D1078751

o/p

The Hodder Book of Christian Quotations

By the same author

QUOTES AND ANECDOTES FOR PREACHERS AND TEACHERS
ASSEMBLE TOGETHER
THROUGH THE YEAR WITH POPE JOHN PAUL II

The Hodder Book of Christian Quotations

Compiled by Tony Castle

HODDER AND STOUGHTON
London Sydney Auckland Toronto

British Library Cataloguing in Publication Data

The Hodder book of Christian quotations.
  1. Christianity   2. Quotations.
  I. Castle, Tony
  808.88'2   PN6084.R3

  ISBN 0-340-32339-6
  ISBN 0-340-32338-8 Pbk

Dedicated to my daughters, Helena, Louise and Angela.

INTRODUCTION

Many years ago, when I was learning the art of public speaking, I started a small collection of useful sayings and inspiring quotations. They totalled no more than a hundred and were arranged thematically in an old school book. That modest interest and pastoral aid was the origin and basis of this present compilation. In collecting the material gathered here the approach has remained practical and pastoral, with the down-to-earth needs of preachers, teachers and writers foremost in mind. The reader, driven by curiosity or seeking spiritual nourishment, will also benefit from the 4,110 quotations arranged under 450 theme headings. It should be noted however that given the source or historico-cultural context of a few of the quotations they cannot all be considered *Christian* quotations, but they are all quotations that Christians should ponder and have available for use.

The latter half of the twentieth century seems to be tipped forward to the future. As radio telescopes and satellites probe deep space for other life forms, young people are conditioned through their education, and even their leisure-time activities, to look to the twenty-first century and beyond for enlightenment and excitement. Our age is impatient with the accumulated wisdom of previous generations, who, lacking the micro-chip, are often ignored and even scorned. But the Christian faith has firm roots in history and cherishes the word of God. The quotations in this collection have won a place because they are seen to cast some light upon that truth and the mysteries and exigencies of life.

I have striven to maintain a balance both between quotations from each of the Christian traditions and between ancient and modern sources. Quotations can be found from every century and, where possible, the authors' dates are given in the index to locate the quotation in its own social and historical context.

Much effort has been made to ascribe the quotations correctly and no anonymous material has been accepted.

A great debt of gratitude is due to Miss Georgette Butcher (formerly Manageress of the Scripture Union book shop, London) for her valuable help and advice. I would like to say thank you too to Sheila Taylor who typed the manuscript.

Tony Castle

ABANDONMENT
(See also PROVIDENCE, TRUST and WILL OF GOD)

A1
The Lord doesn't want the first place in my life, he wants all of my life.
HOWARD AMERDING

A2
The greatness of a man's power is the measure of his surrender.
WILLIAM BOOTH

A3
There is but one thing to do: to purify our hearts, to detach ourselves from creatures, and abandon ourselves entirely to God.
JEAN PIERRE DE CAUSSADE

A4
While he strips of everything the souls who give themselves absolutely to him, God gives them something which takes the place of all; of light, wisdom, life and force: this gift is his love.
JEAN PIERRE DE CAUSSADE

A5
God is the master of the scenes; we must not choose what part we shall act; it concerns us only to be careful that we do it well, always saying, 'If this please God, let it be as it is.'
JEREMY TAYLOR

ABILITY
(See also TALENTS)

A6
If people knew how hard I have to work to gain my mastery, it would not seem wonderful at all.
MICHELANGELO BUONARROTI

A7
The winds and waves are always on the side of the ablest navigators.
EDWARD GIBBON

A8
Alas for those who never sing, but die with all their music in them.
OLIVER WENDELL HOLMES

A9
It is a fine thing to have ability, but the ability to discover ability in others is the true test.
ELBERT KIPLING

A10
Behind an able man there are always other able men.
CHINESE PROVERB

A11
Do what you can, with what you have, where you are.
THEODORE ROOSEVELT

A12
A man must not deny his manifest abilities, for that is to evade his obligations.
ROBERT LOUIS STEVENSON

ACCEPTANCE

A13
As in a game of cards, so in the game of life we must play with what is dealt out to us; and the glory consists not so much in winning as in playing a poor hand well
JOSH BILLINGS

A14
To live by the law of Christ and accept him in our hearts is to turn a giant floodlight of hope into our valleys of trouble.
CHARLES R. HEMBREE

1

Achievement

A15

A man can accept what Christ has done without knowing how it works; indeed, he certainly won't know how it works *until* he's accepted it.

C. S. LEWIS

A16

Acceptance says, True, this is my situation at the moment. I'll look unblinkingly at the reality of it. But I'll also open my hands to accept willingly whatever a loving Father sends.

CATHERINE MARSHALL

A17

I have accepted all and I am free. The inner chains are broken as well as those outside.

CHARLES F. RAMUZ

A18

The task ahead of us is to know ourselves as not acceptable. And to accept that knowledge.

SIMON TUGWELL

A19

If we stand in the openings of the present moment, with all the length and breadth of our faculties unselfishly adjusted to what it reveals, we are in the best condition to receive what God is always ready to communicate.

T. C. UPHAM

A20

You are not accepted by God because you deserve to be, or because you have worked hard for Him; but because Jesus died for you.

COLIN URQUHART

ACHIEVEMENT
(See also SUCCESS)

A21

Having once decided to achieve a certain task, achieve it at all costs of tedium and distaste. The gain in self-confidence of having accomplished a tiresome labour is immense.

ARNOLD BENNETT

A22

Nothing great was ever achieved without enthusiasm.

RALPH WALDO EMERSON

A23

No great thing is created suddenly, any more than a bunch of grapes or a fig. If you tell me that you desire a fig, I answer you that there must be time. Let it first blossom, then bear fruit, then ripen.

EPICTETUS

A24

I am only one, but still I am one. I cannot do everything, but still I can do something; and because I cannot do everything, I will not refuse to do something that I can do.

EDWARD EVERETT HALE

A25

We judge ourselves by what we feel capable of doing; others judge us by what we have done.

HENRY W. LONGFELLOW

A26

Praise the ripe field not the green corn.

IRISH PROVERB

A27

Four steps to achievement. Plan purposefully. Prepare prayerfully. Proceed positively. Pursue persistently.

WILLIAM A. WARD

ACTIVE LIFE

A28

Happy persons seldom think of happiness. They are too busy losing

their lives in the meaningful sacrifices of service.
DAVID AUGSBURGER

A29
We do the works, but God works in us the doing of the works.
ST. AUGUSTINE OF HIPPO

A30
Christian action should be defined as an action of God mediated through a person.
ANTHONY BLOOM

A31
I do not believe in a fate that falls on men however they act; but I do believe in a fate that falls on men unless they act.
G. K. CHESTERTON

A32
Action may not always bring happiness; but there is no happiness without action.
BENJAMIN DISRAELI

A33
Love's secret is always to be doing things for God, and not to mind because they are such very little ones.
FREDERICK W. FABER

A34
It is possible to be so active in the service of Christ as to forget to love him.
P. T. FORSYTH

A35
Our problem is not that we take refuge from action in spiritual things, but that we take refuge from spiritual things in action.
MONICA FURLONG

A36
We ascend to the heights of contemplation by the steps of the active life.
POPE ST. GREGORY I

A37
A Christian should always remember that the value of his good works is not based on their number and excellence, but on the love of God which prompts him to do these things.
ST. JOHN OF THE CROSS

A38
Act well at the moment, and you have performed a good action to all eternity.
JOHANN K. LAVATER

A39
The Christian who tugs on the oars hasn't time to rock the boat.
AUSTIN ALEXANDER LEWIS

A40
Our own actions are our security, not others' judgments.
ENGLISH PROVERB

A41
To live is not merely to breathe; it is to act.
JEAN JACQUES ROUSSEAU

A42
The princes among us are those who forget themselves and serve mankind.
WOODROW WILSON

ADAM
(See also FALL OF MAN and ORIGINAL SIN)

A43
Oh, he didn't believe in Adam or Eve,
He put no faith therein;
His doubts began with the fall of man,
And he laughed at original sin.
HILAIRE BELLOC

A44
The man without a navel still lives in me.
SIR THOMAS BROWNE

A45
Adam, whiles he spake not, had paradise at will.
WILLIAM LANGLAND

A46
When Adam delved and Eve span, who was then a gentleman?
ENGLISH PROVERB

A47
Adam ate the apple and our teeth still ache.
HUNGARIAN PROVERB

A48
Adam and Eve had many advantages, but the principal one was that they escaped teething.
MARK TWAIN

A49
Adam was but human – this explains it all. He did not want the apple for the apple's sake; he wanted it only because it was forbidden. The mistake was in not forbidding the serpent – then he would have eaten the serpent.
MARK TWAIN

A50
I sometimes think that if Adam and Eve had been merely engaged, she would not have talked with the serpent; and the world had been saved an infinity of misery.
H. G. WELLS

ADOPTION
(See also BAPTISM)

A51
Out adoptive sonship is in its supernatural reality a reflection of the sonship of the Word. God has not communicated to us the whole of his nature but a participation of it.
R. GARRIGOU-LAGRANGE

A52
Christians are made, not born.
ST. JEROME

A53
The Spirit is the Spirit of adoption, since He is the Spirit received in baptism, whereby Christians are adopted into the household of God as joint-heirs with Christ.
ALAN RICHARDSON

A54
For children to be baptised implies that they be brought into a whole new set of relationships with the triune God: sons and daughters of the *Father*, reborn in the likeness of Christ, the *Son of God*, to be his faithful witnesses, united to him and adopted by the *Father* through the power of the *Spirit*.
MARK SEARLE

ADORATION
(See also PRAISE and WORSHIP)

A55
At my devotion I love to use the civility of my knee, my hat and hand.
SIR THOMAS BROWNE

A56
If we would understand Divine things, we must cultivate an attitude of humble adoration. Who does not begin by kneeling down, runs every possible risk.
ERNEST HELLO

A57
It is magnificent to be clothed like the lilies of the field . . . but the supreme glory is to be nothingness in adoration.
SØREN KIERKEGAARD

A58
Man is most truly himself, as the Eastern Church well knows, not

when he toils but when he adores.
And we are learning more and
more that all innocent joy in life
may be a form of adoration.

VIDA P. SCUDDER

A59
To pray is less than to adore.

CLARENCE WALWORTH

ADVERSITY
(See also AFFLICTION and
SUFFERING)

A60
Take the cross *he* sends, as it is,
and not as *you* imagine it to be.

CORNELIA CONNELLY

A61
God instructs the heart not by
ideas, but by pains and
contradictions.

JEAN PIERRE DE CAUSSADE

A62
There is no education like
adversity.

BENJAMIN DISRAELI

A63
Adversity is the trial of principle.
Without it a man hardly knows
whether he is honest or not.

HENRY FIELDING

A64
No man is fit to comprehend
heavenly things who hath not
resigned himself to suffer
adversities for Christ.

THOMAS À KEMPIS

A65
Adversity not only draws people
together but brings forth that
beautiful inward friendship, just as
the cold winter forms ice-figures on
the window-panes which the
warmth of the sun effaces.

SØREN KIERKEGAARD

A66
Adversity is the diamond dust
Heaven polishes its jewels with.

ROBERT LEIGHTON

A67
The hardness of God is kinder than
the softness of men, and his
compulsion is our liberation.

C. S. LEWIS

A68
It has done me good to be
somewhat parched by the heat and
drenched by the rain of life.

HENRY WORDSWORTH LONGFELLOW

A69
Adversity is not necessarily an evil.
Beethoven composed his deepest
music after becoming totally deaf.
Pascal set down his most searching
observations about God and man,
life and death, in brief intervals of
release from a prostrating illness.

ROBERT MCCRACKEN

A70
Adversity makes a man wise, not
rich.

ENGLISH PROVERB

A71
Many can bear adversity, but few
contempt.

ENGLISH PROVERB

A72
The stars are constantly shining,
but often we do not see them until
the dark hours.

EARL RINEY

A73
As sure as ever God puts his
children in the furnace he will be in
the furnace with them.

CHARLES H. SPURGEON

A74
Too much sunshine in life makes a
desert.

GUSTAV J. WHITE

ADVICE

A75
Whenever my advice is followed I confess that I always feel oppressed with a greater burden of responsibility, and I can never be confident, and always await the outcome with anxiety.

ST. BERNARD OF CLAIRVAUX

A76
Advice is seldom welcome; and those who want it the most always like it the least.

LORD CHESTERFIELD

A77
Advice is like snow; the softer it falls, the longer it dwells upon, and the deeper it sinks into the mind.

SAMUEL TAYLOR COLERIDGE

A78
To ask advice is in nine cases out of ten to tout for flattery.

JOHN CHURTON COLLINS

A79
To profit from good advice requires more wisdom than to give it.

JOHN CHURTON COLLINS

A80
An honest man may take a fool's advice.

JOHN DRYDEN

A81
No gift is more precious than good advice.

DESIDERIUS ERASMUS

A82
He that won't be counselled can't be helped.

BENJAMIN FRANKLIN

A83
I have often heard that it is more safe to hear and to take counsel than to give it.

THOMAS À KEMPIS

A84
He who builds according to every man's advice will have a crooked house.

DANISH PROVERB

A85
No one wants advice – only corroboration.

JOHN STEINBECK

AFFLICTION
(See also ADVERSITY and SUFFERING)

A86
One and the same violence of affliction proves, purifies and melts the good, and condemns, wastes and casts out the bad.

ST. AUGUSTINE OF HIPPO

A87
God measures out affliction to our need.

ST. JOHN CHRYSOSTOM

A88
The truly loving heart loves God's good pleasure not in consolations only, but, and especially, in afflictions also.

ST. FRANCIS DE SALES

A89
Affliction can be a treasure. Absolutely functional, it triggers life's greatest insights and accomplishments.

FRED GREVE

A90
Strength is born in the deep silence of long-suffering hearts, not amid joy.

FELICIA HEMANS

A91
Afflictions are but the shadow of God's wings.

GEORGE MACDONALD

A92
Whenever I find myself in the cellar
of affliction, I always look about
for the wine.
SAMUEL RUTHERFORD

A93
The Lord gets his best soldiers out
of the highlands of affliction.
CHARLES H. SPURGEON

AFTERLIFE
(See also ETERNITY and
IMMORTALITY)
A94
I cannot conceive that (God) could
make such a species as the human
merely to live and die on this earth.
If I did not believe in a future state,
I should believe in no God.
JOHN ADAMS

A95
Those who hope for no other life
are dead even for this.
JOHANN WOLFGANG VON GOETHE

A96
I know as much about the afterlife
as you do – nothing. I must wait
and see.
WILLIAM RALPH INGE

A97
Before I started working with dying
patients, I did not believe in a life
after death. I now believe in a life
after death, beyond a shadow of a
doubt.
ELIZABETH KUEBLER-ROSS

A98
The seed dies into a new life, and
so does man.
GEORGE MACDONALD

A99
The only ultimate disaster that can
befall us is to feel ourselves at
home on this earth.
MALCOLM MUGGERIDGE

A100
Those who live in the Lord never
see each other for the last time.
GERMAN PROVERB

A101
We maintain that after life has
passed away, thou still remainest in
existence, and look forward to a
day of judgment, and according to
thy deserts, art assigned to misery
or bliss.
QUINTUS TERTULLIAN

A102
I have never seen what to me
seemed an atom of proof that there
is a future life. And yet – I am
strongly inclined to expect one.
MARK TWAIN

AGE and AGES OF MAN
(See also OLD AGE and
YOUTH)
A103
To know how to grow old is the
master work of wisdom, and one of
the most difficult chapters in the
great art of living.
HENRI FRÉDÉRIC AMIEL

A104
They shall grow not old, as we that
are left grow old. Age shall not
weary them, nor the years
condemn. At the going down of the
sun and in the morning we will
remember them.
LAURENCE BINYON

A105
To grow old is to pass from passion
to compassion.
ALBERT CAMUS

A106
The old may be out-run but not
out-reasoned.
GEOFFREY CHAUCER

A107
You know you're getting old when

the candles cost more than the cake.

BOB HOPE

A108
Forty is the old age of youth; fifty the youth of old age.

VICTOR HUGO

A109
The evening of a well-spent life brings its lamps with it.

JOSEPH JOUBERT

A110
The older the fiddle the sweeter the tune.

ENGLISH PROVERB

A111
The old forget, the young don't know.

GERMAN PROVERB

A112
The old age of an eagle is better than the youth of a sparrow.

GREEK PROVERB

A113
For the ignorant, old age is as winter; for the learned, it is a harvest.

JEWISH PROVERB

A114
The young man who has not wept is a savage; the old man who will not laugh is a fool.

GEORGE SANTAYANA

A115
A man of fifty is responsible for his face.

FRANK L. STANTON

A116
No wise man ever wished to be younger.

JONATHAN SWIFT

A117
None are so old as those who have outlived enthusiasm.

HENRY DAVID THOREAU

AGNOSTICISM
(See also DOUBT and UNBELIEF)

A118
The mystery of the beginning of all things is insoluble by us; and I for one must be content to remain an agnostic.

CHARLES DARWIN

A119
Agnosticism simply means that a man shall not say he knows or believes that for which he has no grounds for professing to believe.

THOMAS HENRY HUXLEY

A120
Agnosticism solves not, but merely shelves the mysteries of life. When agnosticism has done its withering work in the mind of man, the mysteries remain as before; all that has been added to them is a settled despair.

VINCENT MCNABB

A121
Agnosticism leads inevitably to moral indifference. It denies us all power to esteem or to understand moral values, because it severs our spiritual contact with God who alone is the source of all morality.

THOMAS MERTON

A122
I do not see much difference between avowing that there is no God, and implying that nothing definite can for certain be known about him.

JOHN HENRY NEWMAN

A123
The agnostic's prayer: 'O God, if there is a god, save my soul, if I have a soul.'

JOSEPH ERNEST RENAN

ALMS
(See also GIFTS AND GIVING)

A124
It is possible to give without loving, but it is impossible to love without giving.
RICHARD BRAUNSTEIN

A125
The more he cast away the more he had.
JOHN BUNYAN

A126
We make a living by what we get, ✗ but we make a life by what we give.
SIR WINSTON CHURCHILL

A127
Our prayers and fastings are of less avail, unless they are aided by almsgiving.
ST. CYPRIAN

A128
Alms are but the vehicles of prayer.
JOHN DRYDEN

A129
Alms never make poor.
ENGLISH PROVERB

A130
The little alms are the best alms.
FRENCH PROVERB

A131
Offer your prayers and alms and do all things according to the Gospel of our Lord.
TEACHING OF THE TWELVE APOSTLES

AMBITION

A132
Ambition is like hunger; it obeys no law but its appetite.
JOSH BILLINGS

A133
Well is it known that ambition can creep as well as soar.
EDMUND BURKE

A134
All ambitions are lawful except those which climb upward on the miseries or credulities of mankind.
JOSEPH CONRAD

A135
Ambition is the mind's immodesty.
SIR WILLIAM DAVENANT

A136
Most of the trouble in the world is caused by people wanting to be important.
T. S. ELIOT

A137
Nothing is humbler than ambition when it is about to climb.
BENJAMIN FRANKLIN

A138
Hew not too high lest the chip fall in thine eye.
JOHN HEYWOOD

A139
Ambition is pitiless; any merit that it cannot use it finds despicable.
JOSEPH JOUBERT

A140
Most people would suceed in small things if they were not troubled by great ambitions.
HENRY WORDSWORTH LONGFELLOW

A141
Every eel hopes to become a whale.
GERMAN PROVERB

A142
Ambition destroys its possessor.
HEBREW PROVERB

A143
You may get to the very top of the ladder, and then find it has not been leaning against the right wall.
A. RAINE

A144
You cannot be anything if you want to be everything.
SOLOMON SCHECHTER

ANGELS

A145
The servants of Christ are protected by invisible, rather than visible, beings. But if these guard you, they do so because they have been summoned by your prayers.
ST. AMBROSE

A146
Angels mean messengers and ministers. Their function is to execute the plan of divine providence, even in earthly things.
ST. THOMAS AQUINAS

A147
Angels can fly because they take themselves lightly.
G. K. CHESTERTON

A148
There are nine orders of angels, to wit, angels, archangels, virtues, powers, principalities, dominations, thrones, cherubim and seraphim.
POPE ST. GREGORY I

A149
They take different forms at the bidding of their master, God, and thus reveal themselves to men and unveil the divine mysteries to them.
ST. JOHN OF DAMASCUS

A150
An angel is a spiritual creature created by God without a body, for the services of Christendom and of the Church.
MARTIN LUTHER

A151
Millions of spiritual creatures walk the earth unseen, both when we sleep and when we awake.
JOHN MILTON

A152
The question of how many angels could dance on the point of a pin no longer is absurd in molecular physics, with its discovery of how broad that point actually is, and what a part invisible electronic 'messengers' play in the dance of life.
LEWIS MUMFORD

A153
Man is neither angel nor beast; and the misfortune is that he who would act the angel acts the beast.
BLAISE PASCAL

A154
In these days you must go to Heaven to find an angel.
POLISH PROVERB

ANGER

A155
Anger is quieted by a gentle word just as fire is quenched by water.
JEAN PIERRE CAMUS

A156
There is no sin nor wrong that gives a man such a foretaste of Hell in this life as anger and impatience.
ST. CATHERINE OF SIENA

A157
There is a holy anger, excited by zeal, which moves us to reprove with warmth those whom our mildness failed to correct.
JEAN BAPTISTE DE LA SALLE

A158
Anger is never without a reason, but seldom with a good one.
BENJAMIN FRANKLIN

A159
Anger is one of the sinews of the soul. He who lacks it hath a maimed mind.
THOMAS FULLER

A160
To be angry is to revenge the fault of others upon ourselves.
ALEXANDER POPE

A161
Anger is often more hurtful than the injury that caused it.
AMERICAN PROVERB

A162
Anger and haste hinder good counsel.
ENGLISH PROVERB

A163
People who fly into a rage always make a bad landing.
WILL ROGERS

A164
He that would be angry and sin not must not be angry with anything but sin.
THOMAS SECKER

ANIMALS

A165
A robin redbreast in a cage
puts all heaven in a rage.
A skylark wounded in the wing
doth make a cherub cease to sing.
He who shall hurt the little wren
shall never be beloved by men.
WILLIAM BLAKE

A166
Monkeys are superior to men in this: when a monkey looks into a mirror, he sees a monkey.
MALCOLM DE CHAZAL

A167
Swans have an air of being proud, stupid, and mischievous – three qualities that go well together.
DENIS DIDEROT

A168
Animals are such agreeable friends – they ask no questions, they pass no criticisms.
GEORGE ELIOT

A169
A cat can be trusted to purr when she is pleased, which is more than can be said about human beings.
WILLIAM RALPH INGE

A170
I tend to be suspicious of people whose love of animals is exaggerated; they are often frustrated in their relationships with humans.
CAMILLA KOFFLER

A171
When an animal has nothing to do, it goes to sleep. When a man has nothing to do, he may ask questions.
BERNARD J. F. LONERGAN

A172
No animal admires another animal.
BLAISE PASCAL

A173
In training animals and children, the same principles apply; be fair, be firm, be fun.
BARBARA WOODHOUSE

ANXIETY
(See also WORRY)

A174
Drones make more noise than bees, but all they make is the wax, not the honey. Those who torment themselves with eagerness and anxiety do little, and that badly.
ST. FRANCIS DE SALES

A175
Anxiety is the natural result when our hopes are centred in anything short of God and his will for us.
BILLY GRAHAM

A176
Anxiety is not only a pain which we must ask God to assuage but also a weakness we must ask him to pardon – for he's told us to take no care for the morrow.
C. S. LEWIS

A177
Anxiety does not empty tomorrow of its sorrows, but only empties today of its strength.
CHARLES H. SPURGEON

A178
Beware of anxiety. Next to sin, there is nothing that so troubles the mind, strains the heart, distresses the soul and confuses the judgment.
WILLIAM ULLATHORNE

APATHY
(See also INDIFFERENCE)

A179
The hottest places in Hell are reserved for those who in time of great moral crisis maintain their neutrality.
DANTE ALIGHIERI

A180
The only thing necessary for the triumph of evil is for good men to do nothing.
EDMUND BURKE

A181
Science may have found a cure for most evils; but it has found no remedy for the worst of them all – the apathy of human beings.
HELEN KELLER

A182
Bad officials are elected by good citizens who do not vote.
GEORGE JEAN NATHAN

APPRECIATION
(See also GRATITUDE and THANKSGIVING)

A183
The deepest principle in human nature is the craving to be appreciated.
WILLIAM JAMES

A184
Brains are like hearts – they go where they are appreciated.
ROBERT McNAMARA

A185
I have yet to find the man, however exalted his station, who did not do better work and put forth greater effort under a spirit of approval than under a spirit of criticism.
CHARLES M. SCHWAB

A186
The best things in life are appreciated most after they have been lost.
ROY L. SMITH

A187
Next to excellence is the appreciation of it.
WILLIAM MAKEPEACE THACKERAY

ARCHITECTURE

A188
It has been said that Gothic architecture represents the soul aspiring to God, and the Renaissance or Romanesque architecture represents God tabernacling with men.
ROBERT H. BENSON

A189
Architecture is frozen music.
JOHANN WOLFGANG VON GOETHE

A190
One of the big problems for an architect in our time is that for a hundred and fifty years men have been building churches as if a church could not belong to our time. A church has to look as if it were left over from some other age. I think that such an assumption is based on an implicit confession of atheism – as if God did not belong to all ages and as if religion were really only a pleasant,

necessary social formality, preserved from past time in order to give our society an air of respectability.

THOMAS MERTON

A191
However my reason may go with Gothic, my heart has ever gone with Grecian.

JOHN HENRY NEWMAN

A192
Varieties of uniformities make complete beauty.

CHRISTOPHER WREN

ART

A193
The aim of art is to represent not the outward appearance of things, but their inward significance.

ARISTOTLE

A194
Art is the signature of man.

G. K. CHESTERTON

A195
There has never been a boy painter, nor can there be. The art requires a long apprenticeship, being mechanical as well as intellectual.

JOHN CONSTABLE

A196
Where the spirit does not work with the hand there is no art.

LEONARDO DA VINCI

A197
One always has to spoil a picture a little bit, in order to finish it.

DELACROIX

A198
Art is a collaboration between God and the artist, and the less the artist does the better.

ANDRÉ GIDE

A199
All art is propaganda, for it is in fact impossible to do anything, to make anything, which is not expressive of 'value'.

ERIC GILL

A200
What is the work of art? A word made flesh. That is the truth, in the clearest sense of the text. A word, that which emanates from the mind. Made flesh; a thing, a thing seen, a thing known, the immeasurable translated into terms of the measurable. From the highest to the lowest that is the substance of works of art.

ERIC GILL

A201
Art is nothing more than the shadow of humanity.

HENRY JAMES

A202
Art is the gift of God, and must be used unto his glory.

HENRY WORDSWORTH LONGFELLOW

A203
Art is beauty made a sacrament. Art is finite human expression made infinite by love.

VINCENT MCNABB

A204
Art is the telling of truth, and is the only available method for telling of certain truths.

IRIS MURDOCH

A205
The novel is practically a Protestant form of art; it is a product of the free mind, of the autonomous individual.

GEORGE ORWELL

A206
A good spectator also creates.

SWISS PROVERB

A207
All great art is the expression of man's delight in God's work, not his own.

JOHN RUSKIN

A208
We should comport ourselves with the masterpieces of art as with exalted personages – stand quietly before them and wait till they speak to us.

ARTHUR SCHOPENHAUER

ASCETICISM
(See also SELF-DENIAL)

A209
The sacrifice most acceptable to God is complete renunciation of the body and its passions. This is the only real piety.

ST. CLEMENT OF ALEXANDRIA

A210
We can only reach the delicate truth of mysticism through the commonplace sincerities of asceticism.

FREDERICK W. FABER

A211
The true ascetic counts nothing his own save his harp.

JOACHIM OF FLORA

A212
The only asceticism known to Christian history is one that multiplies desire till the ascetic with something like divine avarice covets a kingdom beyond even the stars.

VINCENT McNABB

ATHEISM
(See also UNBELIEF)

A213
A little philosophy inclineth a man's mind to atheism, but depth in philosophy bringeth men's minds about to religion.

FRANCIS BACON

A214
Atheism is rather in the lip than in the heart of man.

FRANCIS BACON

A215
Where there is no God, there is no man.

NIKOLAI BERDYAEV

A216
A man cannot become an atheist merely by wishing it.

NAPOLEON BONAPARTE

A217
Nobody talks so constantly about God as those who insist there is no God.

HEYWOOD BROUN

A218
An atheist is a man without any invisible means of support.

JOHN BUCHAN

A219
There are no atheists in fox-holes.

WILLIAM T. CUMMINGS

A220
Some are atheists only in fair weather.

THOMAS FULLER

A221
Every effort to prove there is no God is in itself an effort to reach for God.

CHARLES EDWARD LOCKE

A222
If Christianity cannot be based on atheism one must nevertheless acknowledge that the challenge of atheism is a constant safeguard against idolatry.

JOHN MACQUARRIE

A223
Atheism thrives where religion is most debated.
WELSH PROVERB

A224
To believe means to recognise that we must wait until the veil shall be removed. Unbelief prematurely unveils itself.
EUGEN ROSENSTOCK-HUESSY

A225
The worst moment for the atheist is when he is really thankful and has nobody to thank.
DANTE GABRIEL ROSSETTI

A226
Christianity founds hospitals, and atheists are cured in them, never knowing that they owe their cure to Christ.
WILLIAM TEMPLE

A227
An atheist is a man who believes himself an accident.
FRANCIS THOMPSON

A228
The religion of the atheist has a God-shaped blank at its heart.
H. G. WELLS

ATONEMENT
(See also RECONCILIATION)
A229
Christ's Passion is the true and proper cause of the forgiveness of sins.
ST. THOMAS AQUINAS

A230
For the sake of each of us he laid down his life – worth no less than the universe. He demands of us in return our lives for the sake of each other.
ST. CLEMENT OF ALEXANDRIA

A231
In the cross, God descends to bear in his own heart the sins of the world. In Jesus, he atones at unimaginable cost to himself.
WOODROW A. GEIER

A232
A great many people are trying to make peace, but that has already been done. God has not left it for us to do; all we have to do is to enter into it.
DWIGHT L. MOODY

A233
When God pardons, he consigns the offence to everlasting forgetfulness.
MERV. ROSELL

A234
A heavy guilt rests upon us for what the whites of all nations have done to the coloured peoples. When we do good to them, it is not benevolence – it is atonement.
ALBERT SCHWEITZER

ATTRIBUTES OF GOD
A235
God is that, the greater than which cannot be conceived.
ST. ANSELM OF CANTERBURY

A236
God alone knows the depths and the riches of his Godhead, and divine wisdom alone can declare his secrets.
ST. THOMAS AQUINAS

A237
We can know what God is not, but we cannot know what he is.
ST. AUGUSTINE OF HIPPO

A238
God is within all things, but not included; outside all things, but not

excluded; above all things, but not beyond their reach.

POPE ST. GREGORY I

A239
Change and decay in all around I see;
O thou, who changest not, abide with me.

HENRY FRANCIS LYTE

A240
The attributes of God, though intelligible to us on their surface yet, for the very reason that they are infinite, transcend our comprehension, when they are dwelt upon, when they are followed out, and can only be received by faith.

JOHN HENRY NEWMAN

A241
The word 'God' is a theology in itself, indivisibly one, inexhaustibly various, from the vastness and the simplicity of its meaning.

JOHN HENRY NEWMAN

A242
To him no high, no low, no great, no small; he fills, he bounds, connects and equals all!

ALEXANDER POPE

A243
A comprehended God is no God at all.

GERHARD TERSTEEGEN

A244
One might lay it down as a postulate: all conceptions of God which are incompatible with a movement of pure charity are false. All other conceptions of him, in varying degrees, are true.

SIMONE WEIL

AUTHORITY

A245
No authority has power to impose error, and if it resists the truth, the truth must be upheld until it is admitted.

JOHN ACTON

A246
The man who cannot control himself becomes absurd when he wants to rule over others.

ISAAC ARAMA

A247
It is right to submit to higher authority whenever a command of God would not be violated.

ST. BASIL

A248
Cast away authority, and authority shall forsake you!

ROBERT H. BENSON

A249
I am convinced that people are open to the Christian message if it is seasoned with authority and proclaimed as God's own Word.

BILLY GRAHAM

A250
Authority is not a short way to the truth; it is the only way to many truths; and for men on earth, it is the only way to divine truths.

VINCENT MCNABB

A251
Men desire authority for its own sake that they may bear a rule, command and control other men, and live uncommanded and uncontrolled themselves.

SIR THOMAS MORE

A252
If you accept the authority of Jesus in your life, then you accept the authority of His words.

COLIN URQUHART

BAPTISM

B1

No athlete is admitted to the contest of virtue, unless he has first been washed of all stains of sins and consecrated with the gift of heavenly grace.

ST. AMBROSE

B2

According to the New Testament, all men have in principle received baptism long ago, namely on Golgotha, at Good Friday and Easter.

OSCAR CULLMAN

B3

If any man receive not baptism, he hath no salvation; except only martyrs, who even without water receive the kingdom.

ST. CYRIL OF JERUSALEM

B4

When the Church baptises a child, that action concerns me, for that child is thereby connected to that which is my head too, and ingrafted into that body whereof I am a member.

JOHN DONNE

B5

You have been baptised, but think not that you are straightway a Christian . . . The flesh is touched with salt: what then if the mind remains unsalted? The body is anointed, yet the mind remains unanointed. But if you are buried with Christ within, and already practise walking with Him in newness of life, I acknowledge you as a Christian.

DESIDERIUS ERASMUS

B6

Baptism signifies that the old Adam in us is to be drowned by daily sorrow and repentance, and perish with all sins and evil lusts; and that the new man should daily come forth again and rise, who shall live before God in righteousness and purity forever.

MARTIN LUTHER

B7

Baptism points back to the work of God, and forward to the life of faith.

J. A. MOTYER

B8

In baptism, the direction is indicated rather than the arrival.

FREDERICH REST

B9

Baptism seemed such an integral part of New Testament Christianity and I couldn't imagine a droplet of water dribbled on my head when I was a baby could be a proper substitute for that adult symbol of submission and obedience.

CLIFF RICHARD

B10

After their baptism in the Holy Spirit Christians walk in newness of life, the life of the new creation, the life of the Age to Come.

ALAN RICHARDSON

B11

Baptise as follows: After first explaining all these points, baptise in the name of the Father and of the Son and of the Holy Spirit, in running water. But if you have no running water, baptise in other water; and if you cannot in cold, then in warm. But if you have neither, pour water on the head three times in the name of the Father and of the Son and of the Holy Spirit.

TEACHING OF THE TWELVE APOSTLES

B12

Happy is our sacrament of water,

in that by washing away the sins of our early blindness, we are set free and admitted into eternal life . . . But we, little fishes, after the example of our ICHTHYS (Jesous Christos Theou Uios Soter: Jesus Christ Son of God Saviour) are born in water, nor have we safety in any other way than by permanently abiding in water.

QUINTUS TERTULLIAN

B13
The Passover provides the day of most solemnity for baptism, for then was accomplished our Lord's Passion, and into it we are baptised.

QUINTUS TERTULLIAN

BEATITUDES

B14
If the Sermon on the Mount is the précis of all Christian doctrine, the eight beatitudes are the précis of the whole of the Sermon on the Mount.

JACQUES B. BOSSUET

B15
Blessed is he who does good to others and desires not that others should do good to him.

BROTHER GILES

B16
Jesus clothes the beatitudes with his own life.

CARL F. HENRY

B17
The more we live and try to practise the Sermon on the Mount, the more shall we experience blessing.

MARTYN LLOYD-JONES

B18
It is not written, blessed is he that feedeth the poor, but he that considereth the poor. A little

thought and a little kindness are often worth more than a great deal of money.

JOHN RUSKIN

B19
The beatitudes are a call to us to see ourselves, to live with ourselves, in a way that probably does not come easily to most of us.

SIMON TUGWELL

BEAUTY

B20
Beauty and the beautiful – these are one and the same in God.

ST. THOMAS AQUINAS

B21
Beauty is indeed a good gift of God; but that the good may not think it a great good, God dispenses it even to the wicked.

ST. AUGUSTINE OF HIPPO

B22
Wherever ugliness is kept at bay, there the Spirit of God, who is the God of Beauty, is doing His creative and re-creative labour.

DONALD COGGAN

B23
When beauty fires the blood, how love exalts the mind.

JOHN DRYDEN

B24
Beauty is the mark God sets upon virtue.

RALPH WALDO EMERSON

B25
Though we travel the world over to find the beautiful, we must carry it with us or we find it not.

RALPH WALDO EMERSON

B26
Spring is God thinking in gold, laughing in blue, and speaking in green.

FRANK JOHNSON

B27
A thing of beauty is a joy for ever.
JOHN KEATS

B28
God's fingers can touch nothing but
to mould it into loveliness.
GEORGE MACDONALD

B29
Beauty is the radiance of truth; the
fragrance of goodness.
VINCENT MCNABB

B30
If you want a golden rule that will
fit everybody, this is it: Have
nothing in your houses that you do
not know to be useful, or believe to
be beautiful.
WILLIAM MORRIS

B31
Beauty may have fair leaves, yet
bitter fruit.
ENGLISH PROVERB

B32
The crow thinketh her own birds
fairest in the wood.
ENGLISH PROVERB

B33
Beauty without virtue is a flower
without perfume.
FRENCH PROVERB

B34
The saying that beauty is but skin
deep is but a skin-deep saying.
HERBERT SPENCER

BEHAVIOUR
(See also COURTESY and
MANNERS)

B35
The sum of behaviour is to retain a
man's own dignity, without
intruding upon the liberty of
others.
FRANCIS BACON

B36
We are turning out machines that
act like men, and men that act like
machines.
ERICH FROMM

B37
The quality of moral behaviour
varies in inverse ratio to the
number of human beings involved.
ALDOUS HUXLEY

B38
Would to God we had behaved
ourselves well in this world, even
for one day.
THOMAS À KEMPIS

B39
Strive to be like a well-regulated
watch, of pure gold, with open
face, busy hands and full of good
works.
DAVID NEWQUIST

BELIEF
(See also CONVICTION and
FAITH)

B40
A belief is not true because it is
useful.
HENRI FRÉDÉRIC AMIEL

B41
If you believe in the Gospel what
you like, and reject what you don't
like, it is not the Gospel you
believe, but yourself.
ST. AUGUSTINE OF HIPPO

B42
Understanding is the reward of
faith. Therefore seek not to
understand that you may believe,
but believe that you may
understand.
ST. AUGUSTINE OF HIPPO

B43
Man is what he believes.
ANTON CHEKHOV

B44

The point of having an open mind, like having an open mouth, is to close it on something solid.

G. K. CHESTERTON

B45

He that will believe only what he can fully comprehend must have a very long head or a very short creed.

CHARLES CALEB COLTON

B46

Belief consists in accepting the affirmations of the soul; unbelief in denying them.

RALPH WALDO EMERSON

B47

You never know how much you really believe anything until its truth or falsehood becomes a matter of life and death to you.

C. S. LEWIS

B48

Believing in God means getting down on your knees.

MARTIN LUTHER

B49

It is as absurd to argue men, as to torture them, into believing.

JOHN HENRY NEWMAN

B50

There are three roads to belief: reason, habit, revelation.

BLAISE PASCAL

B51

Believe not all that you see nor half what you hear.

ENGLISH PROVERB

B52

To believe means to recognise that we must wait until the veil shall be removed. Unbelief prematurely unveils itself.

EUGEN ROSENSTOCK-HUESSY

BEREAVEMENT

(See also DEATH and GRIEF)

B53

The true way to mourn the dead is to take care of the living who belong to them.

EDMUND BURKE

B54

The house of mourning teaches charity and wisdom.

ST. JOHN CHRYSOSTOM

B55

A deep plunge into the waters of sorrow is the hopefullest way of getting through them on one's daily road of life again. No one can help another very much in these crises of life; but love and sympathy count for something.

THOMAS HENRY HUXLEY

B56

A man's dying is more the survivors' affair than his own.

THOMAS MANN

B57

You cannot prevent the birds of sorrow from flying over your head, but you can prevent them from building nests in your hair.

CHINESE PROVERB

B58

Those who live in the Lord never see each other for the last time.

GERMAN PROVERB

B59

Ah, why should we wear black for the guests of God.

JOHN RUSKIN

B60

But, oh, for the touch of a vanished hand,
And the sound of a voice that is still!

ALFRED, LORD TENNYSON

BIBLE
(See also SCRIPTURE)

B61
In the Old Testament the New lies hidden, in the New Testament the Old is laid open.

ST. AUGUSTINE OF HIPPO

B62
In the twentieth century our highest praise is to call the Bible 'the World's Best-Seller'. And it has come to be more and more difficult to say whether we think it is a best-seller because it is great, or vice versa.

D. BOORSTIN

B63
The Bible is a window in this prison-world, through which we may look into eternity.

T. DWIGHT

B64
The word of God is in the Bible as the soul is in the body.

P. T. FORSYTH

B65
What you bring away from the Bible depends to some extent on what you carry to it.

OLIVER WENDELL HOLMES

B66
Lay hold on the Bible until the Bible lays hold on you.

WILLIAM H. HOUGHTON

B67
Men do not reject the Bible because it contradicts itself but because it contradicts them.

E. PAUL HOVEY

B68
England has two books, the Bible and Shakespeare. England made Shakespeare but the Bible made England.

VICTOR HUGO

B69
If a man's Bible is coming apart, it is an indication that he himself is fairly well put together.

JAMES JENNINGS

B70
The Bible is an inexhaustible fountain of all truths. The existence of the Bible is the greatest blessing which humanity ever experienced.

IMMANUEL KANT

B71
If thou knewest the whole Bible by heart, and the sayings of all the philosophers, what would it profit thee without the love of God and without grace?

THOMAS À KEMPIS

B72
The Bible is alive, it speaks to me; it has feet, it runs after me; it has hands, it lays hold on me.

MARTIN LUTHER

B73
The Bible was written for a man with a head upon his shoulders.

MARTIN LUTHER

B74
One of the many divine qualities of the Bible is this, that it does not yield its secrets to the irreverent and censorious.

J. I. PACKER

B75
We must not only pause to reflect upon passages from the Bible, but upon 'slices of life', too, relating them together, and to the will of the Risen Christ for us.

MICHEL QUOIST

B76
If a man is not familiar with the Bible, he has suffered a loss which he had better make all possible haste to correct.

THEODORE ROOSEVELT

21

B77
We need never tremble *for* the word of God, though we may tremble *at* it and the demands which it makes upon our faith and courage.
WILLIAM ROBERTSON SMITH

B78
When you have read the Bible, you will know it is the word of God, because you will have found it the key to your own heart, your own happiness and your own duty.
WOODROW WILSON

BIGOTRY
(See also SPIRITUAL BLINDNESS)

B79
Wisdom never has made a bigot, but learning has.
JOSH BILLINGS

B80
Bigotry may be roughly defined as the anger of men who have no opinions.
G. K. CHESTERTON

B81
The mind of a bigot is like the pupil of the eye; the more light you pour upon it, the more it will contract.
OLIVER WENDELL HOLMES

B82
The experience of many ages proves that men may be ready to fight to the death, and to persecute without pity, for a religion whose creed they do not understand, and whose precepts they habitually disobey.
THOMAS B. MACAULAY

B83
Bigotry is the infliction of our own unproved first principles on others, and treating others with scorn or hatred for not accepting them.
JOHN HENRY NEWMAN

B84
Men never do evil so completely and cheerfully as when they do it from religious conviction.
BLAISE PASCAL

B85
No physician can cure the blind in mind.
JEWISH PROVERB

B86
If we believe absurdities we shall commit atrocities.
FRANÇOIS MARIE VOLTAIRE

BIRTH

B87
Those who are born drive out those who preceded them. But there, in the hereafter, we shall all live on together. There will be no successors there, for neither will there be departures.
ST. AUGUSTINE OF HIPPO

B88
If you grieve for the dead, mourn also for those who are born into the world; for as the one thing is of nature, so is the other too of nature.
ST. JOHN CHRYSOSTOM

B89
Birth is the beginning of death.
THOMAS FULLER

B90
Our birth made us mortal, our death will make us immortal.
ENGLISH PROVERB

B91
He who is born, yells; he who dies is silent.
RUSSIAN PROVERB

BISHOP
(See also CLERGY)

B92
'For you, I am Bishop,' said St.

Augustine to his people, 'but with you, I am a Christian. The first is an office accepted, the second a grace received; one a danger, the other safety. If then I am gladder by far to be redeemed with you than I am to be placed over you, I shall, as the Lord commanded, be more completely your servant.'

ST. AUGUSTINE OF HIPPO

B93
Whoever is sent by the Master to run his house, we ought to receive him as we would receive the Master himself. It is obvious, therefore, that we ought to regard the bishop as we would the Lord himself.

ST. IGNATIUS OF ANTIOCH

B94
The bishop is the chief of the priests . . . For he ordains priests and deacons. He has power over all ranks of the clergy; he points out what each one should do.

ST. ISIDORE OF SEVILLE

B95
To be a bishop (sacerdos) is much, to deserve to be one is more.

ST. JEROME

B96
A bishop should die preaching.

JOHN JEWEL

B97
The very conception of Israel or the Church as a flock involves the institution of pastoral rule and oversight; the flock must have shepherds who rule it and feed it under the ultimate supervision of the Chief Shepherd himself.

ALAN RICHARDSON

B98
Now hear an allusion: a mitre, you know, is divided above, but united below. If this you consider, our emblem is right; the bishops divide, but the clergy unite.

JONATHAN SWIFT

BLASPHEMY

B99
Blasphemy itself could not survive religion; if anyone doubts that, let him try to blaspheme Odin.

G. K. CHESTERTON

B100
There is nothing worse than blasphemy.

ST. JOHN CHRYSOSTOM

B101
All great truths begin as blasphemies.

GEORGE BERNARD SHAW

BLESSING

B102
Our real blessings often appear to us in the shape of pains, losses and disappointments; but let us have patience, and we soon shall see them in their proper figures.

JOSEPH ADDISON

B103
Blessedness consists in the accomplishment of our desires, and in our having only regular desires.

ST. AUGUSTINE OF HIPPO

B104
Prosperity is the blessing of the Old Testament; adversity is the blessing of the New.

FRANCIS BACON

B105
Reflect upon your present blessings, of which every man has many; not on your past misfortunes, of which all men have some.

CHARLES DICKENS

B106
Never undertake anything for which you wouldn't have the courage to ask the blessings of heaven.
GEORGE C. LICHTENBERG

B107
It is not God's way that great blessings should descend without the sacrifice first of great sufferings.
JOHN HENRY NEWMAN

B108
Blessings ever wait on virtuous deeds.
ENGLISH PROVERB

B109
Blessings we enjoy daily, and for the most of them, because they be so common, men forget to pay their praises. But let not us, because it is a sacrifice so pleasing to him who still protects us, and gives us flowers, and showers, and meat and content.
IZAAK WALTON

B110
The more we count the blessings we have, the less we crave the luxuries we haven't.
WILLIAM A. WARD

BLINDNESS, SPIRITUAL
(See also BIGOTRY, DARKNESS and LIGHT)

B111
Blind men should judge no colours.
JOHN HEYWOOD

B112
The devil is ready to put out men's eyes that are content willing to wax blind.
SIR THOMAS MORE

B113
None so blind as those who won't see.
ENGLISH PROVERB

B114
When the blind man carries the banner, woe to those who follow.
FRENCH PROVERB

BLOOD

B115
Let us fix our gaze on the blood of Christ and realise how precious it is to the Father, seeing that it was poured out for our salvation.
POPE ST. CLEMENT I

B116
Human blood is all of one colour.
THOMAS FULLER

B117
Blood is thicker than water.
ENGLISH PROVERB

B118
It is His 'blood', the symbol of the laying down of His life, which can cleanse us from our sins today.
JOHN R. W. STOTT

B119
We multiply whenever we are mown down by you; the blood of Christians is seed.
QUINTUS TERTULLIAN

BODY AND SOUL
(See also WHOLENESS)

B120
Despise the flesh, for it passes away; be solicitous for your soul which will never die.
ST. BASIL

B121
The body is a vital source of gratification which we ignore or dismiss only at the risk of violating our integrity.
JACK DOMINIAN

B122
We take excellent care of our bodies, which we have for only a lifetime; yet we let our souls shrivel, which we will have for eternity.

BILLY GRAHAM

B123
The soul, like the body, lives by what it feeds on.

JOSIAH GILBERT HOLLAND

B124
Even a cursory reading of the New Testament leaves a convincing impression that Jesus was typically Hebrew in his view of man: he did not divide man into body and soul, but he saw him as a whole person.

FRANCIS MACNUTT

B125
The body is sooner dressed than the soul.

ENGLISH PROVERB

B126
What soap is for the body, tears are for the soul.

JEWISH PROVERB

B127
Conscience is the voice of the soul, as the passions are the voice of the body. No wonder they often contradict each other.

JEAN JACQUES ROUSSEAU

B128
Body and soul are twins: God only knows which is which.

CHARLES A. SWINBURNE

B129
Body and soul are not two substances but one. They are man becoming aware of himself in two different ways.

C. F. VON WEIZSACKER

BOREDOM

B130
We are seldom tiresome to ourselves.

SAMUEL JOHNSON

B131
One cure for boredom is to forget yourself through activities which bring you in touch with people and ideas outside yourself.

BLANCHE MCKEOUN

B132
The average male gets his living by such depressing devices that boredom becomes a sort of natural state to him.

HENRY L. MENCKEN

B133
Is not life a hundred times too short for us to bore ourselves.

FRIEDRICH NIETZSCHE

B134
There is nothing so insupportable to man as complete repose, without passion, occupation, amusement, care. Then it is that he feels his nothingness, his isolation, his insufficiency, his dependence, his impotence, his emptiness.

BLAISE PASCAL

B135
We often forgive those who bore us, but we cannot forgive those whom we bore.

FRANÇOIS DE LA ROCHEFOUCAULD

B136
The most bored people in life are not the underprivileged but the overprivileged.

FULTON J. SHEEN

BREAD
(See also COMMUNION, HOLY and EUCHARIST)

B137
Therefore you hear that as often as

sacrifice is offered, the Lord's death, the Lord's resurrection, the Lord's ascension and the remission of sins is signified, and will you not take the Bread of Life daily? He who has a wound needs medicine. The wound is that we are under sin; the medicine is the heavenly and venerable Sacrament.

ST. AMBROSE

B138
The question of bread for myself is a material question; but the question of bread for my neighbour, for everybody, is a spiritual and a religious question.

NIKOLAI BERDYAEV

B139
The history of man from the beginning has been the history of the struggle for daily bread.

JESUS DE CASTRO

B140
Here is bread, which strengthens man's heart, and therefore called the staff of life.

MATTHEW HENRY

B141
When God gives us bread, men will supply the butter.

YIDDISH PROVERB

B142
Bread is worth all, it is the staff of life.

ENGLISH PROVERB

B143
He who turns up his nose at his work quarrels with his bread and butter.

CHARLES H. SPURGEON

BROKENNESS

B144
God can never make us wine if we object to the fingers he uses to crush us with. If God would only use his own fingers, and make us broken bread and poured out wine in a special way! But when he uses someone whom we dislike, or some set of circumstances to which we said we would never submit, and makes those the crushers, we object.

OSWALD CHAMBERS

B145
God creates out of nothing. Therefore until a man is nothing, God can make nothing out of him.

MARTIN LUTHER

B146
Broken bones well set become stronger.

ENGLISH PROVERB

B147
We must be broken into life.

CHARLES E. RAVEN

B148
Brokenness is not revival; it is a vital and indispensable step toward it.

ARTHUR WALLIS

B149
How else but through a broken heart may the Lord Christ enter in.

OSCAR WILDE

BROTHERHOOD
(See also COMMUNITY)

B150
Men became what they are, sons of God, by becoming what they are, brothers of their brothers.

MARTIN BUBER

B151
The mystic bond of brotherhood makes all men one.

THOMAS CARLYLE

B152
Until you have become really, in actual fact, the brother of

everyone, brotherhood will not come to pass.

FEODOR DOSTOEVSKI

B153
There is no brotherhood of man without the fatherhood of God.

HENRY MARTYN FIELD

B154
If you really believe in the brotherhood of man, and you want to come into its fold, you've got to let everyone else in too.

OSCAR HAMMERSTEIN

B155
It is through fraternity that liberty is saved.

VICTOR HUGO

B156
The world has narrowed into a neighbourhood before it has broadened into a brotherhood.

LYNDON B. JOHNSON

B157
Human brotherhood is not just a goal. It is a condition on which our way of life depends.

JOHN F. KENNEDY

B158
The race of mankind would perish from the earth did they cease to aid each other.

SIR WALTER SCOTT

B159
In all my travels the thing that has impressed me most is the universal brotherhood of man – what there is of it.

MARK TWAIN

BUSINESS

B160
The society of money and exploitation has never been charged, so far as I know, with

assuring the triumph of freedom and justice.

ALBERT CAMUS

B161
Do other men for they would do you. That's the true business precept.

CHARLES DICKENS

B162
Make yourself a seller when you are buying, and a buyer when you are selling, and then you will sell and buy justly.

ST. FRANCIS DE SALES

B163
Business is the salt of life.

ENGLISH PROVERB

B164
The buyer needs a hundred eyes, the seller but one.

ITALIAN PROVERB

B165
To my mind the best investment a young man starting out in business could possibly make is to give all his time, all his energies to work, just plain, hard work.

CHARLES M. SCHWAB

B166
I think that there is nothing, not even crime, more opposed to poetry, to philosophy, ay, to life itself than this incessant business.

HENRY DAVID THOREAU

B167
Business underlies everything in our national life, including our spiritual life. Witness the fact that in the Lord's Prayer the first petition is for daily bread. No one can worship God or love his neighbour on an empty stomach.

WOODROW WILSON

CAPITALISM
(See also BUSINESS)

C1
All the denominations have fallen prey to the capitalist machine. With what remnant of moral authority can we demand structural change if our own institutes are linked to the old structures?

HELDER CAMARA

C2
What horror has the world come to when it uses profit as the prime incentive in human progress, and competition as the supreme law of economics?

HELDER CAMARA

C3
The inherent vice of capitalism is the unequal sharing of blessings, the inherent vice of socialism is the equal sharing of miseries.

SIR WINSTON CHURCHILL

C4
The fear of capitalism has compelled socialism to widen freedom, and the fear of socialism has compelled capitalism to increase equality.

WILL DURANT

C5
Capital as such is not evil; it is its wrong use that is evil.

MOHANDAS GANDHI

C6
It is just that any man who does service to society and increases the general wealth should himself have a due share of the increased public riches, provided always that he respects the laws of God and the rights of his neighbour.

POPE PIUS XI

C7
Under capitalism man exploits man; under socialism the reverse is true.

POLISH PROVERB

CATHOLIC

C8
The Church has four marks, being one, holy, catholic or universal, and strong or lasting.

ST. THOMAS AQUINAS

C9
For the whole Church which is throughout the whole world possesses one and the same faith.

ST. IRENAEUS

C10
The fact of the missions reveals the Church's faith in herself as the catholic unity of mankind.

J. C. MURRAY

C11
It seems to me that catholicity is not only one of the notes of the Church, but, according to the divine purposes, one of its securities.

JOHN HENRY NEWMAN

C12
True catholicity is commensurate with the wants of the human mind; but persons are often to be found who are surprised that they cannot persuade all men to follow them, and cannot destroy dissent, by preaching a portion of the divine system, instead of the whole of it.

JOHN HENRY NEWMAN

C13
Locality, nationality, particularity are essential marks of the universal Church; the local congregation is the embodiment at a given place and time of the Church of all the world.

ALAN RICHARDSON

CHANGE
(See also REFORM)

C14
All great changes are irksome to the human mind, especially those which are attended with great dangers and uncertain effects.
JOHN ADAMS

C15
We can change, slowly and steadily, if we set our will to it.
ROBERT H. BENSON

C16
We must all obey the great law of change. It is the most powerful law of nature.
EDMUND BURKE

C17
He who shall introduce into public affairs the principles of primitive Christianity will change the face of the world.
BENJAMIN FRANKLIN

C18
There is danger in reckless change; but greater danger in blind conservation.
HENRY GEORGE

C19
There is nothing permanent except change.
HERACLITUS

C20
In a higher world it is otherwise; but here below to live is to change, and to be perfect is to have changed often.
JOHN HENRY NEWMAN

C21
The more change, the more of the same old thing.
FRENCH PROVERB

C22
Those who cannot change their minds cannot change anything.
GEORGE BERNARD SHAW

CHARACTER
(See also PERSONALITY)

C23
Character is better than ancestry, and personal conduct is of more importance than the highest parentage.
DR. BARNARDO

C24
At death, if at any time, we see ourselves as we are, and display our true characters.
ROBERT H. BENSON

C25
Just as good literature and good art raise and ennoble character, so bad literature and bad art degrade it.
DONALD COGGAN

C26
A man is what he thinks about all day long.
RALPH WALDO EMERSON

C27
A character, no more than a fence, can be strengthened by whitewash.
PAUL FROST

C28
The discipline of desire is the background of character.
JOHN LOCKE

C29
Character is what you are in the dark.
DWIGHT L. MOODY

C30
Reputation is what men and women think of us. Character is what God and the angels know of us.
THOMAS PAINE

C31
You cannot carve rotten wood.
CHINESE PROVERB

C32
A man never shows his own character so plainly as by the way

he describes another's.

JEAN PAUL RICHTER

C33

Men best show their character in trifles, where they are not on their guard.

ARTHUR SCHOPENHAUER

C34

Character is not in the mind. It is in the will.

FULTON J. SHEEN

C35

Character is a by-product, it is produced in the great manufacture of daily duty.

WOODROW WILSON

CHARITY
(See also LOVE of NEIGHBOUR)

C36

Charity is the form, mover, mother and root of all the virtues.

ST. THOMAS AQUINAS

C37

Charity is that with which no man is lost, and without which no man is saved.

ST. ROBERT BELLARMINE

C38

No sound ought to be heard in the Church but the healing voice of Christian charity.

EDMUND BURKE

C39

Charity is the pure gold which makes us rich in eternal wealth.

JEAN PIERRE CAMUS

C40

Charity begins at home, and justice begins next door.

CHARLES DICKENS

C41

This is charity, to do all, all that we can.

JOHN DONNE

C42

To love our neighbour in charity is to love God in man.

ST. FRANCIS DE SALES

C43

Perhaps with charity one shouldn't think. Charity like love should be blind.

GRAHAM GREENE

C44

All other gifts of God and works of man are common to good and bad, to the elect and the reprobate, but the gift of charity belongs only to the good and the elect.

WALTER HILTON

C45

True charity means returning good for evil – always.

MARY MAZZARELLO

C46

He who has charity is far from all sin.

POLYCARP

C47

Charity and pride do both feed the poor.

ENGLISH PROVERB

C48

It is certain that God cannot, will not, never did, reject a charitable man in his greatest needs and in his most passionate prayers; for God himself is love, and every degree of charity that dwells in us is the participation of the Divine Nature.

JEREMY TAYLOR

CHASTITY
(See also MODESTY and PURITY)

C49

Do not say that you have chaste minds if you have unchaste eyes, because an unchaste eye is the

messenger of an unchaste heart.
ST. AUGUSTINE OF HIPPO

C50
The essence of chastity is not the suppression of lust, but the total orientation of one's life towards a goal. Without such a goal, chastity is bound to become ridiculous. Chastity is the sine qua non of lucidity and concentration.
DIETRICH BONHOEFFER

C51
To be chaste is to have the body in the keeping of the heart. Their divorce is the one thing which in the end makes unchastity.
FRANCIS H. BRADLEY

C52
Chastity is the longed for house of Christ and the earthly heaven of the heart.
ST. JOHN CLIMACUS

C53
Vigilance and prayer are the safeguards of chastity.
JEAN BAPTISTE DE LA SALLE

C54
If anyone is able to persevere in chastity to the honour of the flesh of the Lord, let him do so in all humility.
ST. IGNATIUS OF ANTIOCH

C55
The virtue of chastity does not mean that we are insensible to the urge of concupiscence, but that we subordinate it to reason and the law of grace, by striving wholeheartedly after what is noblest in human and Christian life.
POPE PIUS XII

C56
We Christians regard a stain upon our chastity as more dreadful than any punishment, or even than death itself.
QUINTUS TERTULLIAN

CHEERFULNESS
(See also CONTENTMENT, HAPPINESS and JOY)

C57
Cheerfulness and content are great beautifiers, and are famous preservers of good looks.
CHARLES DICKENS

C58
Cheerfulness is among the most laudable virtues. It gains you the good will and friendship of others. It blesses those who practise it and those upon whom it is bestowed.
B. C. FORBES

C59
A cheerful look makes a dish a feast.
GEORGE HERBERT

C60
Christian cheerfulness is that modest, hopeful and peaceful joy which springs from charity and is protected by patience.
WILLIAM ULLATHORNE

C61
Cheerfulness in most cheerful people is the rich and satisfying result of strenuous discipline.
EDWIN PERCY WHIPPLE

CHILDREN
(See also FAMILY)

C62
I cannot bear the crying of children, but when my child cries, I don't hear.
ANTON CHEKHOV

C63
Children are our most valuable natural resource.
HERBERT HOOVER

C64
One laugh of a child will make the holiest day more sacred still.
ROBERT G. INGERSOLL

C65
You can learn many things from children. How much patience you have, for instance.
FRANKLIN P. JONES

C66
Children have more need of models than of critics.
JOSEPH JOUBERT

C67
The one thing children wear out faster than shoes is parents.
JOHN PLOMP

C68
Children should be seen and not heard.
ENGLISH PROVERB

C69
Children suck the mother when they are young, and the father when they are old.
ENGLISH PROVERB

C70
The best brought-up children are those who have seen their parents as they are. Hypocrisy is not the parents' first duty.
GEORGE BERNARD SHAW

C71
Children are very adept at comprehending modern statistics. When they say, 'Everyone else is allowed to,' it is usually based on a survey of one.
PAUL SWEENEY

C72
As the twig is bent the tree inclines.
PUBLIUS VIRGIL

C73
Give me a child for the first seven years, and you may do what you like with him afterwards.
FRANCIS XAVIER

C74
Children can forgive their parents for being wrong, but weakness sends them elsewhere for strength.
LEONTINE YOUNG

CHOICE
(See also FREE WILL)

C75
The strongest principle of growth lies in human choice.
GEORGE ELIOT

C76
In darkness there is no choice. It is light that enables us to see the differences between things; and it is Christ who gives us light.
AUGUSTUS W. HARE

C77
When you have to make a choice and don't make it, that is in itself a choice.
WILLIAM JAMES

C78
The power of choosing good or evil is within the reach of all.
ORIGEN OF ALEXANDRIA

CHRISTIAN
(See also DISCIPLESHIP)

C79
All diseases of Christians are to be ascribed to demons.
ST. AUGUSTINE OF HIPPO

C80
A Christian is someone who shares the sufferings of God in the world.
DIETRICH BONHOEFFER

C81
If you were arrested for being a Christian, would there be enough evidence to convict you?
DAVID OTIS FULLER

C82
Being a Christian is more than just
an instantaneous conversion – it is
a daily process whereby you grow
to be more and more like Christ.
BILLY GRAHAM

C83
Christian life is the life of Christ in
man and man in Christ.
ROMANO GUARDINI

C84
A Christian is not his own master,
since all his time belongs to God.
ST. IGNATIUS OF ANTIOCH

C85
To be a Christian is the great thing,
not merely to seem one. And
somehow or other those please the
world most who please Christ least.
ST. JEROME

C86
A true Christian may be almost
defined as one who has a ruling
sense of God's presence within
him.
JOHN HENRY NEWMAN

C87
To be like Christ is to be a
Christian.
WILLIAM PENN

C88
The Christian should resemble a
fruit tree, not a Christmas tree!
For the gaudy decorations of a
Christmas tree are only tied on,
whereas fruit grows on a fruit tree.
JOHN R. W. STOTT

C89
No one is wise, no one is faithful,
no one excels in dignity, but the
Christian; and no one is a Christian
but he who perseveres even to the
end.
QUINTUS TERTULLIAN

CHRISTIANITY

C90
Two things about the Christian
religion must surely be clear to
anybody with eyes in his head. One
is that men cannot do without it;
the other, that they cannot do with
it as it is.
MATTHEW ARNOLD

C91
The essential fact of Christianity is
that God thought all men worth the
sacrifice of his Son.
WILLIAM BARCLAY

C92
Christianity has died many times
and risen again; for it had a God
who knew the way out of the grave.
G. K. CHESTERTON

C93
He who begins by loving
Christianity better than truth will
proceed by loving his own sect or
church better than Christianity and
end in loving himself better than
all.
SAMUEL TAYLOR COLERIDGE

C94
The essence of Christianity is
simply and solely belief in the
unification of the world in God
through the Incarnation.
P. TEILHARD DE CHARDIN

C95
Christianity is completed Judaism,
or it is nothing.
BENJAMIN DISRAELI

C96
The great part of Christianity is
wholeheartedly to want to become
a Christian.
DESIDERIUS ERASMUS

C97
It is unnatural for Christianity to be
popular.
BILLY GRAHAM

C98

There is no more profound or more dangerous enemy to Christianity than anything which shrinks it and makes it narrow.

ABBÉ HUVELIN

C99

Christianity is the highest perfection of humanity.

SAMUEL JOHNSON

C100

Organised Christianity has probably done more to retard the ideals that were its founder's than any other agency in the world.

RICHARD LE GALLIENNE

C101

Christianity, if false, is of no importance, and if true, of infinite importance. The one thing it cannot be is moderately important.

C. S. LEWIS

C102

True Christianity is love in action.

DAVID O. MCKAY

C103

Christianity is more than a doctrine. It is Christ Himself, living in those whom He has united to Himself in One Mystical Body.

THOMAS MERTON

C104

For a religion to be true it must have knowledge of our nature. It must know it greatness and its meaning, and the cause of both. What religion but Christianity knows that?

BLAISE PASCAL

C105

Christianity is like electricity. It cannot enter a person unless it can pass through.

RICHARD C. RAINES

C106

Christ cannot live his life today in this world without our mouth, without our eyes, without our going and coming, without our heart. When we love, it is Christ loving through us. This is Christianity.

LEON JOSEPH SUENENS

C107

The primary declaration of Christianity is not 'This do!' but 'This happened!'

EVELYN UNDERHILL

C108

Christianity can be condensed into four words: admit, submit, commit and transmit.

SAMUEL WILBERFORCE

CHRISTMAS
(See also INCARNATION)

C109

The fact of Jesus' coming is the final and unanswerable proof that God cares.

WILLIAM BARCLAY

C110

The character of the Creator cannot be less than the highest He has created, and the highest is that babe born to Mary on that first Christmas morning.

A. IAN BURNETT

C111

It is good to be children sometimes, and never better than at Christmas, when its mighty Founder was a child Himself.

CHARLES DICKENS

C112

Christmas is the season for kindling the fire of hospitality in the hall, the genial flame of charity in the heart.

WASHINGTON IRVING

C113
To us Christians, the first
Christmas Day is the solstice or
bottleneck of history. Things got
worse till then, ever since we had
lost paradise; things are to get
better since then, till we reach
paradise once more. History is
shaped like an X.
RONALD A. KNOX

C114
You can never truly enjoy
Christmas until you can look up
into the Father's face and tell him
you have received his Christmas
gift.
JOHN R. RICE

C115
The simple shepherds heard the
voice of an angel and found their
Lamb; the wise men saw the light
of a star and found their Wisdom.
FULTON J. SHEEN

C116
Christmas is the day that holds all
time together.
ALEXANDER SMITH

C117
A good many people with houses
half empty on Christmas Eve have
blamed the little innkeeper of
Bethlehem because his place was
full.
ROY L. SMITH

C118
The coming of Christ by way of a
Bethlehem manger seems strange
and stunning. But when we take
him out of the manger and invite
him into our hearts, then the
meaning unfolds and the
strangeness vanishes.
NEIL C. STRAIT

C119
After all, Christmas is but a big
love affair to remove the wrinkles
of the year with kindly
remembrances.
JOHN WANAMAKER

CHURCH
(See also COMMUNION OF
SAINTS)
C120
He cannot have God for his father
who refuses to have the Church for
his mother.
ST. AUGUSTINE OF HIPPO

C121
The Church of Christ is not an
institution; it is a new life with
Christ and in Christ, guided by the
Holy Spirit.
SERGIUS BULGAKOV

C122
Every man may err, but not the
whole gathered together; for the
whole hath a promise.
ROBERT H. BENSON

C123
What matters in the Church is not
religion but the form of Christ, and
its taking form amidst a band of
men.
DIETRICH BONHOEFFER

C124
Wherever we see the Word of God
purely preached and heard, there a
Church of God exists, even if it
swarms with many faults.
JOHN CALVIN

C125
The purpose of the Church in the
world is to be the worshipping and
witnessing spearhead of all that is
in accordance with the will of God
as it has been revealed in Jesus
Christ.
DONALD COGGAN

C126
The Church is the family of God. It

is seen in miniature in each family.
JOHN FERGUSON

C127
The Church of Christ is the world's
only social hope and the sole
promise of world peace.
SIR DOUGLAS HAIG

C128
The Church is in Christ as Eve was
in Adam.
RICHARD HOOKER

C129
God pity the nation whose factory
chimneys rise higher than her
church spires.
JOHN KELMAN

C130
The Church is the only institution
in the world that has lower
entrance requirements than those
for getting on a bus.
WILLIAM LAROE

C131
God never intended his Church to
be a refrigerator in which to
preserve perishable piety. He
intended it to be an incubator in
which to hatch converts.
F. LINCICOME

C132
The Church is failing in her mission
if her dual conception of sin and
joy are defective and inadequate.
MARTYN LLOYD-JONES

C133
It may take a crucified Church to
bring a crucified Christ before the
eyes of the world.
WILLIAM E. ORCHARD

C134
The Church is an anvil that has
worn out many hammers.
ENGLISH PROVERB

C135
He who is near the church is often
far from God.
FRENCH PROVERB

C136
The Church is not a finished,
solidly built and furnished house,
in which all that changes is the
successive generations who live in
it. The Church is a living reality
which has had a history of its own
and still has one.
KARL RAHNER

C137
The Christian Church is the one
organisation in the world that exists
purely for the benefit of
non-members.
WILLIAM TEMPLE

C138
Where three are gathered together,
there is a Church, even though they
be laymen.
QUINTUS TERTULLIAN

CITIZEN
(See also CIVIC DUTY)

C139
The health of a democratic society
may be measured by the quality of
functions performed by private
citizens.
ALEXIS DE TOCQUEVILLE

C140
Morality is the very soul of good
citizenship.
JOHN IRELAND

C141
Citizens pay their taxes, and then
they abdicate. They have lost their
skills as citizens; they have
contracted them out to public
employees.
E. S. SAVAS

C142
Whatever makes men good

Christians makes them good citizens.

DANIEL WEBSTER

CIVIC DUTY
(See also CITIZEN)

C143
No personal consideration should stand in the way of performing a public duty.

ULYSSES S. GRANT

C144
When a man assumes a public trust, he should consider himself as public property.

THOMAS JEFFERSON

C145
No better citizen is there, whether in time of peace or war, than the Christian who is mindful of his duty; but such a one should be ready to suffer all things, even death itself, rather than abandon the cause of God or of the Church.

POPE LEO XIII

C146
The worth of a state, in the long run, is the worth of the individuals composing it.

JOHN STUART MILL

CIVILISATION
(See also CULTURE)

C147
The test of every civilisation is the point below which the weakest and most unfortunate are not allowed to fall.

HERBERT HENRY ASQUITH

C148
Religion is the main determining element in the formation of a culture or civilisation.

HILAIRE BELLOC

C149
Civilisation in the best sense merely means the full authority of the human spirit over all externals.

G. K. CHESTERTON

C150
Intelligent discontent is the mainspring of civilisation.

EUGENE V. DEBS

C151
No true civilisation can be expected permanently to continue which is not based on the great principles of Christianity.

TYRON EDWARDS

C152
The true test of civilisation is, not the census, nor the size of cities, nor the crops, but the kind of man that the country turns out.

RALPH WALDO EMERSON

C153
What has destroyed every previous civilisation has been the tendency to the unequal distribution of wealth and power.

HENRY GEORGE

C154
The true civilisation is where every man gives to every other every right that he claims for himself.

ROBERT G. INGERSOLL

C155
We must each of us be humbled by this fresh wind of the Spirit that has come to lift us up from the nadir our civilisation has reached.

GEORGE MacLEOD

C156
What is called Western civilisation is in an advanced stage of decomposition.

MALCOLM MUGGERIDGE

C157
A visitor from Mars could easily pick out the civilised nations. They

have the best implements of war.
HERBERT V. PROCHNOW

C158
Civilisation is always in danger
when those who have never
learned to obey are given the right
to command.
FULTON J. SHEEN

C159
Civilisation is a movement and not
a condition, a voyage and not a
harbour.
ARNOLD TOYNBEE

C160
All that is best in the civilisation of
today is the fruit of Christ's
appearance among men.
DANIEL WEBSTER

CLERGY
(See also BISHOP and
PRIESTHOOD)

C161
Too many clergymen have become
keepers of an aquarium instead of
fishers of men – and often they are
just swiping each other's fish.
M. S. AUGSBURGER

C162
There is not in the universe a more
ridiculous, nor a more
contemptible animal, than a proud
clergyman.
HENRY FIELDING

C163
People expect the clergy to have
the grace of a swan, the friendliness
of a sparrow, the strength of an
eagle, and the night hours of an
owl – and some people expect such
a bird to live on the food of a
canary.
EDWARD JEFFREY

C164
That clergyman soon becomes an
object of contempt who being often

asked out to dinner never refuses
to go.
ST. JEROME

C165
I have always considered a
clergyman as the father of a larger
family than he is able to maintain.
SAMUEL JOHNSON

C166
The greatest clerks be not the
wisest men.
ENGLISH PROVERB

C167
The duty of the clergyman is to
remind people in an eloquent
manner of the existence of God.
JOHN RUSKIN

C168
Popular religion may be summed
up as respect for ecclesiastics.
BARUCH DE SPINOZA

COMFORT
(See also HOPE)

C169
God does not comfort us to make
us comfortable, but to make us
comforters.
JOHN HENRY JOWETT

C170
All human comfort is vain and
short.
THOMAS À KEMPIS

C171
Comfort in tribulation can be
secured only on the sure ground of
faith holding as true the words of
Scripture and the teaching of the
Church.
SIR THOMAS MORE

C172
The comforter's head never aches.
ENGLISH PROVERB

C173
Comfort is better than pride.
FRENCH PROVERB

COMMANDMENTS
(See also LAW)

C174
What else are the laws of God written in our hearts but the very presence of the Holy Ghost?
ST. AUGUSTINE OF HIPPO

C175
No man can break any of the Ten Commandments. He can only break himself against them.
G. K. CHESTERTON

C176
The Ten Commandments, completed by the evangelical precepts of justice and charity, constitute the framework of individual and collective survival.
POPE JOHN XXIII

C177
I am not sure whether ethical absolutes exist. But I am sure that we have to act as if they existed or civilisation perishes.
ARTHUR KOESTLER

C178
The Ten Commandments, when written on tablets of stone and given to man did not then first begin to belong to him; they had their existence in man and lay as a seed hidden in the form and make of his soul.
WILLIAM LAW

COMMUNICATION
(See also CONVERSATION, MEDIA and TALK)

C179
The best argument is that which seems merely an explanation.
DALE CARNEGIE

C180
The freedom to communicate also requires in a Christian community not only a response of integrity but one of love.
JACK DOMINIAN

C181
The way from God to a human heart is through a human heart.
SAMUEL GORDON

C182
Good words quench more than a bucket of water.
GEORGE HERBERT

C183
The most immutable barrier in nature is between one man's thoughts and another's.
WILLIAM JAMES

C184
Communication is something so simple and difficult that we can never put it in simple words.
T. S. MATTHEWS

COMMUNION, HOLY
(See also BREAD and EUCHARIST)

C185
A soul can do nothing that is more pleasing to God than to communicate in a state of grace.
ST. ALPHONSUS LIGUORI

C186
We eat the Body of Christ that we may be able to be partakers of eternal life.
ST. AMBROSE

C187
Christ is so united to us in the sacrament of Communion that he acts as if he were ourselves.
MARTIN LUTHER

C188
Holy Communion is the shortest and safest way to heaven.
POPE ST. PIUS X

C189
The heart preparing for Communion should be as a crystal vial filled with clear water in which the least mote of uncleanness will be seen.

ELIZABETH SETON

C190
The bread and wine of Communion are visible, tangible emblems of Christ's body given and blood shed on the cross for our sins.

JOHN R. W. STOTT

C191
The reality of our communion with Christ and in him with one another is the increase of love in our hearts.

WILLIAM TEMPLE

COMMUNION OF SAINTS
(See also CHURCH)

C192
The union of men with God is the union of men with one another.

ST. THOMAS AQUINAS

C193
In God and in his Church there is no difference between living and dead, and all are one in the love of the Father. Even the generations yet to be born are part of this one divine humanity.

SERGIUS BULGAKOV

C194
In that Mystical Body, thanks to the communion of saints, no good can be done, no virtue practised by individual members, without its contributing something also to the salvation of all.

POPE PIUS XII

C195
The primary and full Bride of Christ never is, nor can be, the individual man at prayer, but only this complete organism of all faithful people throughout time and space.

FRIEDRICH VON HUGEL

COMMUNISM

C196
Beware of invoking the fear of Communism as an excuse for avoiding a change in the structures which confine millions of the sons of God in a sub-human condition.

HELDER CAMARA

C197
Communism is the Franciscan movement without the moderating balance of the Church.

G. K. CHESTERTON

C198
Radio talks, pamphlets, pious aspirations are not going to defeat Communism – the only answer to it is a just social order.

JOSEPH FITZSIMMONS

C199
One does not have to keep bad governments in to keep Communists out.

JOHN K. GALBRAITH

C200
Society cannot leap into Communism from Capitalism without going through a socialist stage of development. Socialism is the first stage to Communism.

NIKITA S. KHRUSHCHEV

C201
Communism is not love. Communism is a hammer which we use to crush the enemy. We are always revolutionists and never reformers.

MAO TSE-TUNG

C202
One of the analogies between Communism and Roman Catholicism is that only the

'educated' are completely orthodox.

GEORGE ORWELL

C203
Socialism is workable only in heaven where it isn't needed, and in hell where they've got it.

CECIL PALMER

C204
Communism is by its nature anti-religious. It considers religion as 'the opiate of the people' because the principles of religion which speak of a life beyond the grave dissuade the proletariat from the dream of a soviet paradise which is of this world.

POPE PIUS XI

C205
The Communist Party cannot be neutral towards religion. It stands for science, and all religion is opposed to science.

JOSEPH STALIN

C206
So we, who are united in mind and soul, have no hesitation about sharing property. All is commun among us – except our wives.

QUINTUS TERTULLIAN

C207
Communism is an ideal that can be achieved only when people cease to be selfish and greedy and when everyone receives according to his needs from communal production. But that is a long way off.

MARSHAL TITO

C208
Communism is a religion and only as we see it as a religion, though a secular religion, will we understand its power.

ELTON TRUEBLOOD

COMMUNITY
(See also FAMILY)

C209
Community is viable if it is the outgrowth of a deep involvement in a purpose which is other than, or above, that of being a community.

BRUNO BETTELHEIM

C210
The individual man himself does not have the essence of man in himself as a moral or a thinking being. The essence of man is found only in the community, in the unity of man with man.

LUDWIG FEUERBACH

C211
The community stagnates without the impulse of the individual. The impulse dies away without the sympathy of the community.

WILLIAM JAMES

C212
Man, the social being, naturally, and in the sense helplessly, depends on his communities. Sundered from them, he has neither worth nor wit, but wanders in waste places, and, when he returns finds the lonely house of his individual life empty, swept, and garnished.

JOSIAH ROYCE

C213
Community life brings a painful revelation of our limitations, weaknesses and darkness, the unexpected discovery of the monsters within us is hard to accept.

JEAN VANIER

COMPASSION
(See also PITY)

C214
Compassion will cure more sins

than condemnation.
HENRY WARD BEECHER

C215
We must learn to regard people less in the light of what they do or omit to do, and more in the light of what they suffer.
DIETRICH BONHOEFFER

C216
Man may dismiss compassion from his heart, but God will never.
WILLIAM COWPER

C217
God tempers the wind to the shorn lamb.
HENRI ESTIENNE

C218
Man is never nearer the Divine than in his compassionate moments.
JOSEPH H. HERTZ

C219
The existence of compassion in man proves the existence of compassion in God.
CHRISTOPHER HOLLIS

C220
Though our saviour's Passion is over, his compassion is not.
WILLIAM PENN

C221
One heart is mirror to another.
JEWISH PROVERB

C222
The compassion that you see in the kind-hearted is God's compassion: he has given it to them to protect the helpless.
SRI RAMAKRISHNA

C223
Compassion is the basis of all morality.
ARTHUR SCHOPENHAUER

C224
When a man has compassion for others, God has compassion for him.
THE TALMUD

COMPROMISE

C225
All government – indeed, every human benefit and enjoyment, every virtue and every prudent act – is founded on compromise and barter.
EDMUND BURKE

C226
An appeaser is one who feeds a crocodile – hoping it will eat him last.
SIR WINSTON CHURCHILL

C227
Everything yields. The very glaciers are viscous, or regulate into conformity, and the stiffest patriots falter and compromise.
RALPH WALDO EMERSON

C228
Life cannot subsist in society but by reciprocal concessions.
SAMUEL JOHNSON

C229
Better bend than break.
SCOTTISH PROVERB

CONCEIT
(See also PRIDE and VANITY)

C230
Conceit is God's gift to little men.
BRUCE BARTON

C231
Conceit is the most incurable disease that is known to the human soul.
HENRY WARD BEECHER

C232
The world tolerates conceit from

those who are successful, but not from anybody else.

JOHN BLAKE

C233

Talk to a man about himself and he will listen for hours.

BENJAMIN DISRAELI

C234

I've never any pity for conceited people, because I think they carry their comfort about with them.

GEORGE ELIOT

C235

Failures are usually the most conceited of men.

D. H. LAWRENCE

C236

Conceit may puff a man up, but never prop him up.

JOHN RUSKIN

CONFESSION
(See also RECONCILIATION)

C237

The confession of evil works is the first beginning of good works.

ST. AUGUSTINE OF HIPPO

C238

Daily in one's prayer, with tears and sighs, to confess one's past sins to God; to amend those sins for the future.

ST. BENEDICT

C239

Our brother has been given to us to help us. He hears the confession of our sins in Christ's stead and he forgives our sins in Christ's name.

DIETRICH BONHOEFFER

C240

It is better for a man to confess his sins than to harden his heart.

POPE ST. CLEMENT I

C241

Confession is the first step to repentance.

EDMUND GAYTON

C242

For him who confesses, shams are over and realities have begun.

WILLIAM JAMES

C243

A fault confessed is a new virtue added to a man.

JAMES S. KNOWLES

C244

That which you confess today, you will perceive tomorrow.

COVENTRY PATMORE

C245

Open confession is good for the soul.

SCOTTISH PROVERB

CONFIDENCE
(See also TRUST)

C246

The greater and more persistent your confidence in God, the more abundantly you will receive all that you ask.

ST. ALBERT THE GREAT

C247

Confidence as an outgoing act is directness and courage in meeting the facts of life, trusting them to bring instruction and support to a developing self.

JOHN DEWEY

C248

In sorrow and suffering, go straight to God with confidence, and you will be strengthened, enlightened and instructed.

ST. JOHN OF THE CROSS

C249

Confidence in others' honesty is no light testimony to one's own integrity.

MICHEL DE MONTAIGNE

C250

Confidence is a plant of slow growth.

ENGLISH PROVERB

C251
Confidence begets confidence.
LATIN PROVERB

C252
Our confidence in Christ does not make us lazy, negligent, or careless, but on the contrary it awakens us, urges us on, and makes us active in living righteous lives and doing good. There is no self-confidence to compare with this.
ULRICH ZWINGLI

CONFIRMATION

C253
The Holy Spirit gave at the font all that is needed for innocence: at confirmation he gives an increase for grace, for in this world those who survive through the different stages of life, must walk among dangers and invisible enemies.
FAUSTUS

C254
The bishop . . . after pouring oil and laying his hand on his head shall say: I anoint thee with holy oil in God the Father Almighty and Christ Jesus and the Holy Ghost.
ST. HIPPOLYTUS

C255
As to the anointing of neophytes, it is clear that this cannot be done by any save the bishop.
POPE ST. INNOCENT I

C256
Confirmation is the sacrament of the common priesthood of the laity.
GERALD VANN

CONFLICT

C257
All men have in them an instinct for conflict: at least, all healthy men.
HILAIRE BELLOC

C258
You are but a poor soldier of Christ if you think you can overcome without fighting, and suppose you can have the crown without the conflict.
ST. JOHN CHRYSOSTOM

C259
When one ceases from conflict, whether because he has won, because he has lost, or because he cares no more for the game, the virtue passes out of him.
CHARLES H. COOLEY

C260
I am sure that most of us, looking back, would admit that whatever we have achieved in character we have achieved through conflict.
J. WALLACE HAMILTON

C261
No doubt there are other important things in life besides conflict, but there are not many other things so inevitably interesting. The very saints interest us most when we think of them as engaged in a conflict with the Devil.
ROBERT LYND

CONFORMITY
(See also ORTHODOXY)

C262
We should not conform with human traditions to the extent of setting aside the command of God.
ST. BASIL

C263
For one man who thanks God that he is not as other men there are a thousand to offer thanks that they are as other men, sufficiently as others to escape attention.
JOHN DEWEY

C264
We cannot help conforming ourselves to what we love.
ST. FRANCIS DE SALES

C265
We would know mankind better if we were not so anxious to resemble one another.
JOHANN WOLFGANG VON GOETHE

C266
To deny self is to become a nonconformist. The Bible tells us not to be conformed to this world either physically or intellectually or spiritually.
BILLY GRAHAM

C267
The essence of true holiness consists in conformity to the nature and will of God.
SAMUEL LUCAS

C268
We are half ruined by conformity; but we should be wholly ruined without it.
CHARLES D. WARNER

CONSCIENCE
(See also FREE WILL)
C269
Conscience and reputation are two things. Conscience is due to yourself, reputation to your neighbour.
ST. AUGUSTINE OF HIPPO

C270
Conscience illuminated by the presence of Jesus Christ in the heart must be the guide of every man.
ROBERT H. BENSON

C271
A good conscience is a mine of wealth. And in truth, what greater riches can there be, what thing more sweet than a good conscience?
ST. BERNARD OF CLAIRVAUX

C272
A sleeping pill will never take the place of a clear conscience.
EDDIE CANTOR

C273
Conscience is the royalty and prerogative of every private man.
JOHN DRYDEN

C274
Most of us follow our conscience as we follow a wheelbarrow. We push it in front of us in the direction we want to go.
BILLY GRAHAM

C275
What we call conscience is the voice of Divine love in the deep of our being, desiring union with our will.
J. P. GREAVES

C276
The testimony of a good conscience is the glory of a good man; have a good conscience and thou shalt ever have gladness.
THOMAS À KEMPIS

C277
My conscience is captive to the Word of God.
MARTIN LUTHER

C278
Conscience is nearer to me than any other means of knowledge.
JOHN HENRY NEWMAN

C279
All too often a clear conscience is merely the result of a bad memory.
ANCIENT PROVERB

C280
There is no pillow so soft as a clear conscience.
FRENCH PROVERB

C281
A bad conscience is a snake in one's heart.
YIDDISH PROVERB

C282
Conscience is the voice of the soul, as the passions are the voice of the body. No wonder they often contradict each other.
JEAN JACQUES ROUSSEAU

C283
Conscience warns us as a friend before it punishes us as a judge.
KING STANISLAS I

C284
Labour to keep alive in your breast that little spark of celestial fire called conscience.
GEORGE WASHINGTON

CONSERVATION
(See also ECOLOGY and NATURE)

C285
Such prosperity as we have known it up to the present is the consequence of rapidly spending the planet's irreplaceable capital.
ALDOUS HUXLEY

C286
Government cannot close its eyes to the pollution of waters, to the erosion of soil, to the slashing of forests any more than it can close its eyes to the need for slum clearance and schools.
FRANKLIN D. ROOSEVELT

C287
Man is a complex being; he makes deserts bloom – and lakes die.
GIL STERN

CONTEMPLATION
(See also MEDITATION and MYSTICISM)

C288
The contemplation of God is promised to us as the goal of all our acts and the eternal consummation of all our joys.
ST. AUGUSTINE OF HIPPO

C289
Too late I loved you, O beauty so ancient yet ever new! Too late I loved you! And, behold, you were within me, and I out of myself and there I searched for you.
ST. AUGUSTINE OF HIPPO

C290
If we hope to move beyond the superficialities of our culture – including our religious culture – we must be willing to go down into the recreating silences, into the inner world of contemplation.
RICHARD FOSTER

C291
To live according to the spirit is to think, speak and act according to the virtues that are in the spirit, and not according to the sense and sentiments which are in the flesh.
ST. FRANCIS DE SALES

C292
He that contemplates hath a day without night.
GEORGE HERBERT

C293
Contemplation is nothing else but a secret, peaceful, and loving infusion of God, which, if admitted, will set the soul on fire with the Spirit of love.
ST. JOHN OF THE CROSS

C294
Seek in reading and thou shalt find in meditation; knock in prayer and it shall be opened to thee in contemplation.
ST. JOHN OF THE CROSS

C295
We become contemplatives when God discovers Himself in us.
THOMAS MERTON

C296
The love which we bear to others remains the mark of the authenticity of our contemplation.
ROGER SCHUTZ

C297
The acts of contemplation are four: to seek after God, to find Him, to feel His sacred touch in the soul, and to be united with Him and to enjoy Him.
WILLIAM ULLATHORNE

CONTENTMENT
(See also CHEERFULNESS, HAPPINESS and JOY)

C298
The utmost we can hope for in this world is contentment.
JOSEPH ADDISON

C299
Contentment is a pearl of great price, and whoever procures it at the expense of ten thousand desires makes a wise and a happy purchase.
JOHN BALGUY

C300
True contentment is a real, even an active, virtue – not only affirmative but creative. It is the power of getting out of any situation all there is in it.
G. K. CHESTERTON

C301
I am always content with what happens, for I know that what God chooses is better than what I choose.
EPICTETUS

C302
Those who face that which is actually before them, unburdened by the past, undistracted by the future, these are they who live, who make the best use of their lives; these are those who have found the secret of contentment.
ALBAN GOODIER

C303
It is right to be contented with what we have, but never with what we are.
JAMES MACKINTOSH

C304
Better a handful of dry dates and content therewith than to own the Gate of Peacocks and be kicked in the eye by a broody camel.
ARAB PROVERB

C305
A contented mind is a continual feast.
ENGLISH PROVERB

C306
When we cannot find contentment in ourselves it is useless to seek it elsewhere.
FRANÇOIS DE LA ROCHEFOUCAULD

C307
Contentment with the divine will is the best remedy we can apply to misfortune.
WILLIAM TEMPLE

CONTROVERSY

C308
Controversy, for the most part, disfigures the question it seeks to elucidate.
FREDERICK W. FABER

C309
Controversy equalises fools and wise men in the same way – and the fools know it.
OLIVER WENDELL HOLMES

C310
Nothing dies harder than a
theological difference.
RONALD A. KNOX

C311
Half the controversies in the world
are verbal ones; and could they be
brought to a plain issue, they would
be brought to a prompt
termination.
JOHN HENRY NEWMAN

C312
When men understand each other's
meaning, they see, for the most
part, that controversy is either
superfluous or hopeless.
JOHN HENRY NEWMAN

CONVERSATION
(See also TALK)

C313
The mark of good conversation is
that every member of the company
takes part in it, and that all discuss
the same theme.
JOHN ERSKINE

C314
Be at peace regarding what is said
or done in conversations: for if
good, you have something to praise
God for, and if bad, something in
which to serve God by turning your
heart away from it.
ST. FRANCIS DE SALES

C315
The marvellous thing about good
conversation is that it brings to
birth so many half-realised
thoughts of our own – besides
sowing the seeds of innumerable
other thought-plants.
DAVID GRAYSON

C316
Be humble and gentle in your
conversation; and of few words, I
charge you; but always pertinent
when you speak.
WILLIAM PENN

C317
Though conversing face to face,
their hearts have a thousand miles
between them.
CHINESE PROVERB

C318
What a strange scene if the surge of
conversation could suddenly ebb
like the tide, and show us the real
state of people's minds.
SIR WALTER SCOTT

C319
Ultimately the bond of all
companionship, whether in
marriage or in friendship, is
conversation.
OSCAR WILDE

CONVERSION

C320
Conversion has to materialise in
small actions as well as in great.
ROBERT H. BENSON

C321
The Church is a house with a
hundred gates: and no two men
enter at exactly the same angle.
G. K. CHESTERTON

C322
Conversion may occur in an
instant, but the process of coming
from sinfulness into a new life can
be a long and arduous journey.
CHARLES COLSON

C323
Conversion is but the first step in
the divine life. As long as we live
we should more and more be
turning from all that is evil, and to
all that is good.
TYRON EDWARDS

C324
No inferior form of energy can be
simply converted into a superior
form unless at the same time a

source of higher value lends its support.

CARL GUSTAV JUNG

C325
Every story of conversion is the story of a blessed defeat.

C. S. LEWIS

C326
Knox once remarked that the Church gets on by hook or crook, by the hook of the fisherman and the crook of the shepherd.

ARNOLD LUNN

C327
I went to Africa that I might be able to sin to my heart's content. I was a wild beast on the coast of Africa till the Lord caught and tamed me.

JOHN NEWTON

C328
Nothing is more expensive than a start.

FRIEDRICH NIETZSCHE

C329
Men often mistake their imagination for the promptings of their heart, and believe they are converted the moment they think of conversion.

BLAISE PASCAL

C330
A good beginning makes a good ending.

ENGLISH PROVERB

C331
It is better to begin in the evening than not at all.

ENGLISH PROVERB

C332
For a web begun, God sends thread.

ITALIAN PROVERB

CONVICTION
(See also BELIEF)

C333
Conviction, were it never so excellent, is worthless till it convert itself into conduct.

THOMAS CARLYLE

C334
Never, for sake of peace and quiet, deny your own experience or convictions.

DAG HAMMARSKJOLD

C335
Convictions are the mainsprings of action, the driving powers of life. What a man lives are his convictions.

FRANCIS C. KILLEY

C336
Every man, wherever he goes, is encompassed by a cloud of comforting convictions, which move with him like flies on a summer day.

BERTRAND RUSSELL

C337
As life goes on we discover that certain thoughts sustain us in defeat, or give us victory, whether over ourselves or others, and it is these thoughts, tested by passion, that we call convictions.

W. B. YEATS

COURAGE

C338
Mere physical courage – the absence of fear – simply is not worth calling bravery. It's the bravery of the tiger, not the moral bravery of the man.

ROBERT H. BENSON

C339
Have plenty of courage. God is stronger than the Devil. We are on

the winning side.

JOHN CHAPMAN

C340
Courage is almost a contradiction in terms. It means a strong desire to live taking the form of a readiness to die.

G. K. CHESTERTON

C341
To see what is right, and not to do it, is want of courage.

CONFUCIUS

C342
Most acts of assent require far more courage than most acts of protest, since courage is clearly a readiness to risk self-humiliation.

NIGEL DENNIS

C343
Courage is a virtue only insofar as it is directed by prudence.

FRANÇOIS FENELON

C344
Fear can keep a man out of danger, but courage can support him in it.

THOMAS FULLER

C345
Courage is grace under pressure.

ERNEST HEMINGWAY

C346
Have courage for the great sorrows of life, and patience for the small ones. And when you have laboriously accomplished your daily task, go to sleep in peace. God is awake.

VICTOR HUGO

C347
Courage consists not in hazarding without fear, but being resolutely minded in a just cause.

PLUTARCH

C348
To a brave heart nothing is impossible.

FRENCH PROVERB

C349
It is better to live one day as a lion than a hundred years as a sheep.

ITALIAN PROVERB

C350
Courage consists not in blindly overlooking danger, but in seeing it and conquering it.

JEAN PAUL RICHTER

COURTESY
(See also BEHAVIOUR and MANNERS)

C351
The grace of God is in courtesy.

HILAIRE BELLOC

C352
Nothing is more becoming in a great man than courtesy and forbearance.

MARCUS TULLIUS CICERO

C353
Know, most dearly beloved brother, that courtesy is one of the properties of God, who gives His sun and rain to the just and the unjust by courtesy; and courtesy is the sister of charity, by which hatred is vanquished and love is cherished.

ST. FRANCIS OF ASSISI

C354
There is a politeness of the heart, and it is allied to love. It produces the most agreeable politeness of outward behaviour.

JOHANN WOLFGANG VON GOETHE

C355
Genuine courtesy is a splinter from the true cross.

JOHN ANDREW HOLMES

C356
The habit of courtesy, when once acquired, is almost impossible to get rid of.

ROBERT LYND

C357
Courtesy on one side only lasts not long.
ENGLISH PROVERB

C358
The courteous learns his courtesy from the discourteous.
TURKISH PROVERB

C359
Politeness is to human nature what warmth is to wax.
ARTHUR SCHOPENHAUER

C360
Hail the small sweet courtesies of life, for smooth do they make the road of it.
LAURENCE STERNE

COVETOUSNESS
(See also ENVY)

C361
Nothing lies on our hands with such uneasiness as time. Wretched and thoughtless creatures! In the only place where covetousness were a virtue we turn prodigals.
JOSEPH ADDISON

C362
Covetousness often starves other vices.
ENGLISH PROVERB

C363
Abundance consists not so much in material possessions, but in an uncovetous spirit.
JOHN SELDEN

C364
Covetousness is both the beginning and end of the devil's alphabet – the first vice in corrupt nature that moves, and the last which dies.
ROBERT SOUTH

C365
Covetousness is the root of all evil, the ground of all vice.
LEONARD WRIGHT

CREATION
(See also UNIVERSE)

C366
To create is to bring a thing into existence without any previous material at all to work on.
ST. THOMAS AQUINAS

C367
Thus does the world forget You, its Creator, and falls in love with what You have created instead of with You.
ST. AUGUSTINE OF HIPPO

C368
The probability of life originating from accident is comparable to the probability of the unabridged dictionary resulting from an explosion in a printing shop.
EDWIN CONKLIN

C369
We can in fact get at the Creator only through the world.
THOMAS CORBISHLEY

C370
It is for this we are created: that we may give a new and individual expression of the absolute in our own peculiar character.
ISAAC T. HECKER

C371
We are not our own, any more than what we possess is our own. We did not make ourselves; we cannot be supreme over ourselves. We cannot be our own masters. We are God's property by creation, by redemption, by regeneration.
JOHN HENRY NEWMAN

C372
Posterity will some day laugh at the foolishness of modern materialistic philosophy. The more I study nature, the more I am amazed at the Creator.
LOUIS PASTEUR

C373
We depend upon God every moment for our existence: creatures only remain in being through the constant exercise of His upholding power.
J. I. POWER

C374
It has been said that the highest praise of God consists in the denial of Him by the atheist, who finds creation so perfect that he can dispense with a creator.
MARCEL PROUST

C375
God made us and we wonder at it.
SPANISH PROVERB

C376
God as Creator is concerned about the whole quality of men's lives, not only with the personal conversion, important though that is.
DAVID SHEPPARD

C377
The spiritual interest in the doctrine of Creation lies solely in the assertion of the dependence of all existence upon the will of God.
WILLIAM TEMPLE

CREATIVITY
(See also GENIUS and TALENT)

C378
The greatest mystery of life is that satisfaction is felt not by those who take and make demands but by those who give and make sacrifices. In them alone the energy of life does not fail, and this is precisely what is meant by creativity.
NIKOLAI BERDYAEV

C379
To raise new questions, new possibilities, to regard old problems from a new angle requires creative imagination and marks real advances in science.
ALBERT EINSTEIN

C380
If you would create something, you must be something.
JOHANN WOLFGANG VON GOETHE

C381
Creative life is characterised by spontaneous mutability: it brings forth the unknown, impossible to preconceive.
D. H. LAWRENCE

C382
Creativity is so delicate a flower that praise tends to make it bloom, while discouragement often nips it in the bud. Any of us will put out more and better ideas if our efforts are truly appreciated.
ALEXANDER F. OSBORN

CREEDS
(See also DOGMA)

C383
If you have a Bible creed, it is well; but is it filled out and inspired by Christian love?
J. F. BRODIE

C384
The Athanasian Creed is the most splendid ecclesiastical lyric ever poured forth by the genius of man.
BENJAMIN DISRAELI

C385
A man's liberty to travel is not cramped by signposts: on the contrary, they save his time by showing what roads he must avoid if he wishes to reach his destination. The creeds perform the same function.
C. B. MOSS

C386
The proper question to be asked about any creed is not, 'Is it pleasant?' but, 'Is it true?'
DOROTHY L. SAYERS

C387
There lives more faith in honest doubt,
Believe me, than in half the creeds.
ALFRED, LORD TENNYSON

C388
Truth has never been, can never be, contained in any one creed.
MARY AUGUSTA WARD

CRIME AND PUNISHMENT

C389
Heaven takes care that no man secures happiness by crime.
VITTORIO ALFIERI

C390
Poverty is the mother of crime.
MARCUS AURELIUS

C391
The real significance of crime is in its being a breach of faith with the community of mankind.
JOSEPH CONRAD

C392
Capital punishment is as fundamentally wrong as a cure for crime as charity is wrong as a cure for poverty.
HENRY FORD

C393
Whoever meditates a crime has all the guiltiness of the deed.
DECIMUS JUVENAL

C394
Distrust all men in whom the impulse to punish is powerful.
FRIEDRICH NIETZSCHE

C395
No crime is rooted out once for all.
QUINTUS TERTULLIAN

CRITICISM
(See also ADVICE)

C396
It is ridiculous for any man to criticise the works of another if he has not distinguished himself by his own performance.
JOSEPH ADDISON

C397
A thick skin is a gift from God.
KONRAD ADENAUER

C398
Never forget what a man says to you when he is angry.
HENRY WARD BEECHER

C399
I love criticism just so long as it's unqualified praise.
NOEL COWARD

C400
It is much easier to be critical than to be correct.
BENJAMIN DISRAELI

C401
We resent all criticism which denies us anything that lies in our line of advance.
RALPH WALDO EMERSON

C402
To escape criticism – do nothing, say nothing, be nothing.
ELBERT HUBBARD

C403
You will never be an inwardly religious and devout man unless you pass over in silence the shortcomings of your fellow men, and diligently examine your own weaknesses.
THOMAS À KEMPIS

C404
Criticism is asserted superiority.
HENRY E. MANNING

C405
It is salutary to train oneself to be

no more affected by censure than by praise.

W. SOMERSET MAUGHAM

C406
It is easier to bear some abuse if I reflect, 'I do not deserve this reproach but I do deserve others that have not been made.'

FRANÇOIS MAURIAC

C407
If you want to help other people you have got to make up your mind to write things that some men will condemn.

THOMAS MERTON

C408
Nothing would be done at all, if a man waited till he could do it so well that no one could find fault with it.

JOHN HENRY NEWMAN

CROSS

C409
Our Lord who saved the world through the cross, will only work for the good of souls through the cross.

MADELEINE SOPHIE BARAT

C410
It has been said that the cross is the symbol of absolutely endless expansion; it is never content. It points for ever and ever to four indefinitely receding points.

ROBERT H. BENSON

C411
In the cross of Christ excess in men is met by excess in God, excess of evil is mastered by excess of love.

LOUIS BOURDALOUE

C412
The crosses that we shape for ourselves are always lighter than the ones laid upon us.

JEAN PIERRE CAMUS

C413
The cross cannot be defeated for it is defeat.

G. K. CHESTERTON

C414
We have not to carry the cross of others, but our own.

ST. FRANCIS DE SALES

C415
We do not attach any intrinsic virtue to the cross; this would be sinful and idolatrous. Our veneration is referred to Him who died upon it.

JAMES GIBBONS

C416
Everyone who accepts God in Christ accepts him through the cross.

POPE JOHN PAUL II

C417
In the cross is the height of virtue; in the cross is the perfection of sanctity. There is no health of the soul nor hope of eternal life but in the cross.

THOMAS À KEMPIS

C418
The cross is a way of life; the way of love meeting all hate with love, all evil with good, all negatives with positives.

RUFUS MOSELEY

C419
Bear the cross and do not make the cross bear you.

PHILIP NERI

C420
Crosses are ladders that lead to Heaven.

ENGLISH PROVERB

C421
No cross, no crown.

ENGLISH PROVERB

C422

There are no crown-wearers in Heaven who were not cross-bearers here below.

CHARLES H. SPURGEON

C423

In all our actions, when we come in or go out, when we dress, when we wash, at our meals, before retiring to sleep, we make on our foreheads the sign of the cross. These practices are not committed by a formal law of Scripture, but tradition teaches them, custom confirms them, faith observes them.

QUINTUS TERTULLIAN

C424

What other society has as its symbol a horrifying instrument of torture and death – especially when the marks of that society are meant to be love and peace.

DAVID WATSON

CULTURE

C425

Culture is to know the best that has been said and thought in the world.

MATTHEW ARNOLD

C426

The great law of culture: let each become all that he was created capable of being.

THOMAS CARLYLE

C427

There are moments when one is more ashamed of what is called culture than anyone can ever be of ignorance.

EDWARD V. LUCAS

C428

Those who find beautiful meanings in beautiful things are the cultivated. For these there is hope.

OSCAR WILDE

CUSTOM

(See also TRADITION)

C429

The customs of God's people and the institutions of our ancestors are to be considered as laws. And those who throw contempt on the customs of the Church ought to be punished as those who disobey the law of God.

ST. AUGUSTINE OF HIPPO

C430

Custom is a kind of law, having its origin in usage, which takes the place of law when law fails.

ST. ISIDORE OF SEVILLE

C431

The perpetual obstacle to human advancement is custom.

JOHN STUART MILL

C432

Custom without reason is but ancient error.

ENGLISH PROVERB

C433

Some of the roads most used lead nowhere.

JEWISH PROVERB

C434

Custom will often blind one to the good as well as to the evil effects of any long-established system.

RICHARD WHATELY

CYNICISM

C435

We can destroy ourselves by cynicism and disillusion, just as effectively as by bombs.

KENNETH CLARK

C436

The habit of thinking ill of everything and everyone is tiresome to ourselves and to all around us.

POPE JOHN XXIII

C437
Cynicism is disappointed idealism.
HARRY KEMELMAN

C438
I hate cynicism a great deal worse
than I do the devil, unless,
perhaps, the two were the same
thing.
ROBERT LOUIS STEVENSON

C439
Cynicism is humour in ill-health.
H. G. WELLS

C440
A cynic is a man who knows the
price of everything and the value of
nothing.
OSCAR WILDE

DAILY LIVING
(See also DAY and LIFE)

D1
Consider every day that you are
then for the first time – as it
were – beginning; and always act
with the same fervour as on the first
day you began.
ST. ANTHONY OF PADUA

D2
If a man cannot be a Christian
where he is, he cannot be a
Christian anywhere.
HENRY WARD BEECHER

D3
I find a heaven in the midst of
saucepans and brooms.
STANISLAUS KOSTKA

D4
Relying on God has to begin all
over again every day as if nothing
had yet been done.
C. S. LEWIS

D5
We die daily. Happy those who
daily come to life as well.
GEORGE MACDONALD

D6
Every day is a messenger of God.
RUSSIAN PROVERB

D7
You will become a saint by
complying exactly with your daily
duties.
MARY JOSEPH ROSSELLO

D8
Our task as moral beings is to lead
a 'dying life'; to rest on our oars
would mean a 'living death', a very
different thing.
A. E. TAYLOR

DARKNESS
(See also BLINDNESS and
LIGHT)

D9
It is one thing to be blind, and
another to be in darkness.
COVENTRY PATMORE

D10
To see one's darkness proves the
presence of a great light.
RAOUL PIUS

D11
Don't curse the darkness – light a
candle.
CHINESE PROVERB

D12
The darkest hour is that before the
dawn.
ENGLISH PROVERB

D13
Whate'er my darkness be,
'Tis not, O Lord, of Thee:
The light is Thine alone;
The shadows, all my own.
J. B. TABB

D14
In darkness there is no choice. It is
light that enables us to see the
differences between things; and it
is Christ who gives us light.
C. T. WHITMELL

DAY
(See also DAILY LIVING and TIME)

D15
Write it on your heart that every day is the best day in the year. No man has learned anything rightly until he knows that every day is Doomsday.
RALPH WALDO EMERSON

D16
To sensible men, every day is a day of reckoning.
JOHN W. GARDNER

D17
They deem me mad because I will not sell my days for gold; and I deem them mad because they think my days have a price.
KAHLIL GIBRAN

D18
Better the day, better the deed.
THOMAS MIDDLETON

D19
Be the day never so long, at length cometh evensong.
ENGLISH PROVERB

D20
Every day should be passed as if it were to be our last.
PUBLILIUS SYRUS

DEATH

D21
The foolish fear death as the greatest of evils, the wise desire it as a rest after labours and the end of ills.
ST. AMBROSE

D22
For man is by nature afraid of death and of the dissolution of the body; but there is this most startling fact, that he who has put on the faith of the cross despises even what is naturally fearful, and for Christ's sake is not afraid of death.
ST. ATHANASIUS

D23
Death is but a sharp corner near the beginning of life's procession down eternity.
JOHN AYSCOUGH

D24
Men fear death as children fear to go in the dark; and as that natural fear in children is increased with tales, so is the other.
FRANCIS BACON

D25
Death is the great adventure, beside which moon landings and space trips pale into insignificance.
JOSEPH BAYLY

D26
At death, if at any time, we see ourselves as we are, and display our true characters.
ROBERT H. BENSON

D27
What is death at most? It is a journey for a season: a sleep longer than usual. If thou fearest death, thou shouldest also fear sleep.
ST. JOHN CHRYSOSTOM

D28
The final heartbeat for the Christian is not the mysterious conclusion to a meaningless existence. It is, rather, the grand beginning to a life that will never end.
JAMES DOBSON

D29
Death has nothing terrible which life has not made so. A faithful Christian life in this world is the best preparation for the next.
TYRON EDWARDS

D30
Blessed be God for our sister, the death of the body.
ST. FRANCIS OF ASSISI

D31
Death takes no bribes.
BENJAMIN FRANKLIN

D32
We are not entirely present to ourselves until the day of our death.
LOUIS LAVELLE

D33
If after I depart this vale, you ever remember me and have thought to please my ghost, forgive some sinner and wink your eye at some homely girl.
HENRY L. MENCKEN

D34
Death devours lambs as well as sheep.
ENGLISH PROVERB

D35
To die well is the chief part of virtue.
GREEK PROVERB

D36
A good death does honour to a whole life.
ITALIAN PROVERB

D37
Death does not take the old but the ripe.
RUSSIAN PROVERB

D38
The angel of Death has many eyes.
YIDDISH PROVERB

D39
Death is the side of life which is turned away from us.
RAINER MARIA RILKE

D40
When a man dies he clutches in his hands only that which he has given away in his lifetime.
JEAN JACQUES ROUSSEAU

D41
We understand death for the first time when he puts his hand upon one whom we love.
ANNE L. DE STAEL

D42
It is a poor thing for anyone to fear that which is inevitable.
QUINTUS TERTULLIAN

D43
Why is it that we rejoice at a birth and grieve at a funeral? It is because we are not the person involved.
MARK TWAIN

DECEPTION
(See also LYING)

D44
I have met with many that would deceive; who would be deceived, no one.
ST. AUGUSTINE OF HIPPO

D45
Do you hate to be deceived? Then never deceive another.
ST. JOHN CHRYSOSTOM

D46
Human beings seem to have an almost unlimited capacity to deceive themselves, and to deceive themselves into taking their own lies for truth.
R. D. LAING

D47
Indeed, it is not in human nature to deceive others for any long time, without in a measure deceiving ourselves too.
JOHN HENRY NEWMAN

D48
To deceive a deceiver is no deceit.
ENGLISH PROVERB

D49
The wolf will hire himself out very cheaply as a shepherd.
RUSSIAN PROVERB

DECISION
(See also FREE WILL)

D50
The man who insists upon seeing with perfect clearness before he decides never decides.
HENRI FRÉDÉRIC AMIEL

D51
We make our decisions, and then our decisions turn around and make us.
F. W. BOREHAM

D52
Not to decide is to decide.
HARVEY COX

D53
Some persons are very decisive when it comes to avoiding decisions.
BRENDAN FRANCIS

D54
There is a time when we must firmly choose the course we will follow, or the relentless drift of events will make the decision.
HERBERT V. PROCHNOW

D55
No one learns to make right decisions without being free to make wrong ones.
KENNETH SOLLITT

DEED
(See also ACTIVE LIFE)

D56
Our deeds act upon us as much as we act upon them.
GEORGE ELIOT

D57
Deeds done, when viewed in themselves, and not simply as means to ends, are also to be regarded as things made.
ERIC GILL

D58
Everyone knows that it is much harder to turn word into deed than deed into word.
MAXIM GORKY

D59
Deeds are fruits, words are but leaves.
ENGLISH PROVERB

D60
They will be hushed by a good deed who laugh at a wise speech.
FRENCH PROVERB

DEFEAT
(See also FAILURE)

D61
God is never defeated. Though He may be opposed, attacked, resisted, still the ultimate outcome can never be in doubt.
BROTHER ANDREW

D62
There's no defeat in truth, save from within.
HENRY AUSTIN

D63
Defeat is never more assured for an individual than at the moment when he resigns himself to it.
O. A. BATTISTA

D64
It is remarkable that in so many great wars it is the defeated who have won. The people who were left worst at the end of the war were generally the people who were left best at the end of the whole business.
G. K. CHESTERTON

DEMOCRACY
(See also GOVERNMENT and POLITICS)

D65
We are justified, from the point of view of exegesis, in regarding the democratic conception of the state as an expansion of the thought of the New Testament.

KARL BARTH

D66
Democracy doesn't give the average man any real power at all. It swamps him among his fellows – that is to say, it kills his individuality; and his individuality is the one thing he has which is worth anything.

ROBERT H. BENSON

D67
That Christianity is identical with democracy, is the hardest of gospels; there is nothing that so strikes men with fear as the saying that they are all the sons of God.

G. K. CHESTERTON

D68
Democracy is the worst system ever invented – except for all the rest.

SIR WINSTON CHURCHILL

D69
Democracy assumes that there are extraordinary possibilities in ordinary people.

HARRY EMERSON FOSDICK

D70
Democracy always makes for materialism, because the only kind of equality that you can guarantee to a whole people is, broadly speaking, physical.

KATHERINE FULLERTON GEROULD

D71
Democracy is the very child of Jesus' teachings of the infinite worth of every personality.

FRANCIS J. McCONNELL

D72
Man's capacity for justice makes democracy possible. His inclination to injustice makes democracy necessary.

REINHOLD NIEBUHR

DESIRE

D73
For desire never ceases to pray even though the tongue be silent. If ever desiring, then ever praying.

ST. AUGUSTINE OF HIPPO

D74
It is by that which he longs for, that every man knows and apprehends the quality with which he has to serve God.

MARTIN BUBER

D75
To desire to love God is to love to desire Him, and hence to love Him, for love is the root of all desire.

JEAN PIERRE CAMUS

D76
Humble hearts have humble desires.

GEORGE HERBERT

D77
Remove every evil desire and clothe yourself with good and holy desire. For if you are clothed with good desire, you will hate evil desire and bridle it as you please.

SHEPHERD OF HERMAS

D78
Desires are nourished by delays.

ENGLISH PROVERB

D79
He who likes cherries soon learns to climb.

GERMAN PROVERB

D80
They that desire but a few things can be crossed but in a few.
GERMAN PROVERB

D81
None of us ever desired anything more ardently than God desires to bring men to a knowledge of himself.
JOHNN TAULER

D82
If we go down into ourselves we find that we possess exactly what we desire.
SIMONE WEIL

D83
Any unmortified desire which a man allows in will effectually drive and keep Christ out of the heart.
CHARLES WESLEY

DESPAIR

D84
Despair ruins some, presumption many.
BENJAMIN FRANKLIN

D85
I have plumbed the depths of despair and have found them not bottomless.
THOMAS HARDY

D86
I once counselled a man in despair to do what I myself did in similar circumstances: to live for short terms. Come, I said to myself at that time, at any rate you can bear it for a quarter of an hour!
THEODOR HOECKER

D87
Despair is the absolute extreme of self-love. It is reached when a man deliberately turns his back on all help from anyone else in order to taste the rotten luxury of knowing himself to be lost.
THOMAS MERTON

D88
Despair is vinegar from the wine of hope.
AUSTIN O'MALLEY

D89
Despair gives courage to a coward.
ENGLISH PROVERB

D90
It is impossible for that man to despair who remembers that his helper is omnipotent.
JEREMY TAYLOR

DESTINY
(See also PREDESTINATION)

D91
I felt as if I were walking with destiny, and that all my past life had been but a preparation for this hour and this trial.
SIR WINSTON CHURCHILL

D92
Destiny waits in the hand of God, not in the hands of statesmen.
T. S. ELIOT

D93
We are not permitted to choose the frame of our destiny. But what we put into it is ours.
DAG HAMMARSKJOLD

D94
Every man has his own destiny: the only imperative is to follow it, to accept it, no matter where it leads him.
HENRY MILLER

D95
One meets his destiny often in the road he takes to avoid it.
FRENCH PROVERB

DEVIL
(See also SATAN)

D96
The Devil's snare does not catch

you, unless you are first caught by the Devil's bait.

ST. AMBROSE

D97
When the Devil is called the god of this world, it is not because he made it, but because we serve him with our worldliness.

ST. THOMAS AQUINAS

D98
The Devil may also make use of morality.

KARL BARTH

D99
I do not know a description of a devil in literature which does not leave one with some sense of sympathy. Milton's devils are admirable; Dante's devils stir our pity; Goethe's devil makes us feel what a good thing has been wasted. Human nature seems incapable of imagining that which is wholly bad, just because it is not wholly bad itself.

ALBAN GOODIER

D100
The Devil has got to be resisted, not merely deprecated.

MICHAEL GREEN

D101
The Devil cannot lord it over those who are servants of God with their whole heart and who place their hope in Him. The Devil can wrestle with, but not overcome them.

SHEPHERD OF HERMAS

D102
The Devil appeared to St. Bridget and she asked him: 'What is your name?' 'Coldness itself.'

ABBÉ HUVELIN

D103
When you close your eyes to the Devil, be sure that it is not a wink.

JOHN C. KULP

D104
The Devil is a gentleman who never goes where he is not welcome.

JOHN L. LINCOLN

D105
For where God built a church, there the Devil would also build a chapel.

MARTIN LUTHER

D106
Francis Thompson said that the Devil doesn't know how to sing, only how to howl.

VINCENT MCNABB

D107
The Devil dances in an empty pocket.

ENGLISH PROVERB

D108
The Devil paints himself black, but we see him rose-coloured.

FINNISH PROVERB

D109
The Devil's boots don't creak.

SCOTTISH PROVERB

D110
The Devil has three children: pride, falsehood and envy.

WELSH PROVERB

D111
The Devil tries to shake truth by pretending to defend it.

QUINTUS TERTULLIAN

D112
The Devil only tempts those souls that wish to abandon sin and those that are in a state of grace. The others belong to him: he has no need to tempt them.

JOHN VIANNEY

DIGNITY

D113
It is only people of small moral stature who have to stand on their dignity.

ARNOLD BENNETT

D114
To behave with dignity is nothing less than to allow others freely to be themselves.
SOL CHANELES

D115
I know of no case where a man added to his dignity by standing on it.
SIR WINSTON CHURCHILL

D116
What is dignity without honesty?
MARCUS TULLIUS CICERO

D117
Let not a man guard his dignity, but let his dignity guard him.
RALPH WALDO EMERSON

D118
Man is more interesting than men. God made him and not them in his image. Each one is more precious than all.
ANDRÉ GIDE

D119
Scrubbing floors and emptying bedpans has as much dignity as the Presidency.
RICHARD M. NIXON

D120
The easiest way to dignity is humility.
ENGLISH PROVERB

D121
Perhaps the only true dignity of man is his capacity to despise himself.
GEORGE SANTAYANA

DISCIPLESHIP
(See also CHRISTIAN)

D122
Happy are they who know that discipleship simply means the life which springs from grace, and that grace simply means discipleship.
DIETRICH BONHOEFFER

D123
I have inevitably and increasingly been driven to the conclusion, almost against my own will, that for a West European whose life and background and traditions are in terms of Western European Christian civilisation, the only answer lies in the person and life and teaching of Christ.
MALCOLM MUGGERIDGE

D124
On account of him there have come to be many Christs in the world, even all who, like him, loved righteousness and hated iniquity.
ORIGEN OF ALEXANDRIA

D125
The attempts of Christians to be Christians now are almost as ridiculous as the attempts of the first men to be human.
G. A. STUDDERT-KENNEDY

D126
The world around us will recognise us as disciples of Jesus when they see our prayers being answered.
COLIN URQUHART

D127
If we were willing to learn the meaning of real discipleship and actually to become disciples, the Church in the West would be transformed, and the resultant impact on society would be staggering.
DAVID WATSON

DIVINITY OF CHRIST
(See also GOD and JESUS CHRIST)

D128
The Son is the Image of the invisible God. All things that belong to the Father He expresses as the Image; all things that are the

63

Father's He illumines as the splendour of His glory and manifests to us.
St. Ambrose

D129
Just as every human being is one person, that is, a rational soul and body, so, too, is Christ one Person, the Word and Man.
St. Augustine of Hippo

D130
If Socrates would enter the room, we should rise and do him honour. But if Jesus Christ came into the room, we should fall down on our knees and worship Him.
Napoleon Bonaparte

D131
If Jesus Christ is not true God, how could he help us? If he is not true man, how could he help us?
Dietrich Bonhoeffer

D132
I consider the Gospels to be thoroughly genuine; for in them there is the effective reflection of a sublimity which emanated from the Person of Christ; and this is as Divine as ever the divine appeared on earth.
Johann Wolfgang von Goethe

D133
There is one Doctor active in both body and soul, begotten and yet unbegotten, God in man, true Life in death, Son of Mary, and Son of God, first able to suffer and then unable to suffer, Jesus Christ our Lord.
St. Ignatius of Antioch

D134
If the life and death of Socrates were those of a man, the life and death of Jesus were those of God.
Jean Jacques Rousseau

D135
He that cried in the manger, that sucked the paps of a woman, that hath exposed himself to poverty, and a world of inconveniences, is the Son of the Living God, of the same substance with his Father, begotten before all ages, before the morning stars; he is God eternal.
Jeremy Taylor

D136
Jesus acts with the manifest authority of God; he is the creative Word of God. In him we are to see what is the purpose of God in making the world and in making us.
William Temple

D137
They should have known that (Christ) was God. His patience should have proved that to them.
Quintus Tertullian

DOGMA
(See also CREEDS)
D138
No dogmas nail your faith.
Robert Browning

D139
Dogma is the anatomy of thought. As scientists tell you, even a bad doctrine is better than none at all. You can test it, differ from it, your mind has something to bite on. You need the rock to plan the lighthouse.
Joyce Cary

D140
Dogma means the serious satisfaction of the mind. Dogma does not mean the absence of thought, but the end of thought.
G. K. Chesterton

D141
Truths turn into dogmas the moment they are disputed.
G. K. CHESTERTON

D142
Religion cannot but be dogmatic; it ever has been. All religions have had doctrines; all have professed to carry with them benefits which could be enjoyed only on condition of believing the word of a supernatural informant, that is, of embracing some doctrines or other.
JOHN HENRY NEWMAN

DOUBT

D143
Doubt charms me no less than knowledge.
DANTE ALIGHIERI

D144
If only God would give me some clear sign! Like making a large deposit in my name at a Swiss bank.
WOODY ALLEN

D145
Every step toward Christ kills a doubt.
THEODORE CUYLER

D146
Should we feel at times disheartened and discouraged, a confiding thought, a simple movement of heart towards God will renew our powers. Whatever he may demand of us, he will give us at the moment the strength and the courage that we need.
FRANÇOIS FENELON

D147
Doubt is a pain too lonely to know that faith is his twin brother.
KAHLIL GIBRAN

D148
Give me the benefit of your convictions if you have any, but keep your doubts to yourself, for I have enough of my own.
JOHANN WOLFGANG VON GOETHE

D149
Time trieth truth in every doubt.
JOHN HEYWOOD

D150
Doubt comes in at the window when enquiry is denied at the door.
BENJAMIN JOWETT

D151
There are two ways to slide easily through life: to believe everything or to doubt everything; both ways save us from thinking.
ALFRED KORZYBSKI

D152
He is a dull man who is always sure, and a sure man who is always dull.
HENRY L. MENCKEN

D153
Underlying all life is the ground of doubt and self-questioning which sooner or later must bring us face to face with the ultimate meaning of our life.
THOMAS MERTON

D154
Ten thousand difficulties do not make one doubt, as I understand the subject; difficulty and doubt are incommensurate.
JOHN HENRY NEWMAN

D155
When in doubt do nowt.
ENGLISH PROVERB

D156
Who knows nothing doubts nothing.
FRENCH PROVERB

D157
The wise are prone to doubt.
GREEK PROVERB

D158
To believe with certainty we must begin with doubting.
POLISH PROVERB

D159
Our doubts are traitors
And make us lose the good we oft might win
By fearing to attempt.
WILLIAM SHAKESPEARE

D160
There lives more faith in honest doubt, believe me, than in half the creeds.
ALFRED, LORD TENNYSON

D161
Faith keeps many doubts in her pay. If I could not doubt, I should not believe.
HENRY DAVID THOREAU

DUTY

D162
We need to restore the full meaning of that old word, duty. It is the other side of rights.
PEARL BUCK

D163
Exactness in little duties is a wonderful source of cheerfulness.
FREDERICK W. FABER

D164
Do what you can to do what you ought, and leave hoping and fearing alone.
THOMAS HENRY HUXLEY

D165
Let us have faith that right makes might, and in that faith let us to the end dare to do our duty as we understand it.
ABRAHAM LINCOLN

D166
The right, practical divinity is this: believe in Christ, and do your duty in that state of life to which God has called you.
MARTIN LUTHER

D167
You would not think any duty small if you yourself were great.
GEORGE MACDONALD

D168
Duty does not have to be dull. Love can make it beautiful and fill it with life.
THOMAS MERTON

D169
Never think yourself safe because you do your duty in ninety-nine points; it is the hundredth which is to be the ground of your self-denial.
JOHN HENRY NEWMAN

D170
The path of duty lies in what is near at hand, but men seek for it in what is remote.
JAPANESE PROVERB

D171
You will become a saint by complying exactly with your daily duties.
MARY JOSEPH ROSSELLO

D172
Every duty which we omit, obscures some truth which we should have known.
JOHN RUSKIN

D173
God never imposes a duty without giving time to do it.
JOHN RUSKIN

EASTER
(See also RESURRECTION)

E1
The stone at the tomb of Jesus was a pebble to the Rock of Ages inside.
FREDERICK BECK

E2

The great Easter truth is not that we are to live newly after death, but that we are to be new here and now by the power of the resurrection.

PHILLIPS BROOKS

E3

Many meetings and conferences with bishops were held on this point, and all unanimously formulated in their letters the doctrine of the Church for those in every country, that the mystery of the Lord's resurrection from the dead could be celebrated on no day save Sunday, and that on that day alone we should celebrate the end of the paschal feast.

EUSEBIUS OF CAESAREA

E4

Easter says you can put truth in a grave, but it won't stay there.

CLARENCE W. HULL

E5

The night of Easter is spent in keeping the vigil (pervigilia) because of the coming of our King and Lord, that the time of His resurrection may not find us sleeping, but awake. The reason for this night is twofold: either because He then received back His life when He suffered, or because He is later to come for judgment at the same hour at which He arose.

ST. ISIDORE

E6

Easter, like all deep things, begins in mystery and it ends like all high things, in great courage.

BLISS PERRY

E7

At Easter let your clothes be new, or else be sure you will it rue.

ENGLISH PROVERB

ECOLOGY

(See also CONSERVATION and NATURE)

E8

Every flower of the field, every fibre of a plant, every particle of an insect, carries with it the impress of its Maker, and can – if duly considered – read us lectures of ethics or divinity.

THOMAS POPE BLOUNT

E9

An ecologist wants to clean up the world; an environmentalist wants you to clean up your garden.

BILL COPELAND

E10

Due to man's destruction of the forests and woodlands and his pollution of the rivers and air, one species of the animal kingdom per day is lost; goes into extinction. By the 1990s it will be one species an hour!

GERALD DURRELL

E11

The sun, the moon and the stars would have disappeared long ago, had they happened to be within reach of predatory human hands.

HAVELOCK ELLIS

E12

There is a sufficiency in the world for man's need but not for man's greed.

MOHANDAS GANDHI

E13

We won't have a society if we destroy the environment.

MARGARET MEAD

E14

The ground is holy, being even as it came from the Creator. Keep it, guard it, care for it, for it keeps men, guards men, cares for men. Destroy it and man is destroyed.

ALAN PATON

E15

If you want to clear the stream, get the hog out of the spring.

AMERICAN PROVERB

E16

Man has mastered nature, but, in doing that, he has enslaved himself to the new man-made environment that he has conjured up all around him. Man has condemned himself now to live in cities and to make his living by working in factories and offices.

ARNOLD TOYNBEE

ECSTASY
(See also JOY)

E17

The height of love's ecstasy is to have our will not in its own contentment but in God's.

ST. FRANCIS DE SALES

E18

Ecstasy is naught but the going forth of a soul from itself and its being caught up in God, and this is what happens to the soul that is obedient, namely, that it goes forth from itself and from its own desires, and thus lightened, becomes immersed in God.

ST. JOHN OF THE CROSS

E19

For God's sake, mistrust and beware of these states of exaltation and ecstasy. They send you, anyone, swaying so far beyond the centre of gravity in one direction, there is the inevitable swing back with greater velocity in the other direction, and in the end you exceed the limits of your own soul's elasticity, and go smash, like a tower that has swung too far.

D. H. LAWRENCE

E20

The ecstasy of religion, the ecstasy of art, and the ecstasy of love are the only things worth thinking about or experiencing.

DON MARQUIS

E21

I wish I could explain with the help of God, wherein union differs from rapture, or from transport, or from flight of the spirit, as they say, or from a trance, which are all one. I mean that all these are only different names for one and the same thing, which is also called ecstasy.

ST. TERESA OF AVILA

ECUMENISM

E22

The real ecumenical crisis today is not between Catholic and Protestants but between traditional and experimental forms of Church life.

HARVEY COX

E23

I do not want the walls of separation between different orders of Christians to be destroyed, but only lowered, that we may shake hands a little easier over them.

ROWLAND HILL

E24

Church unity is like peace, we are all for it, but we are not willing to pay the price.

DR. VISSER'T HOOFT

E25

Form all together one choir, so that, with the symphony of your feelings and having all taken the tone of God, you may sing with one voice to the Father through Jesus Christ, that He may listen to you

and know you from your chant as
the canticle of His only Son.
St. Ignatius of Antioch

E26
Our divisions prevent our
neighbours from hearing the
Gospel as they should.
John Paul II

E27
Putting all the ecclesiastical corpses
into one graveyard will not bring
about a resurrection.
David M. Lloyd-Jones

E28
Some of us worked long enough in
a shipbuilding district to know that
welding is impossible except the
materials to be joined are at white
heat. When you try to weld them,
they only fall apart.
George F. MacLeod

E29
None understand better the nature
of real distinction than those who
have entered into unity.
Johnn Tauler

EDUCATION
(See also LEARNING)

E30
A teacher affects eternity; he can
never tell where his influence stops.
Henry Adams

E31
To train a citizen is to train a critic.
The whole point of education is
that it should give a man abstract
and eternal standards, by which he
can judge material and fugitive
conditions.
G. K. Chesterton

E32
What greater work is there than
training the mind and forming the
habits of the young.
St. John Chrysostom

E33
Education is the systematic,
purposeful reconstruction of
experience.
John Dewey

E34
The secret of education lies in
respecting the pupil.
Ralph Waldo Emerson

E35
Education is helping the child
realise his potentialities.
Erich Fromm

E36
We must learn to get on in the
world – not in the commercial and
materialistic sense – but as a means
to getting Heavenwards. Any
education which neglects this fact,
and to the extent to which it
neglects it, is false education,
because it is false to man.
Eric Gill

E37
The supreme end of education is
expert discernment in all
things – the power to tell the good
from the bad, the genuine from the
counterfeit, and to prefer the good
and the genuine to the bad and the
counterfeit.
Samuel Johnson

E38
Education without religion, as
useful as it is, seems rather to make
man a more clever devil.
C. S. Lewis

E39
I respect faith, but doubt is what
gets you an education.
Wilson Mizner

E40
Every method of education
founded wholly or in part, on the
denial or forgetfulness of original
sin and grace, and relying solely on

the powers of human nature, is
unsound.

PORE PIUS XI

E41
An education which is not religious
is atheistic; there is no middle way.
If you give to children an account
of the world from which God is left
out, you are teaching them to
understand the world without
reference to God.

WILLIAM TEMPLE

EFFORT
(See also ACTIVE LIFE)

E42
God only asks you to do your best.

ROBERT H. BENSON

E43
The trite objects of human
efforts – possessions, outward
success, luxury – have always
seemed to me contemptible.

ALBERT EINSTEIN

E44
We strain hardest for things which
are almost but not quite within our
reach.

FREDERICK W. FABER

E45
No one knows what is in him till he
tries, and many would never try if
they were not forced to.

BASIL W. MATURIN

E46
Pray to God, but keep rowing to
the shore.

RUSSIAN PROVERB

E47
All effort is in the last analysis
sustained by faith that it is worth
making.

ORDWAY TEAD

EGOISM
(See also CONCEIT AND
SELF-LOVE)

E48
The burden of the absolute ego is
the chief agony of life.

WALDO FRANK

E49
There's only one really nice thing
about egotists, they don't talk
about other people.

PAUL FROST

E50
We talk little if we do not talk
about ourselves.

WILLIAM HAZLITT

E51
There's only one thing that can
keep growing without
nourishment: the human ego.

MARSHALL LUMSDEN

E52
The egoist does not tolerate
egoism.

JOSEPH ROUX

E53
When a man is wrapped up in
himself, he makes a pretty small
package.

JOHN RUSKIN

EMOTION
(See also SENTIMENT)

E54
Emotions should be servants, not
masters – or at least not tyrants.

ROBERT H. BENSON

E55
'What do you think of God?' the
teacher asked. After a pause the
young pupil replied 'He's not a
think, He's a feel'.

PAUL FROST

E56

Emotion may vary in religious experience. Some people are stoical and others are demonstrative, but the feeling will be there. There is going to be a tug at the heart.

BILLY GRAHAM

E57

Trust not to thy feelings, for whatever it be now, it will quickly be changed into another thing.

THOMAS À KEMPIS

E58

The only thing men have not learned to do is to stick up for their own instinctive feelings, against the things they are taught.

D. H. LAWRENCE

E59

Emotion is not the Cinderella of our inner life, to be kept in her place among the cinders in the kitchen. Our emotional life is *us* in a way our intellectual life cannot be.

JOHN MACMURRAY

E60

Each of us makes his own weather, determines the colour of the skies in the emotional universe which he inhabits.

FULTON J. SHEEN

E61

It is so many years before one can believe enough in what one feels even to know what the feeling is.

W. B. YEATS

ENCOURAGEMENT

E62

Encouragement is oxygen to the soul.

GEORGE M. ADAMS

E63

One of the highest of human duties is the duty of encouragement. There is a regulation of the Royal Navy which says: 'No officer shall speak discouragingly to another officer in the discharge of his duties.'

WILLIAM BARCLAY

E64

Correction does much, but encouragement does more. Encouragement after censure is as the sun after a shower.

JOHANN WOLFGANG VON GOETHE

E65

There is a point with me in matters of any size when I must absolutely have encouragement as much as crops rain: afterwards I am independent.

GERARD MANLEY HOPKINS

E66

The deepest principle in human nature is the craving to be appreciated.

WILLIAM JAMES

ENDURANCE

(See also PERSEVERANCE)

E67

Patient endurance is the perfection of charity.

ST. AMBROSE

E68

There remain times when one can only endure. One lives on, one doesn't die, and the only thing that one can do, is to fill one's mind and time as far as possible with the concerns of other people. It doesn't bring immediate peace, but it brings the dawn nearer.

ARTHUR C. BENSON

E69

Nothing great was ever done

without much enduring.
> St. Catherine of Siena

E70
He that endures is not overcome.
> English Proverb

E71
What can't be cured must be endured.
> English Proverb

E72
One can go a long way after one is tired.
> French Proverb

E73
He that can't endure the bad, will not live to see the good.
> Yiddish Proverb

ENEMY
(See also CHARITY and LOVE OF NEIGHBOUR)

E74
Everyone is his own enemy.
> St. Bernard of Clairvaux

E75
The Bible tells us to love our neighbours, and also to love our enemies; probably because they are generally the same people.
> G. K. Chesterton

E76
Love your enemies, for they tell you your faults.
> Benjamin Franklin

E77
If we are bound to forgive an enemy, we are not bound to trust him.
> Thomas Fuller

E78
Love will conquer hate.
> Mohandas Gandhi

E79
I owe much to my friends, but all things considered, it strikes me that I owe even more to my enemies. The real person springs to life under a sting, even better than under a caress.
> André Gide

E80
If you have no enemies, you are apt to be in the same predicament in regard to friends.
> Elbert Hubbard

E81
Where there is no love, pour love in, and you will draw out love.
> St. John of the Cross

E82
Never cease loving a person, and never give up hope for him, for even the Prodigal Son who had fallen most low, could still be saved. The bitterest enemy and also he who was your friend could again be your friend; love that has grown cold can kindle again.
> Søren Kierkegaard

E83
Could we read the secret history of our enemies, we should find in each man's life, sorrow and suffering enough to disarm all hostility.
> Henry Wordsworth Longfellow

E84
Often we attack and make ourselves enemies, to conceal that we are vulnerable.
> Friedrich Nietzsche

E85
An enemy may chance to give good counsel.
> English Proverb

E86
If you would make an enemy, lend a man money, and ask it of him again.
> English Proverb

E87
Love makes all hard hearts gentle
ENGLISH PROVERB

E88
The first duty of love is to listen.
PAUL TILLICH

ENJOYMENT
(See also HAPPINESS and PLEASURE)

E89
Everybody knows how to weep, but it takes a fine texture of mind to know thoroughly how to enjoy the bright and happy things of life.
OLIVER BELL BUNCE

E90
Nobody who looks as though he enjoyed life is ever called distinguished, though he is a man in a million.
ROBERTSON DAVIES

E91
Enjoy what you can and endure what you must.
JOHANN WOLFGANG VON GOETHE

ENTHUSIASM
(See also ZEAL)

E92
Nothing great was ever achieved without enthusiasm.
RALPH WALDO EMERSON

E93
Enthusiasm is the key not only to the achievement of great things but to the accomplishment of anything that is worthwhile.
SAMUEL GOLDWYN

E94
The enthusiastic, to those who are not, are always something of a trial.
ALBAN GOODIER

E95
Be not afraid of enthusiasm; you need it; you can do nothing effectively without it.
FRANCOIS GUIZAT

E96
Enthusiasm finds the opportunities, and energy makes the most of them.
HENRY S. HUSKINS

E97
Apathy can only be overcome by enthusiasm, and enthusiasm can only be aroused by two things; first, an ideal which takes the imagination by storm, and second, a definite intelligible plan for carrying that ideal into practice.
ARNOLD TOYNBEE

E98
Enthusiasm is that temper of the mind in which the imagination has got the better of the judgment.
WILLIAM WARBURTON

ENVY
(See also JEALOUSY)

E99
Show me what a man envies the least in others and I will show you what he has got the most of himself.
JOSH BILLINGS

E100
Envy and fear are the only passions to which no pleasure is attached.
JOHN CHURTON COLLINS

E101
Envy takes the joy, happiness, and contentment out of living.
BILLY GRAHAM

E102
Better be envied than pitied.
JOHN HEYWOOD

E103
Too many Christians envy the sinners their pleasure and the saints their joy, because they don't have either one.

MARTIN LUTHER

E104
Men always hate most what they envy most.

HENRY L. MENCKEN

E105
If envy were a fever, all the world would be ill.

DANISH PROVERB

E106
Envy never enriched any man.

ENGLISH PROVERB

E107
Envy eats nothing but its own heart.

GERMAN PROVERB

E108
Beggars do not envy millionaires, though of course they will envy other beggars who are more successful.

BERTRAND RUSSELL

E109
Envy comes from people's ignorance of, or lack of belief in, their own gifts.

JEAN VANIER

EQUALITY

E110
Equality consists in the same treatment of similar persons.

ARISTOTLE

E111
The only stable state is the one in which all men are equal before the law.

ARISTOTLE

E112
The defect of equality is that we only desire it with our superiors.

HENRY BECQUE

E113
All men are equal on the turf and under it.

GEORGE BENTINCK

E114
In sport, in courage, and the sight of Heaven, all men meet on equal terms.

SIR WINSTON CHURCHILL

E115
Equality is a mortuary word.

CHRISTOPHER FRY

E116
It is not true that some human beings are by nature superior and others inferior. All men are equal in their natural dignity.

POPE JOHN XXIII

E117
All men are born equal but the tough job is to outgrow it.

DON LEARY

E118
Equality is a quantitative term and, therefore, love knows nothing of it. Authority exercised with humility, and obedience accepted with delight are the very lines along which our spirits live.

C. S. LEWIS

E119
All animals are equal, but some animals are more equal than others.

GEORGE ORWELL

E120
Equality begins in the grave.

FRENCH PROVERB

E121
Before God and the bus driver we are all equal.

GERMAN PROVERB

E122
In the public baths, all men are equal.

YIDDISH PROVERB

E123
The Lord so constituted everybody that no matter what colour you are, you require the same amount of nourishment.

WILL ROGERS

E124
Equality of opportunity is an equal opportunity to prove unequal talents.

HERBERT SAMUEL

E125
There is no merit in equality, unless it be equality with the best.

JOHN LANCASTER SPALDING

ERROR
(See also HERESY and MISTAKES)

E126
An error is the more dangerous in proportion to the degree of truth which it contains.

HENRI FRÉDÉRIC AMIEL

E127
It is human to err; it is devilish to remain wilfully in error.

ST. AUGUSTINE OF HIPPO

E128
Who errs and mends, to God himself commends.

MIGUEL DE CERVANTES

E129
One must never confuse error and the person who errs.

POPE JOHN XXIII

E130
Error is just as important a condition of life as truth.

CARL GUSTAV JUNG

E131
It is one thing to show a man that he is in error, and another to put him in possession of truth.

JOHN LOCKE

E132
A wavering or shallow mind does perhaps as much harm to others as a mind that is consistent in error.

JOHN HENRY NEWMAN

E133
To err is human, to forgive divine.

ALEXANDER POPE

E134
Error is always in a hurry.

ENGLISH PROVERB

E135
Who errs and mends, to God himself commends.

ENGLISH PROVERB

E136
An old error is always more popular than a new truth.

GERMAN PROVERB

E137
The error which we hold enquiringly, striving to find what element of fact there be in it, is worth more to us than the truth which we accept mechanically and retain with indifference.

JOHN LANCASTER SPALDING

ETERNITY
(See also AFTERLIFE)

E138
As eternity is the proper measure of permanent being, so time is the proper measure of movement.

ST. THOMAS AQUINAS

E139
The sole purpose of life in time is to gain merit for life in eternity.

ST. AUGUSTINE OF HIPPO

E140
He who has no vision of eternity
will never get a true hold of time.
THOMAS CARLYLE

E141
For a small living, men run a great
way; for eternal life, many will
scarce move a single foot from the
ground.
THOMAS À KEMPIS

E142
There really are two ideas, life
which goes on and life which has
some quality or value in it which
lifts it above time. We might use
'everlasting' for the first idea and
'eternal' for the second.
W. R. MATTHEWS

E143
We have all eternity to celebrate
our victories, but only one short
hour before sunset in which to win
them.
ROBERT MOFFAT

E144
In the presence of eternity, the
mountains are as transient as the
clouds.
ENGLISH PROVERB

E145
The life of faith does not earn
eternal life; it is eternal life. And
Christ is its vehicle.
WILLIAM TEMPLE

E146
He who provides for this life, but
takes no care for eternity, is wise
for a moment, but a fool forever.
JOHN TILLOTSON

ETHICS
(See also MORALITY)

E147
There are no pastel shades in the
Christian ethic.
ARNOLD LOWE

E148
The essence of the ethics of Jesus is
not law, but a relationship of
persons to God.
MICHAEL RAMSEY

E149
The idea of vocation is the central
concept of Christian ethics.
N. H. G. ROBINSON

E150
Ethical behaviour is concerned
above all with human values, not
with legalisms.
A. M. SULLIVAN

E151
An ethical man is a Christian
holding four aces.
MARK TWAIN

EUCHARIST
(See also BREAD and
COMMUNION HOLY)

E152
When it comes to the consecration
of this venerable sacrament, the
priest no longer uses his own
language, but he uses the language
of Christ. Therefore, the word of
Christ consecrates this sacrament.
ST. AMBROSE

E153
The noblest sacrament,
consequently, is that wherein His
Body is really present. The
Eucharist crowns all the other
sacraments.
ST. THOMAS AQUINAS

E154
The appropriateness of the name
'Eucharist' rests upon the giving of
thanks by Jesus at the Last Supper
and upon the character of the rite
itself which is the supreme act of
Christian thanksgiving.
J. G. DAVIES

E155
The sheer stupendous quantity of
the love of God which this ever
repeated action has drawn from
obscure Christian multitudes
through the centuries is in itself an
overwhelming thought.
GREGORY DIX

E156
Let that Eucharist be held valid
which is offered by the bishop or by
one to whom the bishop has
committed this charge.
ST. IGNATIUS OF ANTIOCH

E157
Be zealous, then, in the observance
of one Eucharist. For there is one
Flesh of our Lord, Jesus Christ,
and one Chalice that brings union
in His Blood. There is one altar, as
there is one bishop with the priests
and deacons, who are my fellow
workers. And so, whatever you do,
let it be done in the name of the
Lord.
ST. IGNATIUS OF ANTIOCH

E158
Every Eucharist proclaims the
beginning of the time of God's
salvation.
J. JEREMIAS

E159
The Eucharist is the Church at her
best.
GABRIEL MORAN

E160
The Eucharist is the means
whereby those who once received
the Spirit in baptism are constantly
renewed in the Spirit until their
life's end.
ALAN RICHARDSON

EVANGELISM
(See also MISSION)

E161
The way from God to a human

heart is through a human heart.
SAMUEL GORDON

E162
God will hold us responsible as to
how well we fulfil our
responsibilities to this age and take
advantage of our opportunities.
BILLY GRAHAM

E163
These early Christians (in the Book
of Acts) were led by the Spirit to
the main task of bringing people to
God through Christ, and were not
permitted to enjoy fascinating
sidetracks.
J. B. PHILLIPS

E164
The Church has many tasks but
only one mission.
ARTHUR PRESTON

E165
There is no expeditious road
To pack and label men for God,
And save them by the barrel-load.
FRANCIS THOMPSON

E166
The Church has nothing to do but
to save souls; therefore spend and
be spent in this work. It is not your
business to speak so many times,
but to save souls as you can; to
bring as many sinners as you
possibly can to repentance.
JOHN WESLEY

E167
When social action is mistaken for
evangelism the Church has ceased
to manufacture its own blood cells
and is dying of leukemia.
SHERWOOD WIRT

EVIL
(See also GOOD AND EVIL)

E168
Just as a little fresh water is blown
away by a storm of wind and dust,

in like manner the good deeds, that we think we do in this life, are overwhelmed by the multitude of evils.

ST. BASIL

E169
For evil to triumph, it is only necessary for good men to do nothing.

EDMUND BURKE

E170
It is tempting to deny the existence of evil since denying it obviates the need to fight it.

ALEXIS CARREL

E171
Although it be with truth thou speakest evil, this is also a crime.

ST. JOHN CHRYSOSTOM

E172
If evil is due to ignorance, then all professors should be saints.

RICHARD S. EMRICH

E173
Indifference to evil is more insidious than evil itself; it is more universal, more contagious, more dangerous.

ABRAHAM JESCHEL

E174
Never tell evil of a man, if you do not know it for certainty, and if you know it for a certainty, then ask yourself, 'Why should I tell it?'

JOHANN K. LAVATER

E175
We who live beneath a sky still streaked with the smoke of crematoria, have paid a high price to find out that evil is really evil.

FRANÇOIS MAURIAC

E176
Evil communications corrupt good manners.

MENANDER

E177
Of evil grain, no good seed can come.

ENGLISH PROVERB

E178
One does evil enough when one does nothing good.

GERMAN PROVERB

E179
An evil-speaker differs from an evil-doer only in the lack of opportunity.

MARCUS FABIUS QUINTILIAN

E180
There is some soul of goodness in things evil, would men observingly distil it out.

WILLIAM SHAKESPEARE

E181
The word is grown so bad, that wrens make prey where eagles dare not perch.

WILLIAM SHAKESPEARE

E182
Nature throws a veil either of fear or shame over all evil.

QUINTUS TERTULLIAN

EVOLUTION
(See also SCIENCE)

E183
The evolutionists seem to know everything about the missing link except the fact that it is missing.

G. K. CHESTERTON

E184
Man with all his noble qualities . . . still bears in his bodily frame the indelible stamp of his lowly origin.

CHARLES DARWIN

E185
A creation of evolutionary type (God making things make themselves) has for long seemed to some great minds the most

beautiful form imaginable in which God could act in the universe.
PIERRE TEILHARD DE CHARDIN

E186
If evolution works, how come mothers still have only two hands?
ED. DUSSAULT

E187
In Jesus we see the point in the evolution of the universe when the divine consciousness took possession of a human soul and body and the plan of God in creation from the beginning was revealed.
BEDE GRIFFITHS

E188
Evolution is far more a philosophical concept than a strictly scientific one.
ELTON TRUEBLOOD

EXAMPLE

E189
Example is the school of mankind, and they will learn at no other.
EDMUND BURKE

E190
No man is so insignificant as to be sure his example can do no hurt.
EDWARD CLARENDON

E191
No force the free-born spirit can constrain, but charity and great example gain.
JOHN DRYDEN

E192
People seldom improve when they have no other model but themselves to copy after.
OLIVER GOLDSMITH

E193
It would scarcely be necessary to expound doctrine if our lives were radiant enough. If we behaved like true Christians, there would be no pagans.
POPE JOHN XXIII

F194
Example is always more efficacious than precept.
SAMUEL JOHNSON

E195
There is just one way to bring up a child in the way he should go and that is to travel that way yourself.
ABRAHAM LINCOLN

E196
A holy life will produce the deepest impression. Lighthouses blow no horns; they only shine.
DWIGHT L. MOODY

E197
A child's life is like a piece of paper on which every passer-by leaves a mark.
CHINESE PROVERB

E198
Example is the greatest of all seducers.
FRENCH PROVERB

E199
Precept begins, example accomplishes.
FRENCH PROVERB

E200
Example is not the main thing in influencing others – it is the only thing.
ALBERT SCHWEITZER

E201
I am a part of all that I have met.
ALFRED, LORD TENNYSON

E202
If you try to improve one person by being a good example, you're improving two. If you try to improve someone without being a good example, you won't improve anybody.
JAMES THOM

E203
If you would convince a man that he does wrong, do right. Men will believe what they see. Let them see.
HENRY DAVID THOREAU

E204
Few things are harder to put up with than the annoyance of a good example.
MARK TWAIN

E205
There are two ways of spreading light; to be a candle, or the mirror that reflects it.
EDITH WHARTON

EXISTENCE
(See also LIFE)

E206
To know any man is not merely to be sure of his existence, but to have some conception of what his existence signifies, and what it is for.
PHILLIPS BROOKS

E207
The great majority of men exist but do not live.
BENJAMIN DISRAELI

E208
Man can only find meaning for his existence in something outside himself.
VIKTOR E. FRANKL

E209
The more unintelligent a man is, the less mysterious existence seems to him.
ARTHUR SCHOPENHAUER

E210
Every existing thing is equally upheld in its existence by God's creative love. The friends of God should love him to the point of merging their love into his with regard to all things here below.
SIMONE WEIL

EXPERIENCE

E211
All experience is an arch, to build upon.
HENRY ADAMS

E212
You cannot acquire experience by making experiments. You cannot create experience. You must undergo it.
ALBERT CAMUS

E213
Experience is the best of schoolmasters, only the school fees are heavy.
THOMAS CARLYLE

E214
Nothing which has entered into our experience is ever lost.
WILLIAM ELLERY CHANNING

E215
The years teach much which the days never knew.
RALPH WALDO EMERSON

E216
We cannot afford to forget any experience, even the most painful.
DAG HAMMARSKJOLD

E217
Experience is not what happens to a man. It is what a man does with what happens to him.
ALDOUS HUXLEY

E218
One thorn of experience is worth a whole wilderness of warning.
JAMES RUSSELL LOWELL

E219
Experience is the comb that Nature gives us when we are bald.
BELGIAN PROVERB

E220
Blacksmith's children are not afraid of sparks.
DANISH PROVERB

E221
A new broom sweeps clean, but the old brush knows the corners.
IRISH PROVERB

E222
Experience is always experience of oneself: it cannot, therefore, make others wise.
JOHN LANCASTER SPALDING

E223
To reach something good it is very useful to have gone astray, and thus acquire experience.
ST. TERESA OF AVILA

E224
The long experience of the Church is more likely to lead to correct answers than is the experience of the lone individual.
ELTON TRUEBLOOD

FAILURE
(See also MISTAKES)

F1
Failure sometimes enlarges the spirit. You have to fall back upon humanity and God.
CHARLES H. COOLEY

F2
Show me a thoroughly satisfied man – and I will show you a failure.
THOMAS A. EDISON

F3
One of the reasons mature people stop learning is that they become less and less willing to risk failure.
JOHN W. GARDNER

F4
A failure is a man who has blundered but is not able to cash in the experience.
ELBERT HUBBARD

F5
It is not a disgrace to fail. Failing is one of the greatest arts in the world.
CHARLES KETTERING

F6
When we can begin to take our failures non-seriously, it means we are ceasing to be afraid of them. It is of immense importance to learn to laugh at ourselves.
KATHERINE MANSFIELD

F7
Failure teaches success.
ENGLISH PROVERB

F8
The greatest failure is the failure to try.
WILLIAM A. WARD

FAITH
(See also FAITH AND GOOD WORKS)

F9
Do not rejoice in earthly reality, rejoice in Christ, rejoice in his word, rejoice in his law . . . There will be peace and tranquillity in the Christian heart; but only as long as our faith is watchful; if, however, our faith sleeps, we are in danger.
ST. AUGUSTINE OF HIPPO

F10
For what is faith unless it is to believe what you do not see.
ST. AUGUSTINE OF HIPPO

F11
People only think a thing's worth believing in if it's hard to believe.
ARMIGER BARCLAY

F12
Faith is never identical with piety.
KARL BARTH

F13
Faith is a gift which can be given or withdrawn; it is something infused

Faith

into us, not produced by us.
ROBERT H. BENSON

F14
Those who have the faith of
children have also the troubles of
children.
ROBERT H. BENSON

F15
A faith that cannot survive collision
with the truth is not worth many
regrets.
ARTHUR C. CLARKE

F16
Faith has need of the whole truth.
P. TEILHARD DE CHARDIN

F17
Believe that you have it, and you
have it.
DESIDERIUS ERASMUS

F18
It is cynicism and fear that freeze
life; it is faith that thaws it out,
releases it, sets it free.
HARRY EMERSON FOSDICK

F19
If we really believe in something,
we have no choice but to go
further.
GRAHAM GREENE

F20
For faith is the beginning and the
end is love, and God is the two of
them brought into unity. After
these comes whatever else makes
up a Christian gentleman.
ST. IGNATIUS OF ANTIOCH

F21
Human reason is weak, and may be
deceived, but true faith cannot be
deceived.
THOMAS À KEMPIS

F22
I do not want merely to possess a
faith; I want a faith that possesses
me.
CHARLES KINGSLEY

F23
Faith always shows itself in the
whole personality.
MARTYN LLOYD-JONES

F24
Faith, like light, should always be
simple, and unbending; while love,
like warmth, should beam forth on
every side, and bend to every
necessity of our brethren.
MARTIN LUTHER

F25
Faith is the sight of the inward eye.
ALEXANDER MACLAREN

F26
The deep secret of the mystery of
faith lies in the fact that it is a
'baptism' in the death and sacrifice
of Christ. We can only give
ourselves to God when Christ, by
His grace, dies and rises again
spiritually within us.
THOMAS MERTON

F27
Ultimately, faith is the only key to
the universe. The final meaning of
human existence, and the answers
to the questions on which all our
happiness depends cannot be found
in any other way.
THOMAS MERTON

F28
Faith is illuminative, not operative;
it does not force obedience, though
it increases responsibility; it
heightens guilt, it does not prevent
sin; the will is the source of action.
JOHN HENRY NEWMAN

F29
Belief is a truth held in the mind.
Faith is a fire in the heart.
JOSEPH NEWTON

F30
Faith declares what the senses do
not see, but not the contrary of

what they see. It is above them, not contrary to them.

BLAISE PASCAL

F31
Faith essentially means taking someone at their word.

DAVID WATSON

FAITH AND GOOD WORKS

F32
To be active in works and unfaithful in heart is like raising a beautiful and lofty building on an unsound foundation. The higher the building, the greater the fall. Without the support of faith, good works cannot stand.

ST. AMBROSE

F33
If a man believes and knows God, he can no longer ask, 'What is the meaning of my life?' But by believing he actually lives the meaning of his life.

KARL BARTH

F34
He who would obey the gospel must first be purged of all defilement of the flesh and the spirit that so he may be acceptable to God in the good works of holiness.

ST. BASIL

F35
For faith without works cannot please, nor can good works without faith.

THE VENERABLE BEDE

F36
You do right when you offer faith to God: you do right when you offer works. But if you separate the two, then you do wrong. For faith without works is dead; and lack of charity in action murders faith, just as Cain murdered Abel, so that

God cannot respect your offering.

ST. BERNARD OF CLAIRVAUX

F37
You can do very little with faith, but you can do nothing without it.

NICHOLAS M. BUTLER

F38
You must live with people to know their problems, and live with God in order to solve them.

PETER T. FORSYTH

F39
We must learn that to expect God to do everything while we do nothing is not faith, but superstition.

MARTIN LUTHER KING, JR.

F40
Faith sees by the ears.

ENGLISH PROVERB

F41
All work that is worth anything is done in faith.

ALBERT SCHWEITZER

F42
As the flower is before the fruit, so is faith before good works.

RICHARD WHATELY

F43
Faith is the root of works. A root that produces nothing is dead.

THOMAS WILSON

FALL OF MAN
(See also ADAM and ORIGINAL SIN)

F44
The desire of power in excess caused the angels to fall; the desire of knowledge in excess caused man to fall.

FRANCIS BACON

F45
The fall of man stands as a lie before Beethoven, a truth before Hitler.

GREGORY CORSO

F46
The fruit of the tree of knowledge always drives man from some paradise or other.
WILLIAM R. INGE

F47
Adam whiles he spake not, had paradise at will.
WILLIAM LANGLAND

FAME

F48
The more inward a man's greatness, in proportion to the external show of it, the more substantial, and therefore lasting, his fame.
JOHN AYSCOUGH

F49
Fame always brings loneliness. Success is as ice cold and lonely as the north pole.
VICKI BAUM

F50
All men desire fame. I have never known a single exception to that rule, and I doubt if anyone else has.
HILAIRE BELLOC

F51
A man comes to be famous because he has the matter of fame within him. To seek for, to hunt after fame, is a vain endeavour.
JOHANN WOLFGANG VON GOETHE

F52
If fame is to come only after death, I am in no hurry for it.
MARCUS VALERIUS MARTIAL

F53
All the fame I look for in life is to have lived it quietly.
MICHEL DE MONTAIGNE

F54
For what is fame in itself but the blast of another man's mouth as soon passed as spoken?
SIR THOMAS MORE

F55
All fame is dangerous: good brings envy; bad, shame.
ENGLISH PROVERB

F56
The desire of glory clings even to the best men longer than any other passion.
CAIUS CORNELIUS TACITUS

FAMILY

F57
Wife and children are a kind of discipline of humanity.
FRANCIS BACON

F58
The union of the family lies in love; and love is the only reconciliation of authority and liberty.
ROBERT H. BENSON

F59
Where does the family start? It starts with a young man falling in love with a girl – no superior alternative has yet been found.
SIR WINSTON CHURCHILL

F60
What a father says to his children is not heard by the world, but it will be heard by posterity.
JEAN PAUL EIXHTER

F61
Few are born to do the great work of the world, but the work that all can do is to make a small home circle brighter and better.
GEORGE ELIOT

F62
Every effort to make society sensitive to the importance of the

family is a great service to
humanity.
POPE JOHN PAUL II

F63
No matter how many communes
anybody invents, the family always
creeps back.
MARGARET MEAD

F64
That man will never be unwelcome
to others who makes himself
agreeable to his own family.
FITUS PLAUTUS

F65
Nobody's family can hang out the
sign 'Nothing the matter here.'
CHINESE PROVERB

F66
There are no praises and no
blessings for those who are
ashamed of their families.
JEWISH PROVERB

F67
None but a mule denies his family.
MOROCCAN PROVERB

F68
All happy families resemble one
another; every unhappy family is
unhappy in its own way.
COUNT LEO TOLSTOY

F69
Loving relationships are a family's
best protection against the
challenges of the world.
BERNIE WIEBE

FANATICISM

F70
It is part of the nature of fanaticism
that it loses sight of the totality of
evil and rushes like a bull at the red
cloth instead of at the man who
holds it.
DIETRICH BONHOEFFER

F71
Earth's fanatics make too
frequently heaven's saints.
ELIZABETH BARRETT BROWNING

F72
A fanatic is one who can't change
his mind and won't change the
subject.
SIR WINSTON CHURCHILL

F73
Fanaticism is the false fire of an
overheated mind.
WILLIAM COWPER

F74
There is no strong performance
without a little fanaticism in the
performer.
RALPH WALDO EMERSON

F75
Fanatics seldom laugh. They never
laugh at themselves.
JAMES M. GILLIS

F76
History teaches us that no one feels
so disgustingly certain of victory, or
is so unteachably sure, and immune
to reason, as the fanatic, and that
no one is so absolutely certain of
ultimate defeat.
THEODOR HAECKER

FATHER, GOD THE

F77
If we address him as children, it is
because he tells us he is our Father.
If we unbosom ourselves to him as
a friend, it is because he calls us
friends.
WILLIAM COWPER

F78
The Moslem Faith has ninety-nine
names for God, but 'Our Father' is
not among them.
PAUL FROST

F79
The Father is our Fount and Origin, in whom our life and being is begun.

JOHN OF RUYSBROECK

F80
Whatever may happen to you, God is your Father, and He is interested in you, and that is His attitude towards you.

MARTYN LLOYD-JONES

F81
Our Heavenly Father never takes anything from His children unless He means to give them something better.

GEORGE MUELLER

F82
More than a projection of the qualities of earthly fathers, it is a name that demands its own definition, by the Father Himself, through His Son.

LLOYD JOHN OGILVIE

F83
Be content to be a child, and let the Father proportion out daily to thee what light, what power, what exercises, what straits, what fears, what troubles He sees fit for thee.

I. PENINGTON

F84
God is a kind Father. He sets us all in the places where He wishes us to be employed; and that employment is truly 'Our Father's business'.

JOHN RUSKIN

FATHERHOOD
(See also FAMILY)

F85
There is something ultimate in a father's love, something that cannot fail, something to be believed against the whole world. We almost attribute practical omnipotence to our father in the days of our childhood.

FREDERICK W. FABER

F86
I could not point to any need in childhood as strong as that for a father's protection.

SIGMUND FREUD

F87
It is easier for a father to have children than for children to have a real father.

POPE JOHN XXIII

F88
The father in praising his son extols himself.

CHINESE PROVERB

F89
You have to dig deep to bury your Daddy.

GYPSY PROVERB

F90
The best gift a father can give to his son is the gift of himself – his time. For material things mean little, if there is not someone to share them with.

NEIL C. STRAIT

FAULTS
(See also SIN)

F91
The greatest of faults, I should say, is to be conscious of none.

THOMAS CARLYLE

F92
There is only one way of getting rid of one's faults and that is to acquire the habits contradictory to them.

ERNEST DIMNET

F93
We like to find fault ourselves; but we are never attracted to another man who finds fault. It is the last refuge of our good humour that we like to have a monopoly of censure.

FREDERICK W. FABER

F94
The business of finding fault is very easy, and that of doing better very difficult.
ST. FRANCIS DE SALES

F95
Think of your own faults the first part of the night when you are awake, and of the faults of others the latter part of the night when you are asleep.
CHINESE PROVERB

F96
Faults are thick where love is thin.
DANISH PROVERB

F97
Make peace with men and quarrel with your faults.
RUSSIAN PROVERB

F98
Do not think of the faults of others but of what is good in them and faulty in yourself.
ST. TERESA OF AVILA

F99
A fault which humbles a man is of more use to him than a good action which puffs him up.
THOMAS WILSON

FEAR

F100
If thou hast a fearful thought, share it not with a weakling, whisper it to thy saddle-bow, and ride forth singing.
ALFRED THE GREAT

F101
Fear is never a good counsellor and victory over fear is the first spiritual duty of man.
NIKOLAI BERDYAEV

F102
We must fear God through love,

not love Him through fear.
JEAN PIERRE CAMUS

F103
Servile fear is no honour to God; for what father feels honoured by his son's dread of the rod?
WALTER ELLIOTT

F104
The wise man in the storm prays God, not for safety from danger, but for deliverance from fear. It is the storm within which endangers him, not the storm without.
RALPH WALDO EMERSON

F105
We must not fear fear.
ST. FRANCIS DE SALES

F106
Fear nothing but sin.
GEORGE HERBERT

F107
Fear the Lord, then, and you will do everything well.
SHEPHERD OF HERMAS

F108
All fear is bondage.
ENGLISH PROVERB

F109
Things never go so well that one should have no fear, and never so ill that one should have no hope.
TURKISH PROVERB

F110
The only thing we have to fear is fear itself.
FRANKLIN D. ROOSEVELT

F111
Keep your fears to yourself; share your courage with others.
ROBERT LOUIS STEVENSON

FELLOWSHIP
(See also COMMUNITY and FRIENDSHIP)

F112
Individuals cannot cohere closely

unless they sacrifice something of their individuality.

ROBERT H. BENSON

F113
We are all strings in the concert of his joy.

JACOB BOEHME

F114
The only basis for real fellowship with God and man is to live out in the open with both.

ROY HESSION

F115
To live in prayer together is to walk in love together.

MARGARET MOORE JACOBS

F116
God calls us not to solitary sainthood but to fellowship in a company of committed men.

DAVID SCHULLER

FLATTERY
(See also CONCEIT and VANITY)

F117
Flattery is praise insincerely given for an interested purpose.

HENRY WARD BEECHER

F118
Flattery corrupts both the receiver and giver.

EDMUND BURKE

F119
He who cannot love must learn to flatter.

JOHANN WOLFGANG VON GOETHE

F120
Words really flattering are not those which we prepare but those which escape us unthinkingly.

NINON DE LENELOS

F121
I hate careless flattery, the kind that exhausts you in your effort to believe it.

WILSON MIZNER

F122
In vain does flattery swell a little virtue to a mountain; self-love can swallow it like a mustard seed.

J. PETIT-SENN

F123
What really flatters a man is that you think him worth flattering.

GEORGE BERNARD SHAW

F124
Baloney is the unvarnished lie laid on so thick you hate it. Blarney is flattery laid on so thin you love it.

FULTON J. SHEEN

FOOD
(See also BREAD)

F125
God never sendeth mouth but He sendeth meat.

JOHN HEYWOOD

F126
Strange to see how a good dinner and feasting reconciles everybody.

SAMUEL PEPYS

F127
He who cannot cut the bread evenly cannot get on well with people.

CZECH PROVERB

F128
The way one eats is the way one works.

CZECH PROVERB

F129
When God gives hard bread He gives sharp teeth.

GERMAN PROVERB

FOOLISHNESS

F130
We were deceived by the wisdom of the serpent, but we are freed by the foolishness of God.

ST. AUGUSTINE OF HIPPO

F131
The greatest lesson in life is to know that even fools are right sometimes.
SIR WINSTON CHURCHILL

F132
If fifty million people say a foolish thing, it is still a foolish thing.
ANATOLE FRANCE

F133
Fools and wise folk are alike harmless. It is the half-wise and the half-foolish, who are most dangerous.
JOHANN WOLFGANG VON GOETHE

F134
Suffer fools gladly. They may be right.
HOLBROOK JACKSON

F135
The fellow who is always declaring he's no fool usually has his suspicions.
WILSON MIZNER

F136
Fools rush in where angels fear to tread.
ALEXANDER POPE

F137
Nothing looks so like a man of sense as a fool who holds his tongue.
GERMAN PROVERB

F138
There is no fool who has not his own kind of sense.
IRISH PROVERB

FORGIVENESS
(See also CONFESSION and RECONCILIATION)

F139
'I can forgive, but I cannot forget,' is only another way of saying 'I cannot forgive.'
HENRY WARD BEECHER

F140
There is not one moral virtue that Jesus inculcated but Plato and Cicero did inculcate before him. What then did Christ inculcate? Forgiveness of sins. This alone is the Gospel, and this is the life and immortality brought to life by Jesus.
WILLIAM BLAKE

F141
Forgiveness is man's deepest need and highest achievement.
HORACE BUSHNELL

F142
Nothing in this lost world bears the impress of the Son of God so surely as forgiveness.
ALICE CAREY

F143
The more a man knows, the more he forgives.
CATHERINE THE GREAT

F144
He that cannot forgive others breaks the bridge over which he must pass himself; for every man has need to be forgiven.
THOMAS FULLER

F145
There's no point in burying a hatchet if you're going to put up a marker on the site.
SYDNEY HARRIS

F146
The only true forgiveness is that which is offered and extended even before the offender has apologised and sought it.
SØREN KIERKEGAARD

F147
Everyone says forgiveness is a lovely idea, until they have something to forgive.
C. S. LEWIS

F148
The man who is truly forgiven and knows it, is a man who forgives.
MARTYN LLOYD-JONES

F149
He who forgives ends the quarrel.
AFRICAN PROVERB

F150
The noblest vengeance is to forgive.
ENGLISH PROVERB

F151
They who forgive most shall be most forgiven.
ENGLISH PROVERB

F152
To forgive is beautiful.
GREEK PROVERB

F153
Forgiving the unrepentant is like drawing pictures on water.
JAPANESE PROVERB

F154
Humanity is never so beautiful as when praying for forgiveness or else forgiving another.
JEAN PAUL RICHTER

F155
Only one petition in the Lord's Prayer has any condition attached to it; it is the petition for forgiveness.
WILLIAM TEMPLE

F156
It is very easy to forgive others their mistakes; it takes more grit and gumption to forgive them for having witnessed your own.
JESSAMYN WEST

FREEDOM
(See also FREE WILL and LIBERTY)

F157
One hallmark of freedom is the sound of laughter.
HARRY ASHMORE

F158
The free man is he who does not fear to go to the end of his thought.
LEON BLUM

F159
Freedom! No word was ever spoken that has held greater hope, demanded greater sacrifice, needed more to be nurtured, blessed more the giver . . . or come closer to being God's will on earth.
OMAR N. BRADLEY

F160
No man in this world attains to freedom from any slavery except by entrance into some higher servitude. There is no such thing as an entirely free man conceivable.
PHILLIPS BROOKS

F161
The real problem for the world today is how to preserve freedom, because for most people social justice is more important. People are prepared to abandon freedom for social justice. But then all that happens is that you get a new form of social injustice.
ALBERT CAMUS

F162
God forces no one, for love cannot compel, and God's service, therefore, is a thing of perfect freedom.
HANS DENK

F163
Freedom is not worth having if it does not include the freedom to make mistakes.
MOHANDAS GANDHI

F164
Freedom is to be in possession of oneself.
GEORGE W. F. HEGEL

F165
When people are free to do as they

please, they usually imitate each other.

ERIC HOFFER

F166
It is better for a man to go wrong in freedom than to go right in chains.

THOMAS HENRY HUXLEY

F167
One should never put on one's best trousers to go out to battle for freedom and truth.

HENRIK IBSEN

F168
Freedom is that faculty which enlarges the usefulness of all other faculties.

IMMANUEL KANT

F169
There are two freedoms – the false, where a man is free to do what he likes; the true, where a man is free to do what he ought.

CHARLES KINGSLEY

F170
Men are free when they belong to a living, organic, believing community, active in fulfilling some unfulfilled, perhaps some unrealised purpose.

D. H. LAWRENCE

FREE WILL
(See also FREEDOM and LIBERTY)

F171
We are not constrained by servile necessity, but act with free will, whether we are disposed to virtue or incline to vice.

ST. AMBROSE

F172
There are no galley slaves in the royal vessel of divine love – every man works his oar voluntarily.

JEAN PIERRE CAMUS

F173
God, having placed good and evil in our power, has given us full freedom of choice; he does not keep back the unwilling, but embraces the willing.

ST. JOHN CHRYSOSTOM

F174
We have freedom to do good or evil; yet to make choice of evil, is not to use, but to abuse our freedom.

ST. FRANCIS DE SALES

F175
He who has a firm will moulds the world to himself.

JOHANN WOLFGANG VON GOETHE

F176
People do not lack strength; they lack will.

VICTOR HUGO

F177
He who deliberates fully before taking a step will spend his entire life on one leg.

CHINESE PROVERB

F178
Man is essentially a freedom-event. As established by God, and in his very nature, he is unfinished. He freely determines his own everlasting nature and bears ultimate responsibility for it.

KARL RAHNER

F179
Without our faith in free will the earth would be the scene not only of the most horrible nonsense but also of the most intolerable boredom.

ARTHUR SCHNITZLER

F180
God is omnipotent – but powerless still
To stop my heart from wishing what it will.

ANGELUS SILESIUS

F181
There is no such thing as free will.
The mind is induced to wish this or
that by some cause, and that cause
is determined by another cause,
and so on back to infinity.

BENEDICT DE SPINOZA

F182
You must recognise as brothers
and sisters all who live; and free to
will, free to act, free to enjoy, you
shall know the worth of existence.

RICHARD WAGNER

F183
I think that our power of conscious
origination is where free will comes
in . . . We are continually choosing
between the good and the less
good, whether aware of it or not.

ALFRED NORTH WHITEHEAD

FRIENDSHIP

F184
A friendship that makes the least
noise is very often the most useful;
for which reason I prefer a prudent
friend to a zealous one.

JOSEPH ADDISON

F185
Every man should keep a fair-sized
cemetery, in which to bury the
faults of his friends.

HENRY WARD BEECHER

F186
The essence of a perfect friendship
is that each friend reveals himself
utterly to the other, flings aside his
reserves, and shows himself for
what he truly is.

ROBERT H. BENSON

F187
Friendship is in loving rather than
in being loved.

ROBERT BRIDGES

F188
Friendship is like money, easier
made than kept.

SAMUEL BUTLER

F189
You make more friends by
becoming interested in other
people than by trying to interest
other people in yourself.

DALE CARNEGIE

F190
True friendship is like sound
health, the value of it is seldom
known until it be lost.

CHARLES CALEB COLTON

F191
God evidently does not intend us
all to be rich or powerful or great,
but He does intend us all to be
friends.

RALPH WALDO EMERSON

F192
Friendships begun in this world will
be taken up again, never to be
broken off.

ST. FRANCIS DE SALES

F193
To know someone here or there
with whom you feel there is
understanding in spite of distances
or thoughts unexpressed – that can
make of this earth a garden.

JOHANN WOLFGANG VON GOETHE

F194
Friendship is a disinterested
commerce between equals.

OLIVER GOLDSMITH

F195
True friendship ought never to
conceal what it thinks.

ST. JEROME

F196
It is mutual respect which makes
friendship lasting.

JOHN HENRY NEWMAN

F197
Do not use a hatchet to remove a fly from your friend's forehead.
CHINESE PROVERB

F198
A friend in need is a friend indeed.
ENGLISH PROVERB

F199
Friendship is the marriage of the soul.
FRENCH PROVERB

F200
Hold a true friend with both your hands.
NIGERIAN PROVERB

F201
Blessed is he who hungers for friends – for though he may not realise it, his soul is crying out for God.
HABIB SAHABIB

F202
The impulse of love that leads us to the doorway of a friend is the voice of God within and we need not be afraid to follow it.
AGNES SANFORD

F203
A friend should bear his friend's infirmities.
WILLIAM SHAKESPEARE

F204
No one can develop freely in this world and find a full life without feeling understood by at least one person.
PAUL TOURNIER

F205
True friendship is a plant of slow growth, and must undergo and withstand the shocks of adversity before it is entitled to the appellation.
GEORGE WASHINGTON

FUTURE
(See also TIME)

F206
Most men prefer and strive for the present, we for the future.
ST. AMBROSE

F207
I never think of the future. It comes soon enough.
ALBERT EINSTEIN

F208
The only light upon the future is faith.
THEODOR HOECKER

F209
We should all be concerned about the future because we will have to spend the rest of our lives there.
CHARLES KETTERING

F210
The best thing about the future is that it comes only one day at a time.
ABRAHAM LINCOLN

F211
The most effective way to ensure the value of the future is to confront the present courageously and constructively.
ROLLO MAY

GAMBLING

G1
The Devil invented gambling.
ST. AUGUSTINE OF HIPPO

G2
Gaming, women, and wine, while they laugh they make men pine.
GEORGE HERBERT

G3
Gambling is a disease of barbarians superficially civilised.
WILLIAM R. INGE

G4

Italians come to ruin most
generally in one of three
ways – women, gambling, and
farming. My family chose the
slowest one.

POPE JOHN XXIII

GENEROSITY

G5

Too many people have decided to
do without generosity in order to
practise charity.

ALBERT CAMUS

G6

Generosity is not in giving me that
which I need more than you do, but
it is in giving me that which you
need more than I do.

KAHLIL GIBRAN

G7

If you are not generous with a
meagre income, you will never be
generous with abundance.

HAROLD NYE

G8

The quickest generosity is the best.

ARAB PROVERB

G9

A willing helper does not wait to be
called.

DANISH PROVERB

G10

The hand that gives, gathers.

ENGLISH PROVERB

G11

No one is so generous as he who
has nothing to give.

FRENCH PROVERB

G12

The man who gives little with a
smile gives more than the man who
gives much with a frown.

JEWISH PROVERB

G13

You do not have to be rich to be
generous. If he has the spirit of true
generosity, a pauper can give like a
prince.

CORRINE V. WELLS

GENIUS
(See also CREATIVITY and
TALENTS)

G14

Genius is the ability to think in a
very large number of categories.

HILAIRE BELLOC

G15

The world is always ready to
receive talent with open arms.
Very often it does not know what
to do with genius.

OLIVER WENDELL HOLMES

G16

The principal mark of genius is not
perfection but originality, the
opening of new frontiers.

ARTHUR KOESTLER

G17

Great things are done by devotion
to one idea; there is one class of
geniuses, who would never be what
they are, could they grasp a
second.

JOHN HENRY NEWMAN

G18

Genius makes its way with so much
difficulty, because this lower world
is in the hands of two
omnipotences – that of the wicked
and that of the fools.

JOSEPH ROUX

GENTLENESS
(See also MEEKNESS)

G19

Good manners and soft words have
brought many a difficult thing to
pass.

AESOP

G20
It takes more oil than vinegar to make a good salad.
JEAN PIERRE CAMUS

G21
Nothing appeases an enraged elephant so much as the sight of a little lamb.
ST. FRANCIS DE SALES

G22
Nothing is so strong as gentleness, nothing so gentle as real strength.
ST. FRANCIS DE SALES

G23
If you would reap praise, sow the seeds;
Gentle words and useful deeds.
BENJAMIN FRANKLIN

G24
A real gentleman is a combination of gentle strength and strong gentleness.
GEORGE MONAGHAN

G25
This is the final test of a gentleman: his respect for those who can be of no possible service to him.
WILLIAM L. PHELPS

G26
Kind words don't wear out the tongue.
DANISH PROVERB

G27
Gentle is that gentle does.
ENGLISH PROVERB

G28
A gentle hand may lead the elephant with a hair.
PERSIAN PROVERB

G29
Well bred thinking means kindly and sensitive thoughts.
FRANÇOIS DE LA ROCHEFOUCAULD

GIFTS AND GIVING

G30
What brings joy to the heart is not so much the friend's gift as the friend's love.
ST. AILRED OF RIEVAULX

G31
It is easy to want things from the Lord and yet not want the Lord Himself; as though the gift could ever be preferable to the Giver.
ST. AUGUSTINE OF HIPPO

G32
The more he cast away the more he had.
JOHN BUNYAN

G33
We make a living by what we get, but we make a life by what we give.
SIR WINSTON CHURCHILL

G34
Complete possession is proved only by giving. All you are unable to give possesses you.
ANDRÉ GIDE

G35
God has given us two hands – one for receiving and the other for giving.
BILLY GRAHAM

G36
We must not only give what we *have*; we must also give what we *are*.
DÉSIRÉ JOSEPH MERCIER

G37
He who gives to me teaches me to give.
DANISH PROVERB

G38
Give and spend, and God will send.
ENGLISH PROVERB

G39
He gives twice who gives quickly.
ENGLISH PROVERB

G40
Many look with one eye at what they give and with seven at what they receive.

GERMAN PROVERB

GLORY

G41
Verily, here must the spirit rise to grace, or else neither the body nor it shall there rise to glory.

LANCELOT ANDREWES

G42
Grace is but glory begun, and glory is but grace perfected.

JONATHAN EDWARDS

G43
Provided that God be glorified, we must not care by whom.

ST. FRANCIS DE SALES

G44
The paths of glory lead but to the grave.

THOMAS GRAY

G45
Short is the glory that is given and taken by men; and sorrow followeth ever the glory of this world . . .

. . . But true glory and holy joy is to glory in Thee and not in one's self; to rejoice in Thy name, and not to be delighted in one's own virtue, nor in any creature, save only for Thy sake.

THOMAS À KEMPIS

G46
By faith we know his existence; in glory we shall know his nature.

BLAISE PASCAL

G47
If the glory of God is to break out in your service, you must be ready to go out into the night.

M. BASILEA SCHLINK

GLUTTONY

G48
Gluttony is an emotional escape, a sign something is eating us.

PETER DE VRIES

G49
In general, mankind, since the improvement of cookery, eats twice as much as nature requires.

BENJAMIN FRANKLIN

G50
Gluttony kills more than the sword.

ENGLISH PROVERB

G51
Gluttons dig their graves with their teeth.

JEWISH PROVERB

GOD
(See also ONE GOD and TRINITY)

G52
People who tell me there is no God are like a six-year-old boy saying there is no such thing as passionate love – they just haven't experienced it.

WILLIAM ALFRED

G53
God? The imagination reels.

CHARLES AZNAVOUR

G54
The atheist staring from his attic window is often nearer to God than the believer caught up in his own false image of God.

MARTIN BUBER

G55
What we make in our minds we call God, but in reality He dwells in our hearts.

SIR WINSTON CHURCHILL

G56
Things are all the same in God:
they are God himself.
MEISTER ECKHART

G57
The presence of a superior
reasoning power revealed in the
incomprehensible universe, forms
my idea of God.
ALBERT EINSTEIN

G58
God is not an idea, or a definition
that we have committed to
memory, he is a presence which we
experience in our hearts.
LOUIS EVELY

G59
There are innumerable definitions
of God because his manifestations
are innumerable. They overwhelm
me . . . stun me.
MOHANDAS GANDHI

G60
The world is so empty if one thinks
only of mountains, rivers and
cities, but to know someone here
and there who thinks and feels with
us and who, though distant, is close
to us in spirit, this makes the earth
for us an inhabited garden.
JOHANN WOLFGANG VON GOETHE

G61
We die on the day
when our lives cease to be
illumined
by the steady radiance
renewed daily,
of a wonder,
the source of which
is beyond reason.
DAG HAMMERSKJOLD

G62
There is a native, elemental
homing instinct in our souls which
turns us to God as naturally as the
flower turns to the sun.
RUFUS M. JONES

G63
We know God easily, if we do not
constrain ourselves to define him.
JOSEPH JOUBERT

G64
We expect too much of God, but
He always seems ready.
JOHN F. KENNEDY

G65
The hardness of God is kinder than
the softness of men, and His
compulsion is our liberation.
C. S. LEWIS

G66
Change and decay in all around I
see;
O thou, who changest not, abide
with me.
HENRY FRANCIS LYTE

G67
Two men please God – who serves
Him with all his heart because he
knows Him; who seeks Him with
all his heart because he knows Him
not.
PANIN

G68
If a man is not made for God, why
is he happy only in God? If man is
made for God, why is he opposed
to God?
BLAISE PASCAL

G69
God often visits us, but most of the
time we are not at home.
FRENCH PROVERB

G70
God is an utterable sigh, planted in
the depths of the soul.
JEAN PAUL RICHTER

G71
Anything that makes religion a
second object makes it no object.
He who offers to God a second
place offers him no place.
JOHN RUSKIN

G72

I used to ask God to help me. Then I asked if I might help him. I ended up by asking him to do his work through me.

HUDSON TAYLOR

G73

God is he without whom one cannot live.

COUNT LEO TOLSTOY

G74

If God did not exist, it would be necessary to invent him.

FRANÇOIS M. VOLTAIRE

G75

Religion is the first thing and the last thing, and until a man has found God, and been found by God, he begins at no beginning and works to no end.

H. G. WELLS

GOOD/GOODNESS
(See also GOOD AND EVIL)

G76

Most men are not as good as they pretend to be, or as bad as their enemies paint them.

MORRIS ABRAM

G77

For that which every man seeketh most after, is by him esteemed his greatest good. Which is all one with happiness.

AMICIUS M. S. BOETHIUS

G78

The word *good* has many meanings. For example, if a man were to shoot his grandmother at a range of five hundred yards, I should call him a good shot, but not *necessarily* a good man.

G. K. CHESTERTON

G79

The first condition of human goodness is something to love; the second, something to reverence.

GEORGE ELIOT

G80

It is very hard to be simple enough to be good.

RALPH WALDO EMERSON

G81

We are sometimes so occupied with being good angels that we neglect to be good men and women.

ST. FRANCIS DE SALES

G82

Goodness is something so simple: Always live for others, never to seek one's own advantage.

DAG HAMMARSKJOLD

G83

There is no creature so little and contemptible as not to manifest the goodness of God.

THOMAS À KEMPIS

G84

We must first be made good before we can do good;
we must first be made just before our works can please God.

HUGH LATIMER

G85

An act of goodness, the least act of true goodness, is indeed the best proof of the existence of God.

JACQUES MARITAIN

G86

Good, the more communicated, more abundant grows.

JOHN MILTON

G87

Good and quickly seldom meet.

ENGLISH PROVERB

G88

The cross has revealed to good men that their goodness has not been good enough.

JOHANN H. SCHROEDER

G89
Anyone who proposes to do good must not expect people to roll stones out of his way, but must accept his lot calmly if they even roll a few more upon it.

ALBERT SCHWEITZER

GOOD AND EVIL
(See also EVIL and GOOD)
G90
Non-cooperation with evil is as much a duty as is cooperation with good.

MOHANDAS GANDHI

G91
Good is that which makes for unity; evil is that which makes for separateness.

ALDOUS HUXLEY

G92
Man knows not how to rejoice aright or how to grieve aught, for he understands not the distance that there is between good and evil.

ST. JOHN OF THE CROSS

G93
A good word costs no more than a bad one.

ENGLISH PROVERB

G94
Evil communications corrupt good manners.

ENGLISH PROVERB

G95
One does evil enough when one does nothing good.

GERMAN PROVERB

G96
The first prison I ever saw had inscribed on it, 'Cease to do evil: learn to do well,' but as the inscription was on the outside, the prisoners could not read it. It should have been addressed to the self-righteous free spectator in the street, and should have run 'All have sinned, and fallen short of the glory of God.'

GEORGE BERNARD SHAW

GOSPEL
(See also BIBLE and SCRIPTURE)
G97
Thanks be to the gospel, by means of which we also, who did not see Christ when He came into this world, seem to be with Him when we read His deeds.

ST. AMBROSE

G98
Because it was the message of God to humanity, the gospel could only reveal itself in the simplest of garments.

ADOLF DEISSMANN

G99
Cry the gospel with your whole life.

CHARLES DE FOUCAULD

G100
Talk about the questions of the day; there is but one question, and that is the gospel. It can and will correct everything needing correction.

WILLIAM E. GLADSTONE

G101
The gospel was not good advice but good news.

WILLIAM RALPH INGE

G102
The glory of the gospel is that when the Church is absolutely different from the world, she invariably attracts it.

MARTYN LLOYD-JONES

G103
God writes the gospel not in the Bible alone, but on trees, and flowers, and clouds, and stars.

MARTIN LUTHER

G104
The gospel is neither a discussion or a debate. It is an announcement.
PAUL S. REES

G105
How petty are the books of the philosophers with all their pomp, compared with the Gospels!
JEAN JACQUES ROUSSEAU

G106
Humble and self-forgetting we must be always but diffident and apologetic about the gospel never.
JAMES S. STEWART

G107
Our reading of the gospel story can be and should be an act of personal communion with the living Lord.
WILLIAM TEMPLE

GOSSIP
(See also SCANDAL and TALK)

G108
Truly unexpected tidings make both ears tingle.
ST. BASIL

G109
A real Christian is a person who can give his pet parrot to the town gossip.
BILLY GRAHAM

G110
I am grateful that my worst offences have not been found out. We all complain about gossip, but gossip is merciful to all of us in that it does not know all.
EDGAR W. HOWE

G111
Gossip is vice enjoyed vicariously.
ELBERT HUBBARD

G112
Never listen to accounts of the frailties of others; and if anyone should complain to you of another, humbly ask him not to speak of him at all.
ST. JOHN OF THE CROSS

G113
I always prefer to believe the best of everybody; it saves so much trouble.
RUDYARD KIPLING

G114
If all men knew what each said of the other, there would not be four friends in the world.
BLAISE PASCAL

G115
Whoever gossips to you will gossip of you.
SPANISH PROVERB

GOVERNMENT
(See also DEMOCRACY and POLITICS)

G116
Christianity introduced no new forms of government, but a new spirit, which totally transformed the old ones.
JOHN ACTON

G117
As the happiness of the people is the sole end of government, so the consent of the people is the only foundation of it.
JOHN ADAMS

G118
If therefore, it is natural for man to live in society of many, it is necessary that there exist among men some means by which the group may be governed. For where there are many men together, and each one is looking after his own interest, the group would be broken up and scattered unless there were also someone to take care of what appertains to the common weal.
ST. THOMAS AQUINAS

G119
Government is a contrivance of human wisdom to provide for human wants.
EDMUND BURKE

G120
When one is in office one has no idea how damnable things can feel to the ordinary rank and file of the public.
SIR WINSTON CHURCHILL

G121
All free governments are managed by the combined wisdom and folly of the people.
JAMES A. GARFIELD

G122
No matter how noble the objectives of a government, if it blurs decency and kindness, cheapens human life, and breeds ill will and suspicion – it is an evil government.
ERIC HOFFER

G123
That government is best which governs the least, because its people discipline themselves.
THOMAS JEFFERSON

G124
When a man assumes a public trust, he should consider himself as public property.
THOMAS JEFFERSON

G125
The most successful government is that which leads its subjects to the highest aim by means of the greatest freedom.
VINCENT McNABB

G126
Even a fool can govern if nothing happens.
GERMAN PROVERB

G127
The people's government is made for the people, made by the people, and is answerable to the people.
DANIEL WEBSTER

GRACE

G128
No athlete is admitted to the contest of virtue, unless he has first been washed of all stains of sins and consecrated with the gift of heavenly grace.
ST. AMBROSE

G129
Grace does not destroy nature, it perfects it.
ST. THOMAS AQUINAS

G130
This grace of Christ without which neither infants nor adults can be saved, is not rendered for any merits, but is given gratis, on account of which it is also called grace.
ST. AUGUSTINE OF HIPPO

G131
Let grace be the beginning, grace the consummation, grace the crown.
THE VENERABLE BEDE

G132
There is no such way to attain to a greater measure of grace as for a man to live up to the little grace he has.
PHILLIPS BROOKS

G133
Glory is perfected grace.
MEISTER ECKHART

G134
A state of mind that sees God in everything is evidence of growth in grace and a thankful heart.
CHARLES G. FINNEY

G135
Grace is not sought nor bought nor wrought. It is a free gift of Almighty God to needy mankind.
BILLY GRAHAM

G136
They travel lightly whom God's grace carries.
THOMAS À KEMPIS

G137
All men who live with any degree of serenity live by some assurance of grace.
REINHOLD NIEBUHR

G138
God does not refuse grace to one who does what he can.
LATIN PROVERB

G139
Grace grows best in the winter.
SAMUEL RUTHERFORD

G140
Grace is love that cares and stoops and rescues.
JOHN R. W. STOTT

G141
The burden of life is from ourselves, its lightness from the grace of Christ and the love of God.
WILLIAM ULLATHORNE

G142
Grace is God himself, his loving energy at work within his Church and within our souls.
EVELYN UNDERHILL

GRATITUDE
(See also THANKSGIVING)

G143
A true Christian is a man who never for a moment forgets what God has done for him in Christ, and whose whole comportment and whole activity have their root in the sentiment of gratitude.
JOHN BAILLIE

G144
Ingratitude is the soul's enemy; it empties it of merit, scatters its virtues, and deprives it of graces.
ST. BERNARD OF CLAIRVAUX

G145
Gratitude is heaven itself.
WILLIAM BLAKE

G146
In ordinary life we hardly realise that we receive a great deal more than we give, and that it is only with gratitude that life becomes rich. It is very easy to overestimate the importance of our own achievements in comparison with what we owe others.
DIETRICH BONHOEFFER

G147
Gratitude is not only the greatest of virtues, but the parent of all the others.
MARCUS TULLIUS CICERO

G148
The obligation of gratitude may easily become a trap, and the young are often caught and maimed in it.
ERIC GILL

G149
Thou hast given so much to me . . . Give one thing more – a grateful heart.
GEORGE HERBERT

G150
How happy a person is depends upon the depth of his gratitude.
JOHN MILLER

G151
Gratitude is the heart's memory.
FRENCH PROVERB

G152
One finds little ingratitude so long as one is in a position to grant favours.
FRENCH PROVERB

G153
Gratitude to God makes even a temporal blessing a taste of heaven.

WILLIAM ROMAINE

G154
He who receives a benefit with gratitude repays the first instalment on his debt.

SENECA

G155
Gratitude is not only the memory but the homage of the heart – rendered to God for his goodness.

NATHANIEL PARKER WILLIS

GREATNESS

G156
Greatness after all, in spite of its name, appears to be not so much a certain size as a certain quality in human lives. It may be present in lives whose range is very small.

PHILLIPS BROOKS

G157
There is a great man who makes every man feel small. But the really great man is the man who makes every man feel great.

G. K. CHESTERTON

G158
The price of greatness is responsibility.

SIR WINSTON CHURCHILL

G159
We all go to our graves unknown, worlds of unsuspected greatness.

FREDERICK W. FABER

G160
He who stays not in his littleness, loses his greatness.

ST. FRANCIS DE SALES

G161
It is a grand mistake to think of being great without goodness; and I pronounce it as certain that there was never yet a truly great man that was not at the same time truly virtuous.

BENJAMIN FRANKLIN

G162
Great hopes make great men.

THOMAS FULLER

G163
He who comes up to his own idea of greatness must always have had a very low standard of it in his mind.

WILLIAM HAZLITT

G164
Nothing can make a man truly great but being truly good and partaking of God's holiness.

MATTHEW HENRY

G165
The world is charged with the grandeur of God.

GERARD MANLEY HOPKINS

G166
There is a greatness that can come to all of us, but it is a greatness that comes to us through prayer.

HAROLD LINDSELL

G167
One of the marks of true greatness is the ability to develop greatness in others.

J. C. MACAULAY

G168
It is no sign of intellectual greatness to hold other men cheaply. A great intellect takes for granted that other men are more or less like itself.

HENRY E. MANNING

G169
Persons and things look great at a distance, which are not so when seen close.

JOHN HENRY NEWMAN

G170
Goodness is not tied to greatness,
but greatness to goodness.
GREEK PROVERB

G171
Great without small makes a bad
wall.
GREEK PROVERB

G172
For us the great men are not those
who solved the problems, but those
who discovered them.
ALBERT SCHWEITZER

G173
Be not afraid of greatness: some
are born great, some achieve
greatness and some have greatness
thrust upon 'em.
WILLIAM SHAKESPEARE

GREED
(See also GLUTTONY)

G174
It is an excellent rule to banish
greed beyond the reach of scandal,
and not only to be innocent of it.
ST. BERNARD OF CLAIRVAUX

G175
If you would abolish avarice, you
must abolish its mother, luxury.
MARCUS TULLIUS CICERO

G176
Greed has three facets: love of
things, love of fame, and love of
pleasure; and these can be attacked
directly with frugality, anonymity,
and moderation.
PAUL MARTIN

G177
Greedy folks have long arms.
ENGLISH PROVERB

G178
One of the weaknesses of our age is
our apparent inability to

distinguish our needs from our
greeds.
DON ROBINSON

GRIEF
(See also SADNESS and
SORROW)

G179
There is no greater grief than, in
misery, to recall happier times.
DANTE ALIGHIERI

G180
Genuine grief is like penitence, not
clamorous, but subdued.
JOSH BILLINGS

G181
The true way to mourn the dead is
to take care of the living who
belong to them.
EDMUND BURKE

G182
Grief and death were born of sin,
and devour sin.
ST. JOHN CHRYSOSTOM

G183
There is no grief which time does
not lessen and soften.
MARCUS TULLIUS CICERO

G184
Grief knits two hearts in closer
bonds than happiness ever can, and
common suffering is a far stronger
link than common joy.
ALPHONSE DE LAMARTINE

G185
Grief is the agony of an instant; the
indulgence of grief, the blunder of
a life.
BENJAMIN DISRAELI

G186
Sorrow makes us all children again,
destroys all differences in intellect.
The wisest knows nothing.
RALPH WALDO EMERSON

G187
Happiness is beneficial for the body but it is grief that develops the powers of the mind.
MARCEL PROUST

G188
You cannot prevent the birds of sorrow from flying over your head, but you can prevent them from building nests in your hair.
CHINESE PROVERB

G189
He who would have no trouble in this world must not be born in it.
ITALIAN PROVERB

G190
He that conceals his grief finds no remedy for it.
TURKISH PROVERB

G191
To weep is to make less the depth of grief.
WILLIAM SHAKESPEARE

GROWTH
(See also MATURITY)

G192
In this world, things that are naturally to endure for a long time, are the slowest in reaching maturity.
VINCENT DE PAUL

G193
The great majority of men are bundles of beginnings.
RALPH WALDO EMERSON

G194
Growth is the only evidence of life.
JOHN HENRY NEWMAN

G195
Be not afraid of growing slowly, be afraid only of standing still.
CHINESE PROVERB

G196
What grows makes no noise.
GERMAN PROVERB

G197
I am learning to see I do not know why it is, but everything penetrates more deeply within me, and no longer stops at the place, where until now, it always used to finish.
RAINER MARIA RILKE

G198
He is only advancing in life, whose heart is getting softer, his blood warmer, his brain quicker, and his spirit entering into living peace.
JOHN RUSKIN

G199
Growth begins when we start to accept our own weakness.
JEAN VANIER

GUILT

G200
The act of sin may pass, and yet the guilt remain.
ST. THOMAS AQUINAS

G201
It is better that ten guilty persons escape than one innocent suffer.
WILLIAM BLACKSTONE

G202
Too many of our securities are guilt-edged.
MARIANNE CRISWELL

G203
Guilt has very quick ears to an accusation.
HENRY FIELDING

G204
A guilty conscience needs no accuser.
ENGLISH PROVERB

G205
Man today attempts to escape his guilt through the electrifying effects of consumer society, through seeking different ways of being amused, through the

merchandising of peace by
commercial means.
ROGER SCHUTZ

G206
Every man is guilty of all the good
he didn't do.
FRANÇOIS MARIE VOLTAIRE

HABIT
(See also CUSTOM)

H1
Habits, like fish-hooks, are lots
easier to get caught than uncaught.
FRANK A. CLARK

H2
Two quite opposite qualities
equally bias our minds – habit and
novelty.
JEAN DE LA BRUYÈRE

H3
Habit and routine have an
unbelievable power to waste and
destroy.
HENRI DE LUBAC

H4
We first make our habits, then our
habits make us.
JOHN DRYDEN

H5
But oftentimes if we brace
ourselves with strong energy
against the incitements of evil
habits, we turn even those very evil
habits to the account of virtue.
POPE ST. GREGORY I

H6
Habit is overcome by habit.
THOMAS À KEMPIS

H7
I never knew a man to overcome a
bad habit gradually.
JOHN R. MOTT

H8
The strength of a man's virtue
should not be measured by his

special exertions, but by his
habitual acts.
BLAISE PASCAL

H9
Habit is a shirt made of iron.
CZECH PROVERB

H10
The best way to break a bad habit
is to drop it.
D. S. YODER

HAPPINESS
(See also CONTENTMENT and
JOY)

H11
Happiness is living by inner
purpose, not by outer pressures.
Happiness is a
happening-with-God.
DAVID AUGSBURGER

H12
Happiness consists in the
attainment of our desires, and in
our having only right desires.
ST. AUGUSTINE OF HIPPO

H13
Those who bring sunshine to the
lives of others cannot keep it from
themselves.
JAMES M. BARRIE

H14
If you ever find happiness by
hunting for it, you will find it, as
the old woman did her best
spectacles, safe on her own nose all
the time.
JOSH BILLINGS

H15
Men are made for happiness, and
anyone who is completely happy
has a right to say to himself 'I am
doing God's will on earth.'
ANTON CHEKHOV

H16
Happiness is the practice of the virtues.

ST. CLEMENT OF ALEXANDRIA

H17
The happiest man is he who learns from nature the lesson of worship.

RALPH WALDO EMERSON

H18
It is the chiefest point of happiness that a man is willing to be what he is.

DESIDERIUS ERASMUS

H19
The supreme happiness of life is the conviction of being loved for yourself, or, more correctly, of being loved in spite of yourself.

VICTOR HUGO

H20
God cannot give us happiness and peace apart from himself, because it is not there. There is no such thing.

C. S. LEWIS

H21
Most of us believe in trying to make other people happy only if they can be happy in ways which we approve.

ROBERT S. LYND

H22
A happiness that is sought for ourselves alone can never be found: for a happiness that is diminished by being shared is not big enough to make us happy.

THOMAS MERTON

H23
Happiness is the harvest of a quiet eye.

AUSTIN O'MALLEY

H24
Happiness is neither within us only, or without us; it is the union of ourselves with God.

BLAISE PASCAL

H25
Two happy days are seldom brothers.

BULGARIAN PROVERB

H26
When a man is happy he does not hear the clock strike.

GERMAN PROVERB

H27
Happiness is not a horse; you cannot harness it.

RUSSIAN PROVERB

H28
Happiness is not a state to arrive at, but a manner of travelling.

MARGARET LEE RUNBECK

H29
Happiness is a great love and much serving.

OLIVE SCHREINER

H30
Happiness? That's nothing more than health and a poor memory.

ALBERT SCHWEITZER

H31
Much happiness is overlooked because it doesn't cost anything.

OSCAR WILDE

HATE

H32
Hatred is self-punishment.

HOSEA BALLOU

H33
We hate what we fear and so where hate is, fear is lurking.

CYRIL CONNOLLY

H34
Hatred is like fire; it makes even light rubbish deadly.

GEORGE ELIOT

H35
Love blinds us to faults, but hatred blinds us to virtues.

MOSES IBN EZRA

H36
Hating people is like burning down your own house to get rid of a rat.

HARRY EMERSON FOSDICK

H37
The important thing is not to oneself be poisoned. Now, hatred poisons.

ANDRÉ GIDE

H38
When you visualised a man or a woman carefully, you could always begin to feel pity . . . That was a quality God's image carried with it . . . When you saw the lines at the corners of the eyes, the shape of the mouth, how the hair grew, it was impossible to hate. Hate was just a failure of imagination.

GRAHAM GREENE

H39
These two sins, hatred and pride, deck and trim themselves out as the devil clothed himself in the Godhead. Hatred will be Godlike; pride will be truth. These two are deadly sins: hatred is killing, pride is lying.

MARTIN LUTHER

H40
Hate cannot wise thee worse
Than guilt and shame have made thee.

THOMAS MOORE

H41
Short is the road that leads from fear to hate.

ITALIAN PROVERB

H42
You shall not hate any man; but some you shall admonish, and pray for others, and still others you shall love more than your own life.

TEACHING OF THE TWELVE APOSTLES

HEALING
(See also HEALTH)

H43
The good Instructor, the Wisdom, the Word of the Father, who made man, cares for the whole nature of his creature. The all-sufficient Physician of humanity, the Saviour, heals both our body and soul, which are the proper man.

ST. CLEMENT OF ALEXANDRIA

H44
The prayer that reforms the sinner and heals the sick is an absolute faith that all things are possible to God – a spiritual understanding of Him, an unselfed love.

MARY BAKER EDDY

H45
The temperature of the spiritual life of the Church is the index of her power to heal.

EVELYN FROST

H46
Christian thinkers cannot consider experiences of healing today because of the tacit acceptance of a world view which allows no place for a breakthrough of 'divine power' into the space-time world.

MORTON T. KELSEY

H47
In healing one can concentrate on either of two attributes: the power of God or the love of God. In every healing there is a manifestation of both.

FRANCIS MACNUTT

H48
The healing acts of Jesus were themselves the message that he had come to set men free.

FRANCIS MACNUTT

H49
Stronger than all the evils in the soul is the Word, and the healing power that dwells in him.

ORIGEN OF ALEXANDRIA

H50
Only the Holy Spirit can safely direct our healing power. And if we will listen to the voice of God within, we will be shown for whom to pray.

AGNES SANFORD

H51
Hear further, O man, of the work of resurrection going on in yourself, even though you were unaware of it. For perhaps you have sometimes fallen sick, and lost flesh, and strength, and beauty; but when you received again from God mercy and healing, you picked up again in flesh and appearance and recovered also your strength.

THEOPHILUS OF ANTIOCH

HEALTH
(See also BODY AND SOUL and HEALING)

H52
Health and cheerfulness mutually beget each other.

JOSEPH ADDISON

H53
Half the spiritual difficulties that men and women suffer arise from a morbid state of health.

HENRY WARD BEECHER

H54
Be careful to preserve your health. It is a trick of the devil, which he employs to deceive good souls, to incite them to do more than they are able, in order that they may no longer be able to do anything.

ST. VINCENT DE PAUL

H55
Take care of your health, that it may serve you to serve God.

ST. FRANCIS DE SALES

H56
The secret of the physical well-being of the Christian is the vitality of the divine life welling up within by virtue of his incorporation into Christ.

EVELYN FROST

H57
Do the best you can, without straining yourself too much and too continuously, and leave the rest to God. If you strain yourself too much you'll have to ask God to patch you up. And for all you know, patching you up may take time that it was planned to use some other way.

DON MARQUIS

H58
He who has health has hope; and he who has hope has everything.

ARAB PROVERB

H59
Health is better than wealth.

ENGLISH PROVERB

H60
Health is not valued till sickness comes.

ENGLISH PROVERB

H61
He who has health is rich and does not know it.

ITALIAN PROVERB

H62
All sorts of bodily diseases are produced by half-used minds.

GEORGE BERNARD SHAW

H63
Look at your health: and if you have it, praise God, and value it next to a good conscience.

IZAAK WALTON

HEART

H64
A man's first care should be to avoid the reproaches of his own heart.

JOSEPH ADDISON

H65
To my God, a heart of flame; to my fellow men, a heart of love; to myself, a heart of steel.

ST. AUGUSTINE OF HIPPO

H66
The heart is as divine a gift as the mind; and to neglect it in the search for God is to seek ruin.

ROBERT H. BENSON

H67
Let us learn to cast our hearts into God.

ST. BERNARD OF CLAIRVAUX

H68
A man's heart gets cold if he does not keep it warm by living in it; and a censorious man is one who ordinarily lives out of his own heart.

FREDERICK W. FABER

H69
What a number of the dead we carry in our hearts. Each of us bears his cemetery within.

GUSTAVE FLAUBERT

H70
Plato located the soul of man in the head; Christ located it in the heart.

ST. JEROME

H71
The heart of a good man is the sanctuary of God in this world.

MADAME NECKER

H72
When the heart is crowded, it has most room; when empty, it can find place for no new guest.

AUSTIN O'MALLEY

H73
The heart has its reasons which reason does not understand.

BLAISE PASCAL

H74
When the heart is afire, some sparks will fly out of the mouth.

ENGLISH PROVERB

H75
Nowhere are there more hiding places than in the heart.

GERMAN PROVERB

H76
The capital of Heaven is the heart in which Jesus Christ is enthroned as king.

SADHU SUNDAR SINGH

HEAVEN

H77
If you insist on having your own way, you will get it. Hell is the enjoyment of your own way forever. If you really want God's way with you, you will get it in Heaven.

DANTE ALIGHIERI

H78
Heaven is not to be looked upon only as the reward, but as the natural effect of a religious life.

JOSEPH ADDISON

H79
People sometimes say to youth, 'The world is at your feet!' But this is not true unless Heaven is in your heart.

P. AINSWORTH

H80
Heaven will be the endless portion of every man who has Heaven in his soul.

HENRY WARD BEECHER

H81
To believe in Heaven is not to run

away from life; it is to run towards it.

JOSEPH D. BLINCO

H82
God may not give us an easy journey to the Promised Land, but He will give us a safe one.

ANDREW BONAR

H83
A man's reach should exceed his grasp, or what's a Heaven for?

ROBERT BROWNING

H84
All the way to Heaven is Heaven.

ST. CATHERINE OF SIENA

H85
Heaven means to be one with God.

CONFUCIUS

H86
The main object of religion is not to get a man into Heaven; but to get Heaven into him.

THOMAS HARDY

H87
I would not give one moment of Heaven for all the joys and riches of the world, even if it lasted for thousands and thousands of years.

MARTIN LUTHER

H88
Earth hath no sorrow that Heaven cannot heal.

THOMAS MOORE

H89
Love of Heaven is the only way to Heaven.

JOHN HENRY NEWMAN

H90
Men go laughing to Heaven.

DUTCH PROVERB

H91
If God were not willing to forgive sin Heaven would be empty.

GERMAN PROVERB

H92
Heaven is mine if God says amen.

SPANISH PROVERB

H93
One day, in my despair, I threw myself into a chair in the consulting room and groaned out, 'What a blockhead I was to come out here to doctor savages like these!' Whereupon Joseph quietly remarked, 'Yes, doctor, here on earth you are a great blockhead, but not in Heaven.'

ALBERT SCHWEITZER

H94
Heaven is God and God is in my soul.

ELISABETH DE LA TRINITÉ

HELL

H95
I found the original of my Hell in the world which we inhabit.

DANTE ALIGHIERI

H96
Hell is not to love anymore.

GEORGE BERNANOS

H97
What is Hell? . . . The suffering that comes from the consciousness that one is no longer able to love.

FEODOR DOSTOEVSKI

H98
Hell is truth seen too late – duty neglected in its season.

TYRON EDWARDS

H99
Hell was not prepared for man. God never meant that man would ever go to Hell. Hell was prepared for the devil and his angels, but man rebelled against God and followed the devil.

BILLY GRAHAM

H100
There is nobody will go to Hell for company.
GEORGE HERBERT

H101
Men are not in Hell because God is angry with them: they are in wrath and darkness because they have done to the light, which infinitely flows forth from God, as that man does to the light of the sun who puts out his own eyes.
WILLIAM LAW

H102
The safest road to Hell is the gradual one – the gentle slope, soft underfoot, without sudden turnings, without milestones, without signposts.
C. S. LEWIS

H103
The one principle of Hell is 'I am my own.'
GEORGE MACDONALD

H104
When the world dissolves, all places will be Hell that are not Heaven.
CHRISTOPHER MARLOWE

H105
Heaven would be Hell to an irreligious man.
JOHN HENRY NEWMAN

H106
Heaven for climate; Hell for society.
GERMAN PROVERB

H107
Hell is paved with good intentions and roofed with lost opportunities.
PORTUGUESE PROVERB

H108
Fierce and poisonous animals were created for terrifying man, in order that he might be made aware of the final judgment in Hell.
JOHN WESLEY

HELP

H109
He who sees a need and waits to be asked for help is as unkind as if he had refused it.
DANTE ALIGHIERI

H110
God's help is nearer than the door.
WILLIAM G. BENHAM

H111
A willing helper does not wait to be called.
DANISH PROVERB

H112
Help your brother's boat across, and your own will reach the shore.
HINDU PROVERB

H113
To help all created things, that is the measure of our responsibility; to be helped by all, that is the measure of our hope.
GERALD VANN

HERESY
(See also ERROR)

H114
For you are not to suppose, brethren, that heresies could be produced through any little souls. None save great men have been the authors of heresies.
ST. AUGUSTINE OF HIPPO

H115
We should detest and prohibit in heretics not those common beliefs in which they are with us and not against us, but those divisions of peace contrary to truth by which they are against us and do not follow.
THE VENERABLE BEDE

H116
The heretic is not a man who loves truth too much; no man can love

truth too much. The heretic is a man who loves his truth more than truth itself. He prefers the half-truth that he has found to the whole truth which humanity has found.

G. K. CHESTERTON

H117
Ignorance is the mark of the heathen, knowledge of the true Church, and conceit of the heretics.

ST. CLEMENT OF ALEXANDRIA

H118
A heretic was one who was pertinacious, or sinfully obstinate, in his rejection of revealed doctrine. To speak of a heretic in good faith would have seemed as odd to the medieval thinkers as to speak of a murderer in good faith seems to us.

CHARLES DAVIS

H119
When doctrines meet with general approbation,
it is not heresy, but reformation.

DAVID GARRICK

H120
Heresy is the school of pride.

GEORGE HERBERT

H121
They that approve a private opinion, call it opinion, but they that mislike it, heresy, and yet heresy signifies no more than private opinion.

THOMAS HOBBES

H122
It is a shorter thing, and sooner done, to write heresies, than to answer them.

SIR THOMAS MORE

H123
In reading ecclesiastical history, when I was an Anglican, it used to be forcibly brought home to me how the initial error of what afterwards became heresy was the urging forward some truth against the prohibition of authority at an unseasonable time.

JOHN HENRY NEWMAN

HISTORY

H124
God cannot alter the past, but historians can.

SAMUEL BUTLER

H125
Perhaps history is a thing that would stop happening if God held His breath, or could be imagined as turning away to think of something else.

HERBERT BUTTERFIELD

H126
One of the deepest impulses in man is the impulse to record – to scratch a drawing on a tusk or keep a diary, to collect sagas and heap cairns. This instinct as to the enduring value of the past is, one might say, the very basis of civilisation.

JOHN JAY CHAPMAN

H127
History unfolds itself by strange and unpredictable paths. We have little control over the future; and none at all over the past.

SIR WINSTON CHURCHILL

H128
What are all histories but God manifesting himself.

OLIVER CROMWELL

H129
There is no history; only biography.

RALPH WALDO EMERSON

H130
Man writes histories; goodness is silent. History is, indeed, little

more than the register of the crimes, follies, and misfortunes of mankind.

EDWARD GIBBON

H131
The lesson of history tells us that no state or government devised by man can flourish forever.

BILLY GRAHAM

H132
The historian cannot choose his villains like the poet, nor invent them. At a particular time they are 'given'. Given, as it were, perfectly clearly, by a higher power.

THEODOR HAECKER

H133
The first law of history is not to dare to utter falsehood; the second, not to fear to speak the truth.

POPE LEO XIII

H134
In truth, every event of this world is a type of those that follow, history proceeding forward as a circle ever enlarging.

JOHN HENRY NEWMAN

H135
Hegel was right when he said that we learn from history that men never learn anything from history.

GEORGE BERNARD SHAW

HOLINESS
(See also PERFECTION, SPIRITUAL LIFE and WHOLENESS)

H136
There is no single definition of holiness: there are dozens, hundreds. But there is one I am particularly fond of; being holy means getting up immediately every time you fall, with humility and joy. It doesn't mean never

falling into sin. It means being able to say, 'Yes, Lord, I have fallen a thousand times. But thanks to you I have got up again a thousand and one times.' That's all. I like thinking about that.

HELDER CAMARA

H137
The beauty of holiness has done more, and will do more, to regenerate the world and bring in everlasting righteousness than all the other agencies put together.

THOMAS CHALMERS

H138
All of us can attain to Christian virtue and holiness, no matter in what condition of life we live and no matter what our life-work may be.

ST. FRANCIS DE SALES

H139
Sanctify yourself and you will sanctify society.

ST. FRANCIS OF ASSISI

H140
There is no true holiness without humility.

THOMAS FULLER

H141
In our era the road to holiness necessarily passes through the world of action.

DAG HAMMERSKJOLD

H142
We have become too spiritual in a 'holy' 'holy' sense, whereas we should be Biblically holy – that means facing up to the totality of life, in the power of the Cross.

GEORGE MacLEOD

H143
To know what holiness is you have to be holy.

DONALD NICHOLL

H144
Holiness is not an optional extra to the process of creation but rather the whole point of it.
DONALD NICHOLL

H145
You must be holy in the way God asks you to be holy. God does not ask you to be a Trappist monk or a hermit. He wills that you sanctify the world and your everyday life.
VINCENT PALLOTTI

H146
The serene beauty of a holy life is the most powerful influence in the world next to the power of God.
BLAISE PASCAL

H147
Humour is one of the three H's that link Holiness to Humility.
T. D. ROBERTS

HOLY SPIRIT
(See also HOLY TRINITY and INDWELLING SPIRIT)

H148
Love can be used either as an essential name of the divine nature or as a personal name of a divine person – then it is the proper name of the Holy Ghost, as Word is the proper name of the Son.
ST. THOMAS AQUINAS

H149
The Holy Spirit Himself, which also operates in the prophets, we assert to be an effluence of God, flowing from Him and returning back again like a beam of the sun.
ATHENAGORAS

H150
As 'to be born' is, for the Son, to be from the Father, so, for the Holy Spirit, 'to be the gift of God' is to proceed from Father and Son.
ST. AUGUSTINE OF HIPPO

H151
I should as soon attempt to raise flowers if there were no atmosphere, or produce fruits if there were neither light nor heat, as to regenerate men if I did not believe there was a Holy Ghost.
HENRY WARD BEECHER

H152
The Holy Spirit is the living interiority of God.
ROMANO GUARDINI

H153
The whole future of the human race depends on bringing the individual soul more completely and perfectly under the sway of the Holy Spirit.
ISAAC T. HECKER

H154
Those who have the gale of the Holy Spirit go forward even in sleep.
BROTHER LAWRENCE

H155
The Spirit of God first imparts love; he next inspires hope, and then gives liberty; and that is about the last thing we have in many of our churches.
DWIGHT L. MOODY

H156
Every time we say 'I believe in the Holy Spirit,' we mean that we believe there is a living God able and willing to enter human personality and change it.
J. B. PHILLIPS

HOME
(See also FAMILY)

H157
The strength of a nation is derived from the integrity of its homes.
CONFUCIUS

H158
A home is no home unless it contains food and fire for the mind as well as for the body.
MARGARET FULLER

H159
He is the happiest, be he king or peasant, who finds peace in his home.
JOHANN WOLFGANG VON GOETHE

H160
Home is where the heart is.
PLINY THE ELDER

H161
Better be kind at home than burn incense in a far place.
CHINESE PROVERB

H162
It takes patience to appreciate domestic bliss; volatile spirits prefer unhappiness.
GEORGE SANTAYANA

H163
Happiness is to be found only in the home where God is loved and honoured, where each one loves, and helps, and cares for the others.
THEOPHANE VÉNARD

H164
The home must be in accord with the Church, that all harmful influences be withheld from the souls of children. Where there is true piety in the home, purity of morals reigns supreme.
JOHN VIANNEY

HONESTY
(See also INTEGRITY)

H165
How desperately difficult it is to be honest with oneself. It is much easier to be honest with other people.
EDWARD BENSON

H166
He who says there is no such thing as an honest man, you may be sure is himself a knave.
GEORGE BERKELEY

H167
Honesty is the first chapter of the book of wisdom.
THOMAS JEFFERSON

H168
An honest man's the noblest work of God.
ALEXANDER POPE

H169
Honesty may be dear bought, but can never be an ill pennyworth.
ENGLISH PROVERB

H170
No honest man ever repented of his honesty.
GERMAN PROVERB

H171
I hope I shall possess firmness and virtue enough to maintain what I consider the most enviable of all titles, the character of an honest man.
GEORGE WASHINGTON

H172
Honesty is the best policy; but he who is governed by that maxim is not an honest man.
RICHARD WHATELY

HONOUR

H173
Dignity does not consist in possessing honours, but in deserving them.
ARISTOTLE

H174
Honour is like a rocky island without a landing place; once we leave it we can't get back.
NICOLAS BOILEAU-DESPREAUX

H175
The louder he talked of his honour,
the faster we counted our spoons.
RALPH WALDO EMERSON

H176
When one has to seek the honour
that comes from God only, he will
take the withholding of the honour
that comes from men very quietly
indeed.
GEORGE MACDONALD

H177
Whoever would not die to preserve
his honour would be infamous.
BLAISE PASCAL

H178
He who has lost honour can lose
nothing more.
PUBLILIUS SYRUS

H179
It is better to deserve honours and
not have them than to have them
and not deserve them.
MARK TWAIN

HOPE
(See also ENCOURAGEMENT)
H180
No man is able of himself to grasp
the supreme good of eternal life; he
needs divine help. Hence there is
here a two-fold object, the eternal
life we hoped for, and the divine
help we hope by.
ST. THOMAS AQUINAS

H181
Other men see only a hopeless end,
but the Christian rejoices in an
endless hope.
GILBERT BRENKEN

H182
What oxygen is to the lungs, such is
hope for the meaning of life.
EMIL BRUNNER

H183
As long as matters are really
hopeful, hope is a mere flattery or
platitude; it is only when
everything is hopeless that hope
begins to be a strength at all. Like
all the Christian virtues, it is as
unreasonable as it is indispensable.
G. K. CHESTERTON

H184
Hope is one of the principal springs
that keep mankind in motion.
ANDREW FULLER

H185
The word which God has written
on the brow of every man is Hope.
VICTOR HUGO

H186
Hope is itself a species of
happiness, and perhaps, the chief
happiness which the world affords.
SAMUEL JOHNSON

H187
Hope is the struggle of the soul,
breaking loose from what is
perishable, and attesting her
eternity.
HERMAN MELVILLE

H188
The coffin of every hope is the
cradle of a good experience.
FLORENCE NIGHTINGALE

H189
Hope springs eternal in the human
breast.
ALEXANDER POPE

H190
If it were not for hope the heart
would break.
ENGLISH PROVERB

H191
While there is life there is hope.
LATIN PROVERB

H192
We promise according to our

hopes, and perform according to our fears.

FRANÇOIS DE LA ROCHEFOUCAULD

H193
I am a man of hope, not for human reasons nor from any natural optimism, but because I believe the Holy Spirit is at work in the Church and in the World, even when His name remains unheard.

LEON JOSEPH SUENENS

H194
Hope is the only good that is common to all men; those who have nothing else possess hope still.

THALES

HOSPITALITY

H195
The Christian should offer his brethren simple and unpretentious hospitality.

ST. BASIL

H196
It is a sin against hospitality to open your doors and shut up your countenance.

ENGLISH PROVERB

H197
Hospitality is one form of worship.

JEWISH PROVERB

H198
To give our Lord a perfect hospitality, Mary and Martha must combine.

ST. TERESA OF AVILA

HUMAN CONDITION
(See also ORIGINAL SIN)

H199
The goodness of God knows how to use our disordered wishes and actions, often lovingly turning them to our advantage while always preserving the beauty of His order.

ST. BERNARD OF CLAIRVAUX

H200
We are all as God made us, and oftentimes a great deal worse.

MIGUEL DE CERVANTES

H201
Do you think anything on earth can be done without trouble?

MOHANDAS GANDHI

H202
There is no crime of which one cannot imagine oneself to be the author.

JOHANN WOLFGANG VON GOETHE

H203
The world owes all its onward impulse to men ill at ease. The happy man inevitably confines himself within ancient limits.

NATHANIEL HAWTHORNE

H204
The children of Israel did not find in the manna all the sweetness and strength they might have found in it; not because the manna did not contain them, but because they longed for other meat.

ST. JOHN OF THE CROSS

H205·
He who makes a beast of himself gets rid of the pain of being a man.

SAMUEL JOHNSON

H206
From such crooked wood as that which man is made of, nothing straight can be fashioned.

IMMANUEL KANT

H207
Humanity does not pass through phases as a train passes through a station: being alive, it has the privilege of always moving yet never leaving anything behind.

Whatever we have been, in some sort we are still.

C. S. LEWIS

H208

If there be a God, *since* there is a God, the human race is implicated in some terrible aboriginal calamity. It is out of joint with the purposes of its Creator.

JOHN HENRY NEWMAN

H209

To what shall I compare this life of ours? Even before I can say, 'It is like a lightning flash or a dewdrop,' it is no more.

SENGAI

H210

We are not part of a nice neat creation, set in motion by a loving God; we are part of a mutinous world where rebellion against God is the order of the day.

SAMUEL M. SHOEMAKER

HUMANITY
(See also MAN)

H211

Our humanity were a poor thing were it not for the divinity that stirs within us.

FRANCIS BACON

H212

I know of no rights of race superior to the rights of humanity.

FREDERICK DOUGLAS

H213

It is easier to love humanity as a whole than to love one's neighbour.

ERIC HOFFER

H214

Whenever there is lost the consciousness that every man is an object of concern for us just because he is a man, civilisation and morals are shaken, and the advance to fully developed inhumanity is only a question of time.

ALBERT SCHWEITZER

H215

Only on paper has humanity yet achieved glory, beauty, truth, knowledge, virtue, and abiding love.

GEORGE BERNARD SHAW

HUMANITY OF CHRIST
(See also JESUS CHRIST)

H216

He became what we are that he might make us what he is.

ST. ATHANASIUS

H217

Christ as God is the fatherland where we are going. Christ as man is the way by which we go.

ST. AUGUSTINE OF HIPPO

H218

To know Jesus and Him crucified is my philosophy, and there is none higher.

ST. BERNARD OF CLAIRVAUX

H219

God clothed himself in vile man's flesh so He might be weak enough to suffer woe.

JOHN DONNE

H220

By a Carpenter mankind was created and made, and by a Carpenter meet it was that man should be repaired.

DESIDERIUS ERASMUS

H221

Tell me the picture of Jesus you have reached and I will tell you some important traits about your nature.

OSCAR PFISTER

H222
He is a man who acts like a man.
DANISH PROVERB

H223
'Gentle Jesus, meek and mild,' is a snivelling modern invention, with no warrant in the Gospels.
GEORGE BERNARD SHAW

H224
Poor creature though I be, I am the hand and foot of Christ. I move my hand and my hand is wholly Christ's hand, for deity is become inseparably one with me. I move my foot, and it is aglow with God.
ST. SYMEON THE NEW THEOLOGIAN

H225
God's only Son doth hug humanity into his very person.
EDWARD TAYLOR

H226
Christ did not die a martyr. He died – infinitely more humbly – a common criminal.
SIMONE WEIL

HUMAN NATURE

H227
It will be very generally found that those who will sneer habitually at human nature, and affect to despise it, are among its worst and least pleasant samples.
CHARLES DICKENS

H228
It is human nature to think wisely and act foolishly.
ANATOLE FRANCE

H229
Human nature will find itself only when it fully realises that to be human it has to cease to be beastly or brutal.
MOHANDAS GANDHI

H230
Human action can be modified to some extent, but human nature cannot be changed.
ABRAHAM LINCOLN

H231
Human nature is like a drunk peasant. Lift him into the saddle on one side, over he topples on the other side.
MARTIN LUTHER

H232
Left to itself, human nature tends to death, and utter apostasy from God, however plausible it may look externally.
JOHN HENRY NEWMAN

H233
We were made to be human beings here, and when people try to be anything else, they generally get into some sort of scrapes.
HANNAH WHITHALL SMITH

HUMAN RIGHTS
(See also RIGHT)

H234
Rights that do not flow from duty well performed are not worth having.
MOHANDAS GANDHI

H235
Wherever there is a human being, I see God-given rights inherent in that being, whatever may be the sex or complexion.
WILLIAM L. GARRISON

H236
I am the inferior of any man whose rights I trample under foot.
ROBERT G. INGERSOLL

H237
They have rights who dare maintain them.
JAMES RUSSELL LOWELL

H238
No one can be perfectly free till all

are free, no one can be perfectly moral till all are moral; no one can be perfectly happy till all are happy.

HERBERT SPENCER

H239
A right is worth fighting for only when it can be put into operation.

WOODROW WILSON

HUMILITY
(See also MODESTY)

H240
Pride is the cold mountain peak, sterile and bleak; humility is the quiet valley fertile and abounding in life, and peace lives there.

ANNE AUSTIN

H241
You grow up the day you have your first real laugh at yourself.

ETHEL BARRYMORE

H242
To feel extraordinarily small and unimportant is always a wholesome feeling.

ROBERT H. BENSON

H243
Humility is the mother of salvation.

ST. BERNARD OF CLAIRVAUX

H244
Humility is the truth about ourselves loved.

C. CAREY-ELWES

H245
Humility in oneself is not attractive, though it is attractive in others.

JOHN CHAPMAN

H246
It is always the secure who are humble.

G. K. CHESTERTON

H247
The reason why God is so great a Lover of humility is because He is the great Lover of truth. Now humility is nothing but truth, while pride is nothing but lying.

ST. VINCENT DE PAUL

H248
True humility makes no pretence of being humble, and scarcely ever utters words of humility.

ST. FRANCIS DE SALES

H249
The humble knowledge of yourself is a surer way to God than the deepest search after science.

THOMAS À KEMPIS

H250
In the sight of God no man can look at himself except when he is down on his knees.

FRANÇOIS MAURIAC

H251
If there were no humility in the world, everybody would long ago have committed suicide.

THOMAS MERTON

H252
The humble man receives praise the way a clean window takes the light of the sun. The truer and more intense the light is, the less you see of the glass.

THOMAS MERTON

H253
I used to think that God's gifts were on shelves one above the other and that the taller we grew in Christian character the more easily we could reach them. I now find that God's gifts are on shelves one beneath the other and that it is not a question of growing taller but of stooping lower.

F. B. MEYER

H254
Golden deeds kept out of sight are most laudable.

BLAISE PASCAL

H255
An able yet humble man is a jewel worth a kingdom.

WILLIAM PENN

H256
Too much humility is pride.

GERMAN PROVERB

H257
Don't make yourself so big. You are not so small.

JEWISH PROVERB

H258
Reflect that true humility consists to a great extent in being ready for what the Lord desires to do with you, and happy that He should do it, and in always considering yourselves unworthy to be called His servants.

ST. TERESA OF AVILA

H259
Humility like darkness reveals the heavenly lights.

HENRY DAVID THOREAU

HUMOUR
(See also JOY and LAUGHTER)

H260
A clown may be the first in the Kingdom of Heaven, if he has helped lessen the sadness of human life.

RABBI BAROKA

H261
True humour springs not more from the head than from the heart; it is not contempt, its essence is love.

THOMAS CARLYLE

H262
It is the test of a good religion whether you can make a joke of it.

G. K. CHESTERTON

H263
Whom the gods would make bigots, they first deprive of humour.

JAMES M. GILLIS

H264
There is of course something wrong with a man who is only partly humorous, or is only humorous at times, for humour ought to be a yeast, working through the whole of a man and his bearing.

THEODOR HAECKER

H265
I have never understood why it should be considered derogatory to the Creator to suppose that he has a sense of humour.

WILLIAM RALPH INGE

H266
Humour is the harmony of the heart.

DOUGLAS JERROLD

H267
Humour distorts nothing, and only false gods are laughed off their earthly pedestals.

AGNES PEPPLIER

HUNGER
(See also POVERTY)

H268
There's no sauce in the world like hunger.

MIGUEL DE CERVANTES

H269
There is no reason that the senseless Temples of God should abound in riches, and the living Temples of the Holy Spirit starve for hunger.

ETHELWOLD,
BISHOP OF WINCHESTER

H270
Hunger makes hard beans sweet.
ENGLISH PROVERB

H271
Hungry bellies have no ears.
ENGLISH PROVERB

H272
The road to Jericho today, the road
of the Good Samaritan, runs
through every under-developed
country.
MICHEL QUOIST

HUSBAND
(See also FAMILY and
MARRIAGE)

H273
Being a husband is a full-time job.
That is why so many husbands fail.
They cannot give their entire
attention to it.
ARNOLD BENNETT

H274
Husbands who have the courage to
be tender, enjoy marriages that
mellow through the years.
BRENDAN FRANCIS

H275
The only compliment some
husbands pay their wives is to
marry them.
ARNOLD GLASGOW

H276
To make a good husband, make a
good wife.
JOHN HEYWOOD

H277
And the woman must realise that
the man is a boy always, and will
take his pleasures always as a boy.
He must have his own circle of
fellow-men. That is his way of
pleasure. That is how he escapes.
Sports, games, recreation – he is a
boy again; living a boy's memories
even to old age.
BEDE JARRETT

H278
Marriage is not harmed by seducers
but by cowardly husbands.
SØREN KIERKEGAARD

H279
Husbands are in heaven whose
wives scold not.
ENGLISH PROVERB

H280
In the husband wisdom, in the wife
gentleness.
ENGLISH PROVERB

H281
Christian husband! Imitate St.
Joseph by beginning your day's
work with God, and ending it for
Him. Cherish those belonging to
you as the holy foster father did
Jesus, and be their faithful
protector.
JOHN VIANNEY

HYPOCRISY
(See also DECEPTION)

H282
Don't stay away from church
because there are so many
hypocrites. There's always room
for one more.
ARTHUR R. ADAMS

H283
A bad man is worse when he
pretends to be a saint.
FRANCIS BACON

H284
Hypocrisy – prejudice with a halo.
AMBROSE BIERCE

H285
No man, for any considerable
period, can wear one face to
himself and another to the
multitude, without finally getting
bewildered as to which may be the
true.
NATHANIEL HAWTHORNE

H286
It is no fault of Christianity if a hypocrite falls into sin.

ST. JEROME

H287
Solemn prayers, rapturous devotions, are but repeated hypocrisies unless the heart and mind be conformable to them.

WILLIAM LAW

H288
Better be a sinner than a hypocrite.

DANISH PROVERB

H289
When the fox preaches, look to your geese.

GERMAN PROVERB

H290
Hypocrisy is the homage which vice pays to virtue.

FRANÇOIS DE LA ROCHEFOUCAULD

H291
One may smile, and smile, and be a villain.

WILLIAM SHAKESPEARE

H292
The old-style hypocrite was a person who tried to appear better than he actually was: the new-style hypocrite tries to appear worse than he or she is.

CHARLES TEMPLETON

IDEALISM

I1
There is only one really startling thing to be done with the ideal, and that is to do it.

G. K. CHESTERTON

I2
If we put an absurdly high ideal before us, it ceases to be an ideal at all, because we have no idea of acting upon it.

FREDERICK W. FABER

I3
Men find in Jesus a reflection of their own ideals.

GRANVILLE HICKS

I4
The test of an ideal or rather of an idealist, is the power to hold to it and get one's inspiration from it under difficulties.

OLIVER WENDELL HOLMES

I5
Some men can live up to their loftiest ideals without ever going higher than a basement.

THEODORE ROOSEVELT

I6
Ideals are like the stars – we never reach them, but like the mariners of the sea we chart our course by them.

CARL SCHURZ

IDLENESS

I7
Idleness is the enemy of the soul.

ST. BENEDICT

I8
Sloth, like rust, consumes faster than labour wears.

BENJAMIN FRANKLIN

I9
To have too much to do is for most men safer than to have too little.

HENRY E. MANNING

I10
The devil tempts all but the idle man tempts the devil.

ENGLISH PROVERB

I11
How beautiful it is to do nothing, and then rest afterward.

SPANISH PROVERB

I12
He is not only idle who does

nothing but he is idle who might be better employed.

SOCRATES

I13
To be idle requires a strong sense of personal identity.

ROBERT LOUIS STEVENSON

IDOLATRY

I14
The Church is society's permanent rampart against idolatry. This is the ultimate, in a sense it is the only, sin, the root of all disorder.

AELRED GRAHAM

I15
We easily fall into idolatry, for we are inclined to it by nature; and coming to us by inheritance, it seems pleasant.

MARTIN LUTHER

I16
Christians can be more prone to idolatry than they realise, and their idolatries take the form of fetishism, the devotional attachment to facts, words or concepts which are not themselves final and are not themselves God.

MICHAEL RAMSEY

I17
When men have gone so far as to talk as though their idols have come to life, it is time that someone broke them.

RICHARD H. TAWNEY

I18
Whatever a man seeks, honours, or exalts more than God, this is the god of idolatry.

WILLIAM ULLATHORNE

IGNORANCE

I19
There are more fools than wise men and even in the wise man

himself there is more folly than wisdom.

NICOLAS DE CHAMFORT

I20
A young levite once remarked to his professor: 'God can dispense with my learning.' 'Yes,' was the reply, 'but He has still less need of your ignorance.'

JAMES GIBBONS

I21
There is nothing more frightful than ignorance in action.

JOHANN WOLFGANG VON GOETHE

I22
Ignorance is preferable to error; and he is less remote from truth who believes nothing, than he who believes what is wrong.

THOMAS JEFFERSON

I23
Nothing is so firmly believed as that which is least known.

FRANCIS JEFFREY

I24
We must make up our minds to be ignorant of much, if we would know anything.

JOHN HENRY NEWMAN

I25
Herein is the evil of ignorance, that he who is neither good nor wise is nevertheless satisfied with himself: he has no desire for that of which he feels no want.

SOCRATES

I26
I believe in the forgiveness of sins and the redemption of ignorance.

ADLAI STEVENSON

I27
Not ignorance, but ignorance of ignorance, is the death of knowledge.

ALFRED NORTH WHITEHEAD

IMAGINATION

128
The soul without imagination is
what an observatory would be
without a telescope.
HENRY WARD BEECHER

129
Imagination is not a talent of some
men but is the health of every man.
RALPH WALDO EMERSON

130
He who has imagination without
learning has wings and no feet.
JOSEPH JOUBERT

131
Always be on your guard against
your imagination. How many lions
it creates in our paths, and so
easily! And we suffer so much if we
do not turn a deaf ear to its tales
and suggestions.
GEORGE PORTER

132
Imagination and fiction make up
more than three-quarters of our
real life. Rare indeed are the true
contacts with good and evil.
SIMONE WEIL

IMMORTALITY
(See also AFTERLIFE and
ETERNITY)

133
If there is a sin against life, it lies
perhaps less in despairing of it than
in hoping for another and evading
the implacable grandeur of the one
we have.
ALBERT CAMUS

134
To be immortal is to share in
Divinity.
ST. CLEMENT OF ALEXANDRIA

135
There is nothing innocent or good
that dies and is forgotten: let us

hold to that faith or none.
CHARLES DICKENS

136
Here in this world He bids us
come, there in the next He shall bid
us welcome.
JOHN DONNE

137
Our dissatisfaction with any other
solution is the blazing evidence of
immortality.
RALPH WALDO EMERSON

138
We cannot resist the conviction
that this world is for us only the
porch of another and more
magnificent temple of the Creator's
majesty.
FREDERICK W. FABER

139
The average man does not know
what to do with this life, yet wants
another one that will last forever.
ANATOLE FRANCE

140
Without love immortality would be
frightful and horrible.
THEODOR HAECKER

141
Our Creator would never have
made such lovely days, and have
given us the deep hearts to enjoy
them above and beyond all
thought, unless we were meant to
be immortal.
NATHANIEL HAWTHORNE

142
Surely God would not have created
such a being as man . . . to exist
only for a day! No, no, man was
made for immortality.
ABRAHAM LINCOLN

143
The universe is a stairway leading
nowhere unless man is immortal.
EDGAR YOUNG MULLINS

144
Those who live in the Lord never
see each other for the last time.
GERMAN PROVERB

145
Spring – an experience in
immortality.
HENRY DAVID THOREAU

146
I have never seen what to me
seemed an atom of proof that there
is a future life. And yet – I am
strongly inclined to expect one.
MARK TWAIN

147
There is only one way I can get
ready for immortality, and that is
to love this life, and live it bravely
and cheerfully and as faithfully as I
can.
HENRY VAN DYKE

INCARNATION
(See also CHRISTMAS)

148
I think that the purpose and cause
of the Incarnation was that God
might illuminate the world by his
wisdom and excite it to the love of
himself.
PETER ABELARD

149
In order that the body of Christ
might be shown to be a real body,
he was born of a woman; but in
order that his Godhead might be
made clear he was born of a virgin.
ST. THOMAS AQUINAS

150
The greatness of God was not cast
off, but the slightness of human
nature was put on.
ST. THOMAS AQUINAS

151
Every thought, word, action,
silence, and self-repression in the

incarnate life of the Word of God is
full of spiritual significance and
effectiveness.
ROBERT H. BENSON

152
The Word of God became man that
you also may learn from a man how
a man becomes a God.
ST. CLEMENT OF ALEXANDRIA

153
The Incarnation would be equally a
miracle however Jesus entered the
world.
P. T. FORSYTH

154
If Jesus Christ is God incarnate, no
fuller disclosure of God in terms of
manhood than is given in his
person is conceivable or possible.
CHARLES GORE

155
The Word of God, Jesus Christ, on
account of His great love for
mankind, became what we are in
order to make us what He is
himself.
ST. IRENAEUS

156
The Incarnation is not an event; but
an institution. What Jesus once
took up He never laid down.
VINCENT MCNABB

157
On account of Him there have
come to be many Christs in the
world, even all who, like Him,
loved righteousness and hated
iniquity.
ORIGEN OF ALEXANDRIA

158
We are far too apt to limit and
mechandise the great doctrine of the
Incarnation, which forms the
centre of the Christian faith.
Whatever it may mean, it means at
least this – that in the conditions of

human life we have access, as nowhere else, to the inmost nature of the divine.

A. S. PRINGLE-PATTISON

159
What happened at the Incarnation is that God, the power of nature and history, the logos or principle of the evolutionary process, began to be represented in a new way.

JOHN A. T. ROBINSON

INDEPENDENCE

160
Independence, like honour, is a rocky island without a beach.

NAPOLEON BONAPARTE

161
Let every tub stand upon its own bottom.

JOHN BUNYAN

162
There is a great deal of self-will in the world, but very little genuine independence of character.

FREDERICK W. FABER

163
Christianity promises to make men free; it never promises to make them independent.

WILLIAM RALPH INGE

164
It is tragic how few people ever 'possess their souls' before they die. 'Nothing is more rare in any man,' says Emerson, 'than an act of his own.' It is quite true. Most people are other people. Their thoughts are someone else's opinions, their lives a mimicry, their passions a quotation.

OSCAR WILDE

INDIFFERENCE
(See also APATHY)

165
Holy indifference goes beyond resignation: for it loves nothing except for the love of God's will.

ST. FRANCIS DE SALES

166
The opposite of love is not hate; it is something much worse than that; hate with all its negation and emotion at least takes the other into account; the opposite of love is something much cooler, more pallid, and really much more cruel, the opposite of love is indifference.

WILLIAM HAGUE

167
Most of us have no real loves and no real hatreds. Blessed is love, less blessed is hatred, but thrice accursed is that indifference which is neither one nor the other.

MARK RUTHERFORD

168
The worst sin toward our fellow creatures is not to hate them, but to be indifferent to them.

GEORGE BERNARD SHAW

INDIVIDUALITY

169
The real man is a maze of a million notes: the label is all one note.

HILAIRE BELLOC

170
It is often all our own individuality that hinders us from becoming aware of the individualities of others to their full extent.

JOHANN WOLFGANG VON GOETHE

171
The way of salvation cannot lie in melting people down into a mass, but on the contrary in their

separation and individuation.

THEODOR HAECKER

172
It is because of the devotion or sacrifice of individuals that causes become of value.

JULIAN HUXLEY

173
Every man must do two things alone: he must do his own believing, and his own dying.

MARTIN LUTHER

174
The only ultimate reason why man as man has individual significance is that Christ died for him.

GEORGE F. MACLEOD

175
At bottom every man knows well enough that he is a unique being, only once on this earth; and by no extraordinary chance will such a marvellously picturesque piece of diversity in unity as he is, ever be put together a second time.

FRIEDRICH NIETZSCHE

INDWELLING SPIRIT
(See also SPIRITUAL LIFE)

176
For it is not by themselves being so that men are gods, but they become gods by participation in that one God Who is the true God.

ST. AUGUSTINE OF HIPPO

177
The indwelling of God is this – to hold God ever in memory, His shrine established within us.

ST. BASIL

178
The seed of God is in us. Given an intelligent and hard-working farmer, it will thrive and grow up to God, whose seed it is; and accordingly its fruits will be God-nature. Pear seeds grow into pear trees, nut seeds into nut trees, and God seeds into God.

MEISTER ECKHART

179
The very best and utmost of attainment in this life is to remain still and let God act and speak in thee.

MEISTER ECKHART

180
What lies behind us and what lies before us are tiny matters compared to what lies within us.

RALPH WALDO EMERSON

181
The gift of the Holy Ghost closes the last gap between the life of God and ours . . . When we allow the love of God to move in us, we can no longer distinguish ours and his; he becomes us, he lives us. It is the first fruits of the spirit, the beginning of our being made divine.

AUSTIN FARRER

182
For what is more consoling to a soul on earth than to be withdrawn by grace from the trouble of worldly affairs, from the defilement of desiring and the vanity of loving creatures, into the peace and sweetness of spiritual love, where it inwardly perceives God's presence and is satisfied with the light of His countenance?

WALTER HILTON

183
Your treasure house is within. It contains all you will ever need. Use it fully instead of seeking vainly outside yourself.

HUI HAI

184
The centre of the soul is God, and

when the soul has attained to him according to the whole capacity of its being, and according to the force of its operation, it will have reached the last and deep centre of the soul, which will be when with all its powers it loves and understands and enjoys God.

ST. JOHN OF THE CROSS

185
Too few people have experienced the divine image as the innermost possession of their own souls. Christ only meets them from without, never from within the soul.

CARL GUSTAV JUNG

186
Every time we say, 'I believe in the Holy Spirit,' we mean that we believe that there is a living God able and willing to enter human personality and change it.

J. B. PHILLIPS

187
God is nigh unto thee. He is with thee. He is within thee. There is no good man but hath God within him.

SENECA

188
Father! replenish with Thy grace
This longing heart of mine;
Make it Thy quiet dwelling-place,
Thy sacred inmost shrine!

ANGELUS SILESIUS

INFLUENCE

189
Every life is a profession of faith, and exercises an inevitable and silent influence.

HENRI FRÉDÉRIC AMIEL

190
No man should think himself a zero, and think he can do nothing

about the state of the world.

BERNARD M. BARUCH

191
We live at the mercy of a malevolent word. A sound, a mere disturbance of the air, sinks into our very soul sometimes.

JOSEPH CONRAD

192
Blessed is the influence of one true, loving soul on another.

GEORGE ELIOT

193
He who goes with wolves learns to howl.

SPANISH PROVERB

INNOCENCE

194
Innocence always calls mutely for protection, when we would be so much wiser to guard ourselves against it; innocence is like a dumb leper who has lost his bell, wandering the world, meaning no harm.

GRAHAM GREENE

195
Hold fast to simplicity of heart and innocence. Yes, be as infants who do not know the wickedness that destroys the life of men.

SHEPHERD OF HERMAS

196
Innocence comes in contact with evil and doesn't know it; it baffles temptation; it is protected where no one else is.

BASIL W. MATURIN

197
Innocent actions carry their warrant with them.

ENGLISH PROVERB

I98
What hope is there for innocence if
it is not recognised?

SIMONE WEIL

INSIGHT

I99
A moment's insight is sometimes
worth a life's experience.

OLIVER WENDELL HOLMES

I100
Where man sees but withered
leaves God sees sweet flowers
growing.

ALBERT LAIGHTON

I101
The longer the field of activity the
personality has, the greater will be
its insights into reality.

WILLIAM F. LYNCH

I102
It is not easy to repent of anything
that has given us truer insight.

JOHN LANCASTER SPALDING

I103
One of the first things for which we
have to pray is a true insight into
our condition.

OLIVE WYON

INSPIRATION

I104
Look well into yourself; there is a
source which will always spring up
if you will search there.

MARCUS ANTONIUS

I105
No man was ever great without
some portion of divine inspiration.

MARCUS TULLIUS CICERO

I106
Inspirations never go in for long
engagements; they demand
immediate marriage to action.

BRENDAN FRANCIS

I107
Inspiration is the name of that
all-comprehensive operation of the
Holy Spirit whereby he has
bestowed on the Church a
complete and infallible Scripture.

ABRAHAM KUYPER

I108
The ultimate reason why God has
inspired certain books is that
through them he should be present
in our midst.

HUBERT J. RICHARDS

I109
You ask if inspiration can be lost;
no, when creation has started (then
it goes on like the child in the
womb).

W. B. YEATS

INSTINCT

I110
We know very little indeed about
the inner working of our own
selves. There's instinct, for
instance. We know nothing about
that, except that it is so.

ROBERT H. BENSON

I111
Beasts obey the prescript of their
natures, and live up to the height of
that instinct that Providence hath
given them.

RICHARD POWER

I112
Instinct is a great matter, I was a
coward on instinct.

WILLIAM SHAKESPEARE

I113
Few of us have vitality enough to
make any of our instincts
imperious.

GEORGE BERNARD SHAW

INTEGRITY
(See also HONESTY)

I114
Always vote for a principle, though you vote alone, and you may cherish the sweet reflection that your vote is never lost.

JOHN QUINCY ADAMS

I115
Live so that the preacher can tell the truth at your funeral.

K. BECKSTROM

I116
My worth to God in public is what I am in private.

OSWALD CHAMBERS

I117
He that is good at making excuses is seldom good at anything else.

BENJAMIN FRANKLIN

I118
Integrity without knowledge is weak and useless, and knowledge without integrity is dangerous and dreadful.

SAMUEL JOHNSON

I119
Some people are likeable in spite of their unswerving integrity!

DON MARQUIS

I120
Live among men as if God beheld you;
speak with God as if men were listening.

SENECA

INTELLIGENCE

I121
Intelligence is not something possessed once for all. It is in constant process of forming, and its retention requires constant alertness in observing consequences, and open-minded will to learn and courage in readjustment.

JOHN DEWEY

I122
I do not feel obliged to believe that that same God who has endowed us with sense, reason, and intellect has intended us to forego their use.

GALILEO GALILEI

I123
True intelligence very readily conceives of an intelligence superior to its own; and this is why truly intelligent men are modest.

ANDRÉ GIDE

I124
The more intelligent a man is, the more originality he discovers in men. Ordinary people see no difference between men.

BLAISE PASCAL

I125
Christianity has need of thought that it may come to the consciousness of its real self. For centuries it treasured the great commandment of love and mercy as traditional truth without recognising it as a reason for opposing slavery, witch-burning, torture, and all the other ancient and medieval forms of inhumanity.

ALBERT SCHWEITZER

INTENTION
(See also MOTIVATION)

I126
God looks at the intention of the heart rather than the gifts He is offered.

JEAN PIERRE CAMUS

I127
The consciousness of good intentions is the greatest solace in misfortune.

MARCUS TULLIUS CICERO

I128
One of the most excellent
intentions that we can possibly
have in all our actions, is to do
them because our Lord did them.
ST. FRANCIS DE SALES

I129
Man beholds the face, but God
looks upon the heart. Man
considers the actions, but God
weighs the intentions.
THOMAS À KEMPIS

I130
One often sees good intentions, if
pushed beyond moderation, bring
about very vicious results.
MICHEL DE MONTAIGNE

INVOLVEMENT

I131
Behold the turtle; he makes
progress only when he sticks his
neck out.
JAMES BRYANT CONANT

I132
The Church as a whole must be
concerned with both evangelism
and social action. It is not a case of
either-or; it is both-and. Anything
less is only a partial Gospel, not the
whole counsel of God.
ROBERT D. DE HAAN

I133
Be to the world a sign that while we
as Christians do not have all the
answers, we do know and care
about the questions.
BILLY GRAHAM

JEALOUSY
(See also ENVY)

J1
As to the green-eyed monster
jealousy . . . set on him at once and
poison him with extra doses of
kindness to the person whom he
wants to turn you against.
GEORGE PORTER

J2
Frenzy, heresy, and jealousy,
seldom cured.
ENGLISH PROVERB

J3
In jealousy there is more self-love
than love.
FRANÇOIS DE LA ROCHEFOUCAULD

J4
Moral indignation is jealousy with
a halo.
H. G. WELLS

JESUS CHRIST
(See also DIVINITY OF CHRIST
and HUMANITY OF CHRIST)

J5
Jesus Christ will be Lord of all or
he will not be Lord at all.
ST. AUGUSTINE OF HIPPO

J6
If Jesus Christ is not true God, how
could he *help* us? If he is not true
man, how could he help *us*?
DIETRICH BONHOEFFER

J7
Christ did not love humanity. He
never said that he loved humanity.
He loved men.
G. K. CHESTERTON

J8
As Gregory of Nyssa pictures it,
He entered paradise bringing with
Him His bride, Humanity, whom
He had just wedded on the Cross.
JEAN DANIELOU

J9
Who can deny that Jesus of
Nazareth, the incarnate Son of the
most High God, is the eternal glory
of the Jewish Race?
BENJAMIN DISRAELI

J10
I believe there is no one lovelier,
deeper, more sympathetic and
more perfect than Jesus. I say to
myself that not only is there no one
else like him, but there could never
be any one like him.
FEODOR DOSTOEVSKI

J11
A Christian has a union with Jesus
Christ more noble, more intimate
and more perfect than the
members of a human body have
with their head.
JOHN EUDES

J12
Jesus Christ is God's everything for
man's total need.
RICHARD HALVERSON

J13
Had the doctrines of Jesus been
preached always as pure as they
came from his lips, the whole
civilised world would now have
been Christian.
THOMAS JEFFERSON

J14
We get no deeper into Christ than
we allow him to get into us.
JOHN HENRY JOWETT

J15
In his life Christ is an example,
showing us how to live; in his death
he is a sacrifice, satisfying for our
sins; in his resurrection, a
conqueror; in his ascension, a king;
in his intercession, a high priest.
MARTIN LUTHER

J16
We can hardly think of Jesus Christ
without thinking of the sparrows,
the grass, fig trees, sheep,
VINCENT MCNABB

J17
A radical revolution, embracing
even nature itself, was the
fundamental idea of Jesus.
JOSEPH ERNEST RENAN

J18
I have a great need for Christ; I
have a great Christ for my need.
CHARLES H. SPURGEON

JEWS

J19
The Hebrews have done more to
civilise men than any other nation.
If I were an atheist, and believed in
blind eternal fate, I should still
believe that fate had ordained the
Jews to be the most essential
instrument for civilising the
nations.
JOHN QUINCY ADAMS

J20
To be a Jew is a destiny.
VICKI BAUM

J21
In Israel, in order to be a realist
you must believe in miracles.
DAVID BEN-GURION

J22
If my theory of relativity is proven
successful, Germany will claim me
as a German and France will
declare that I am a citizen of the
world. Should my theory prove
untrue, France will say that I am a
German and Germany will declare
that I am a Jew.
ALBERT EINSTEIN

J23
The pursuit of knowledge for its
own sake, an almost fanatical love
of justice, and a desire for personal
independence – these are features
of the Jewish tradition which make
me thank my stars that I belong to
it.
ALBERT EINSTEIN

J24
The race of the Hebrews is not new but is honoured among all men for its antiquity and is itself well known to all.

EUSEBIUS OF CAESAREA

J25
The Jew's home has rarely been his 'castle'; throughout the ages it has been something far higher – his sanctuary.

JOSEPH H. HERTZ

J26
Spiritually we are all Semites.

POPE PIUS XI

J27
No Jew is a fool, no hare is lazy.

SPANISH PROVERB

J28
Even Moses couldn't get along with the Jews.

YIDDISH PROVERB

J29
No misfortune avoids a Jew.

YIDDISH PROVERB

J30
For others a knowledge of the history of their people is a civic duty, while for Jews it is a sacred duty.

MAURICE SAMUEL

J31
The Jews generally give value. They make you pay; but they deliver the goods. In my experience the men who want something for nothing are invariably Christians.

GEORGE BERNARD SHAW

JOY
(See also HAPPINESS, HUMOUR and LAUGHTER)

J32
Those who bring sunshine to the lives of others cannot keep it from themselves.

JAMES M. BARRIE

J33
To be able to find joy in another's joy, that is the secret of happiness.

GEORGE BERNANOS

J34
Joy is the most infallible sign of the presence of God.

LEON BLOY

J35
We are all strings in the concert of his joy.

JAKOB BOEHME

J36
The joy that Jesus gives is the result of our disposition being at one with his own disposition.

OSWALD CHAMBERS

J37
The life without festival is a long road without an inn

DEMOCRITUS OF ABDERA

J38
It is good if man can bring about that God sings within him.

RABBI ELIMELEKH

J39
When I think upon my God, my heart is so full of joy that the notes dance and leap from my pen; and since God has given me a cheerful heart, it will be pardoned me that I serve Him with a cheerful spirit.

FRANZ JOSEF HAYDN

J40
There is no law which lays it down that you must smile! But you can make a gift of your smile; you can be the heaven of kindness in your family.

POPE JOHN PAUL II

J41
If there is joy in the world, surely
the man of pure heart possesses it.
THOMAS À KEMPIS

J42
Joy is never in our power, and
pleasure is. I doubt whether
anyone who has tasted joy would
ever, if both were in his power,
exchange it for all the pleasure in
the world.
C. S. LEWIS

J43
Joy is the serious business of
heaven.
C. S. LEWIS

J44
Only joyous love redeems.
CATHERINE MARSHALL

J45
One joy dispels a hundred cares.
ORIENTAL PROVERB

J46
Joy is the heavenly 'okay' of the
inner life of power.
AGNES SANFORD

J47
The surest mark of a Christian is
not faith, or even love, but joy.
SAMUEL M. SHOEMAKER

J48
This is the secret of joy. We shall
no longer strive for our own way;
but commit ourselves, easily and
simply, to God's way, acquiesce in
his will and in so doing find our
peace.
EVELYN UNDERHILL

JUDGING OTHERS
(See also JUDGMENT)
J49
We must neither judge nor suspect
evil of our neighbour, without good
grounds.
ST. ALPHONSUS LIGUORI

J50
It is well, when one is judging a
friend, to remember that he is
judging you with the same godlike
and superior impartiality.
ARNOLD BENNETT

J51
When it seems that God shows us
the faults of others, keep on the
safer side. It may be that thy
judgment is false.
ST. CATHERINE OF SIENA

J52
You will not become a saint
through other people's sins.
ANTON CHEKHOV

J53
How rarely we weigh our
neighbour in the same balance in
which we weigh ourselves.
THOMAS À KEMPIS

J54
Our duty is to believe that for
which we have sufficient evidence,
and to suspend judgment when we
have not.
SIR JOHN LUBBOCK

J55
Never a sound judgment without
charity. When man judges man,
charity is less a bounty from our
mercy than just allowance for the
insensible leeway of human
fallibility.
HERMAN MELVILLE

J56
A man's judgment of another
depends more on the judging and
on his passions than on the one
being judged and his conduct.
PAUL TOURNIER

JUDGMENT
(See also JUDGING OTHERS)
J57
For when the judgment is finished,

this heaven and earth shall cease to be, and there will be a new heaven and a new earth. For this world shall pass away by transmutation, not by absolute destruction.
ST. AUGUSTINE OF HIPPO

J58
It may be that the day of judgment will dawn tomorrow; in that case, we shall gladly stop working for a better future. But not before.
DIETRICH BONHOEFFER

J59
If we judge ourselves, we will not be judged by God.
JEAN PIERRE CAMUS

J60
God himself, sir, does not propose to judge man until the end of his days.
SAMUEL JOHNSON

J61
God postpones the collapse and dissolution of the universe (through which the bad angels, the demons, and men would cease to exist), because of the Christian seed, which He knows to be the cause in nature of the World's preservation.
ST. JUSTIN MARTYR

J62
Who judges others condemns himself.
ENGLISH PROVERB

J63
The judgment of God is going on wherever the word of God is being proclaimed; men are judging themselves, according to their acceptance or rejection of the Gospel.
ALAN RICHARDSON

JUSTICE
(See also JUDGMENT)

J64
Justice discards party, friendship, kindred, and is always, therefore, represented as blind.
JOSEPH ADDISON

J65
The rule of justice is plain, namely, that a good man ought not to swerve from the truth, not to inflict any unjust loss on anyone, nor to act in any way deceitfully or fraudulently.
ST. AMBROSE

J66
Let justice be done though the world perish.
ST. AUGUSTINE OF HIPPO

J67
Children are innocent and love justice, while most adults are wicked and prefer mercy.
G. K. CHESTERTON

J68
Justice is truth in action.
BENJAMIN DISRAELI

J69
The perfection of justice implies charity, because we have a right to be loved.
AUSTIN O'MALLEY

J70
The Christian demand for justice does not come from Karl Marx. It comes from Jesus Christ and the Hebrew prophets.
G. BROMLEY OXNAM

J71
Justice and power must be brought together, so that whatever is just may be powerful, and whatever is powerful may be just.
BLAISE PASCAL

J72
One hour of justice is worth a
hundred of prayer.

ARAB PROVERB

J73
In times when the government
imprisons any unjustly, the true
place for a just man is also the
prison.

HENRY DAVID THOREAU

KINDNESS

(See also LOVE)

K1
The greatest thing a man can do for
his Heavenly Father is to be kind to
some of His other children.

HENRY DRUMMOND

K2
Kindness has converted more
sinners than zeal, eloquence and
learning.

FREDERICK W. FABER

K3
There is a grace of kind listening,
as well as a grace of kind speaking.

FREDERICK W. FABER

K4
If you would reap praise, sow the
seeds;
gentle words and useful deeds.

BENJAMIN FRANKLIN

K5
Kindness is the golden chain by
which society is bound together.

JOHANN WOLFGANG VON GOETHE

K6
Wise sayings often fall on barren
ground; but a kind word is never
thrown away.

ARTHUR HELPS

K7
Sign in a little shop: 'Kindness
spoken here.'

MILDRED E. KORDENAT

K8
Kindness which is bestowed on the
good is never lost.

PLATO

K9
One kind word can warm three
winter months.

JAPANESE PROVERB

K10
One can pay back the loan of gold,
but one dies forever in debt to
those who are kind.

MALAYAN PROVERB

K11
To give pleasure to a single heart
by a single kind act is better than a
thousand head-bowings in prayer.

SAADI

K12
Be kind; everyone you meet is
fighting a hard battle.

JOHN WATSON

K13
That best portion of a good man's
life – His little, nameless
unremembered acts of kindness
and of love.

WILLIAM WORDSWORTH

KINGDOM OF GOD

K14
The Kingdom of God will not come
in a day; it will not be left with the
morning milk.

S. PARKES CADMAN

K15
Wherever the bounds of beauty,
truth and goodness are advanced
there the Kingdom comes.

DONALD COGGAN

K16
Is the Kingdom of God a big
family? Yes, in a sense it is. But in
another sense it is a prodigious
biological operation – that of the

Redeeming Incarnation.
P. TEILHARD DE CHARDIN

K17
To accept His Kingdom and to enter in brings blessedness, because the best conceivable thing is that we should be in obedience to the will of God.
C. H. DODD

K18
The Kingdom of God is a kingdom of love; and love is never a stagnant pool.
HENRY W. DU BOSE

K19
To want all that God wants, always to want it, for all occasions and without reservations, this is the Kingdom of God which is all within.
FRANÇOIS FENELON

K20
Wherever God rules over the human heart as King, there is the Kingdom of God established.
PAUL W. HARRISON

K21
The core of all that Jesus teaches about the Kingdom is the immediate apprehension and acceptance of God as King in his own life.
T. W. MASON

K22
In the Gospel, Jesus is *autobasileia*, the Kingdom himself.
ORIGEN OF ALEXANDRIA

K23
Eighty-six years I have served Him, and He has done me no wrong. How can I blaspheme my King who has saved me?
ST. POLYCARP TO HIS EXECUTIONERS

K24
If only we knew how to look at life as God sees it, we should realise that nothing is secular in the world, but that everything contributes to the building of the Kingdom of God.
MICHEL QUOIST

K25
If you do not wish for His kingdom, don't pray for it. But if you do, you must do more than pray for it; you must work for it.
JOHN RUSKIN

K26
Power in complete subordination to love – that is something like a definition of the Kingdom of God.
WILLIAM TEMPLE

K27
There is no structural organisation of society which can bring about the coming of the Kingdom of God on earth, since all systems can be perverted by the selfishness of man.
WILLIAM TEMPLE

K28
Jesus never speaks of the Kingdom of God as previously existing. To him the Kingdom is throughout something new, now first to be realised.
GEERHARDUS VOS

KNOWLEDGE
(See also KNOWLEDGE OF GOD and OMNISCIENCE)

K29
A scrap of knowledge about sublime things is worth more than any amount about trivialities.
ST. THOMAS AQUINAS

K30
Let knowledge be applied to a kind of scaffolding, making it possible for the edifice of charity to rise, to endure for ever, even when

knowledge is done away with.

ST. AUGUSTINE OF HIPPO

K31
The knower and the known are one. Simple people imagine that they should see God, as if He stood there and they here. This is not so. God and I, we are one in knowledge.

MEISTER ECKHART

K32
It is in the matter of knowledge that a man is most haunted with a sense of inevitable limitation.

JOSEPH FARRELL

K33
If you have knowledge, let others light their candles at it.

MARGARET FULLER

K34
Wonder rather than doubt is the root of knowledge.

ABRAHAM JOSHUA HESCHEL

K35
Knowledge without integrity is dangerous and dreadful.

SAMUEL JOHNSON

K36
All men naturally desire to know, but what doth knowledge avail without the fear of God?

THOMAS À KEMPIS

K37
All knowledge is sterile which does not lead to action and end in charity.

DÉSIRÉ JOSEPH MERCIER

K38
Quarry the granite rock with razors, or moor the vessel with a thread of silk; then may you hope with such keen and delicate instruments as human knowledge and human reason to contend against those giants, the passion and the pride of man.

JOHN HENRY NEWMAN

K39
Where there is the tree of knowledge, there is always Paradise: so say the most ancient and the most modern serpents.

FRIEDERICH NIETZSCHE

K40
Knowledge is folly, except grace guide it.

ENGLISH PROVERB

K41
Knowledge without conscience is the ruination of the soul.

FRANCIS RABELAIS

K42
Knowledge unused for the good of others is more vain than unused gold.

JOHN RUSKIN

KNOWLEDGE OF GOD
(See also GOD and OMNISCIENCE)

K43
If by knowledge only, and reason, we could come to God, then none should come but they that are learned and have good wits . . . But God hath made His way 'via Regiam' – the King's Highway.

LANCELOT ANDREWES

K44
God alone knows the depths and the riches of His Godhead, and divine wisdom alone can declare his secrets.

ST. THOMAS AQUINAS

K45
There is but one thing in the world really worth pursuing – the knowledge of God.

ROBERT H. BENSON

K46
By faith we know his existence; in
glory we shall know his nature.
BLAISE PASCAL

K47
The way through to the vision of
the Son of man and the knowledge
of God, which is the heart of
contemplative prayer, is by
unconditional love of the
neighbour, of 'the nearest *Thou* to
hand.'
JOHN A. T. ROBINSON

K48
He truly knows God perfectly that
finds Him incomprehensible and
unable to be known.
RICHARD ROLLE

K49
All living knowledge of God rests
upon his foundation: that we
experience him in our lives as
Will-to-Love.
ALBERT SCHWEITZER

K50
The best way to know God is to
love many things.
VINCENT VAN GOGH

K51
We can no more find a method for
knowing God than for making
God, because the knowledge of
God is God himself dwelling in the
soul. The most we can do is to
prepare for his entry, to get out of
his way, to remove the barriers, for
until God acts in us there is nothing
positive that we can do in this
direction.
ALAN W. WATTS

LAUGHTER
(See also HUMOUR and JOY)
L1
Keep company with the more
cheerful sort of the Godly; there is

no mirth like the mirth of believers.
RICHARD BAXTER

L2
Genuine laughter is the physical
effect produced in the rational
being by what suddenly strikes his
immortal soul as being damned
funny.
HILAIRE BELLOC

L3
A laugh is like a love affair in that it
carries a man completely off his
feet; a laugh is like a creed or a
church in that it asks that a man
should trust himself to it.
G. K. CHESTERTON

L4
Laughter with us is still suspect to
this extent at least, that not yet do
we without a shock think of God
laughing.
ARTHUR G. CLUTTON-BROCK

L5
God cannot be solemn, or he
would not have blessed man with
the incalculable gift of laughter.
SYDNEY HARRIS

L6
Man is the only animal that laughs
and weeps: for he is the only
animal that is struck by the
difference between what things are
and what they might have been.
WILLIAM HAZLITT

L7
Shared laughter creates a bond of
friendship. When people laugh
together, they cease to be young
and old, master and pupils, worker
and driver. They have become a
single group of human beings,
enjoying their existence.
W. GRANT LEE

L8
If you're not allowed to laugh in
Heaven, I don't want to go there.
MARTIN LUTHER

L9
God is the creator of laughter that is good.

PHILO

L10
He is not laughed at that laughs at himself first.

ENGLISH PROVERB

L11
One who is always laughing is a fool, and one who never laughs a knave.

SPANISH PROVERB

LAW
(See also COMMANDMENTS)

L12
All law is directed to the common well-being. From this it draws its force and meaning, and to the extent that it falls short of this it does not oblige in conscience.

ST. THOMAS AQUINAS

L13
The law is reason free from passion.

ARISTOTLE

L14
The law's final justification is in the good it does or fails to do to the society of a given place and time.

ALBERT CAMUS

L15
Probably all laws are useless; for good men do not need laws at all, and bad men are made no better by them.

DEMONAX THE CYNIC

L16
The law, in its majestic equality, forbids the rich as well as the poor to sleep under bridges, to beg in the streets, and to steal bread.

ANATOLE FRANCE

L17
Moral law is more than a test, it is for man's own good. Every law that God has given has been for man's benefit. If man breaks it, he is not only rebelling against God, he is hurting himself.

BILLY GRAHAM

L18
Wherever law ends, tyranny begins.

JOHN LOCKE

L19
Men of most renowned virtue have sometimes by transgressing most truly kept the law.

JOHN MILTON

L20
There is nothing more necessary for the national or international community than respect for the majesty of the law and the salutary thought that the law is also sacred and protected, so that whoever breaks it is punishable and will be punished.

POPE PIUS XII

L21
The beginning and the end of the law is kindness.

JEWISH PROVERB

L22
Nobody has a more sacred obligation to obey the law than those who make the law.

SOPHOCLES

L23
Law is a common, just and stable precept, which has been sufficiently promulgated.

F. SUAREZ

L24
Law never made men a whit more just.

HENRY DAVID THOREAU

LEADERSHIP

L25
There is no worse mistake in public leadership than to hold out false hopes soon to be swept away.

SIR WINSTON CHURCHILL

L26
If in order to succeed in an enterprise, I were obliged to choose between fifty deer commanded by a lion, and fifty lions commanded by a deer, I should consider myself more certain of success with the first group than with the second.

ST. VINCENT DE PAUL

L27
In the simplest terms, a leader is one who knows where he wants to go, and gets up, and goes.

JOHN ERSKINE

L28
A good leader takes a little more than his share of blame; a little less than his share of credit.

ARNOLD H. GLASGOW

L29
The final test of a leader is that he leaves behind him in other men the conviction and the will to carry on.

WALTER LIPPMANN

L30
To command is to serve, nothing more and nothing less.

ANDRÉ MALRAUX

L31
In this world no one rules by mere love; if you are but amiable, you are no hero; to be powerful, you must be strong, and to have dominion you must have a genius for organising.

JOHN HENRY NEWMAN

L32
Beware of the chief seat, because it shifts.

JEWISH PROVERB

L33
Reason and calm judgment are the qualities of a leader.

CAIUS CORNELIUS TACITUS

L34
To be a leader means to have determination. It means to be resolute inside and outside, with ourselves and with others.

LECH WALESA

L35
Leadership is a serving relationship that has the effect of facilitating human development.

TED WARD

LEARNING
(See also EDUCATION)

L36
Anyone who stops learning is old, whether at twenty or eighty. Anyone who keeps learning stays young. The greatest thing in life is to keep your mind young.

HENRY FORD

L37
One of the reasons mature people stop learning is that they become less and less willing to risk failure.

JOHN W. GARDNER

L38
I have learned silence from the talkative, toleration from the intolerant, and kindness from the unkind; yet strange, I am ungrateful to these teachers.

KAHLIL GIBRAN

L39
Learning is not to be blamed, nor the mere knowledge of anything which is good in itself and ordained by God; but a good conscience and

a virtuous life are always to be preferred before it.

THOMAS À KEMPIS

L40
I've known countless people who were reservoirs of learning yet never had a thought.

WILSON MIZNER

L41
He who is afraid of asking is ashamed of learning.

DANISH PROVERB

L42
Learning is the eye of the mind.

ENGLISH PROVERB

LEISURE
(See also PLEASURE)

L43
One ought, every day at least, to hear a little song, read a good poem, see a fine picture, and, if it were possible, to speak a few reasonable words.

JOHANN WOLFGANG VON GOETHE

L44
Leisure, like its sister peace, is among those things which are internally felt rather than seen from the outside.

VERNON LEE

L45
Leisure nourishes the body and the mind.

OVID

L46
To be for one day entirely at leisure is to be for one day an immortal.

CHINESE PROVERB

L47
Too much leisure with too much money has been the dread of societies across the ages. That is when nations cave in from within.

WILLIAM RUSSELL

L48
Life lived amidst tension and business needs leisure. Leisure that re-creates and renews. Leisure should be a time to think new thoughts, not ponder old ills.

NEIL C. STRAIT

L49
He enjoys true leisure who has time to improve his soul's estate.

HENRY DAVID THOREAU

L50
To be able to fill leisure intelligently is the last product of civilisation.

ARNOLD TOYNBEE

LIBERTY
(See also FREEDOM and FREE WILL)

L51
There is no true liberty except the liberty of the happy who cleave to the eternal law.

ST. AUGUSTINE OF HIPPO

L52
The condition upon which God hath given liberty to man is eternal vigilance.

JOHN PHILPOT CURRAN

L53
Freedom is not worth having if it does not connote freedom to err.

MOHANDAS GANDHI

L54
The love of liberty is the love of others; the love of power is the love of ourselves.

WILLIAM HAZLITT

L55
The world has never had a good definition of the word liberty.

ABRAHAM LINCOLN

L56
God grants liberty only to those who love it.

DANIEL WEBSTER

L57
Liberty is the only thing you can't have unless you give it to others.

WILLIAM ALLEN WHITE

LIFE

L58
A blessed life may be defined as consisting simply and solely in the possession of goodness and truth.

ST. AMBROSE

L59
The man who has no inner life is the slave to his surroundings.

HENRI FRÉDÉRIC AMIEL

L60
All life is meeting.

MARTIN BUBER

L61
If, after all, men cannot always make history have a meaning, they can always act so that their own lives have one.

ALBERT CAMUS

L62
One life, a little gleam of time between two eternities.

THOMAS CARLYLE

L63
One person who has mastered life is better than a thousand persons who have mastered only the contents of books, but no one can get anything out of life without God.

MEISTER ECKHART

L64
Is life so wretched? Isn't it rather your hands which are too small, your vision which is muddied? You are the one who must grow up.

DAG HAMMARSKJOLD

L65
Living a good, decent, Christian life is what's important, live that life and the rest will follow.

SPIKE MILLIGAN

L66
Fear not that your life shall come to an end, but rather that it shall never have a beginning.

JOHN HENRY NEWMAN

L67
Life is filled with meaning as soon as Jesus Christ enters into it.

STEPHEN NEILL

L68
Life is a hard fight, a struggle, a wrestling with the principle of evil, hand to hand, foot to foot. Every inch of the way is disputed. The night is given us to take breath and to pray, to drink deep at the fountain of power. The day, to use the strength which has been given us, to go forth to work with it till the evening.

FLORENCE NIGHTINGALE

L69
Life is an onion which one peels crying.

FRENCH PROVERB

L70
The tragedy of life is what dies inside a man while he lives.

ALBERT SCHWEITZER

L71
Life is a flame that is always burning itself out, but it catches fire again every time a child is born.

GEORGE BERNARD SHAW

L72
The only significance of life consists in helping to establish the Kingdom of God; and this can be done only by means of the acknowledgment and profession of the truth by each one of us.

COUNT LEO TOLSTOY

L73

Let us endeavour so to live that when we come to die even the undertaker will be sorry.

MARK TWAIN

L74

After all it is those who have a deep and real inner life who are best able to deal with the 'irritating details of outer life'.

EVELYN UNDERHILL

L75

God wants us to approach life, full of expectancy that God is going to be at work in every situation as we release our faith in Him.

COLIN URQUHART

L76

How melancholy it is that we must often bolster up our will to live and strive by the thought that someone else is in an even worse plight than we are ourselves.

OSCAR WILDE

LIGHT

L77

Light, even though it passes through pollution, is not polluted.

ST. AUGUSTINE OF HIPPO

L78

The first creature of God, in the works of the days, was the light of the sense, the last was the light of reason.

FRANCIS BACON

L79

To the Church, Pentecost brought light, power, joy. There came to each illumination of mind, assurance of heart, intensity of love, fulness of power, exuberance of joy. No one needed to ask if they had received the Holy Ghost. Fire is self-evident. So is power!

SAMUEL CHADWICK

L80

And I saw that there was an Ocean of Darkness and Death; but an infinite Ocean of Light and Love flowed over the Ocean of Darkness; and in that I saw the infinite love of God.

GEORGE FOX

L81

There is more light than can be seen through the window.

RUSSIAN PROVERB

L82

In darkness there is no choice. It is light that enables us to see the differences between things; and it is Christ who gives us light.

C. T. WHITMELL

LITTLE THINGS

L83

From a little spark may burst a mighty flame.

DANTE ALIGHIERI

L84

By gnawing through a dike, even a rat may drown a nation.

EDMUND BURKE

L85

We are too fond of our own will. We want to be doing what we fancy mighty things; but the great point is to do small things, when called to them, in a right spirit.

RICHARD CECIL

L86

Faithfulness in little things is a big thing.

ST. JOHN CHRYSOSTOM

L87

Exactness in little duties is a wonderful source of cheerfulness.

FREDERICK W. FABER

L88
There is nothing small in the service of God.
ST. FRANCIS DE SALES

L89
God does not want us to do extraordinary things; He wants us to do the ordinary things extraordinarily well.
CHARLES GORE

L90
Little things come daily, hourly, within our reach, and they are not less calculated to set forward our growth in holiness than are the greater occasions which occur but rarely. Moreover, fidelity in trifles, and an earnest seeking to please God in little matters, is a test of real devotion and love. Let our aim be to please our dear Lord perfectly in little things, and to attain a spirit of childlike simplicity and dependence.
JEAN NICOLAS GROU

L91
He does most in God's great world who does his best in his own little world.
THOMAS JEFFERSON

L92
We can do little things for God: I turn the cake that is frying on the pan, for love of him; and that done, if there is nothing else to call me, I prostrate myself in worship before him who has given me grace to work; afterwards I rise happier than a king.
BROTHER LAWRENCE

L93
He who is faithful over a few things is a lord of cities. It does not matter whether you preach in Westminster Abbey, or teach a ragged class, so

you be faithful. The faithfulness is all.
GEORGE MACDONALD

L94
There may be living and habitual conversation in heaven, under the aspect of the most simple, ordinary life. Let us always remember that holiness does not consist in doing uncommon things, but in doing everything with purity of heart.
HENRY E. MANNING

L95
Do little things as if they were great, because of the majesty of the Lord Jesus Christ who dwells in thee.
BLAISE PASCAL

L96
Nothing is too little to be ordered by our Father; nothing too little in which to see His hand; nothing, which touches our souls, too little to accept from Him; nothing too little to be done to Him.
EDWARD B. PUSEY

L97
Between the great things we cannot do and the little things we will not do, the danger is that we will do nothing.
H. G. WEAVER

LITURGY
(See also WORSHIP)

L98
If liturgy is to become a reality in the life of the Church it will have to be taken outside the Church precincts and become a formative element in the lives of Christians.
JAMES D. CRICHTON

L99
The liturgy is the 'prayer' of the ecclesiastical community, a

community which is forever moving towards the Lord and striving for a new fullness by continually searching to deepen its faith, strengthen its love, and solidify its hope in a world that is perpetually in a state of flux.

LUCIEN DEISS

L100
Without the worship of the heart liturgical prayer becomes a matter of formal routine.

AELRED GRAHAM

L101
The great danger is that liturgy creates a world of things over against the secular, instead of a vision of the sacredness of the secular.

ERIC JAMES

L102
Great liturgies cannot be manufactured; they grow.

ARNOLD LUNN

L103
It is superstition to found your hopes on ceremonies, but it is pride to refuse to submit to them.

BLAISE PASCAL

L104
Liturgy can only really live, worship can only truly express joy, sorrow, hope, faith and love if it is firmly rooted in the actual lives and experience of the people who are worshipping.

IANTHE PRATT

L105
Liturgy and evangelism are simply the inside and the outside of the one act of 'proclaiming the Lord's death'.

JOHN A. T. ROBINSON

L106
The praise of Christ expressed by the liturgy is effective in so far as it continues to inform the humblest tasks.

ROGER SCHUTZ

LOGIC

L107
Logic is like the sword – those who appeal to it shall perish by it.

SAMUEL BUTLER

L108
Logic never attracts men to the point of carrying them away.

ALEXIS CARREL

L109
One truth does not displace another. Even apparently contradictory truths do not displace one another. Logic is far too coarse to make the subtle distinctions life demands.

D. H. LAWRENCE

L110
In formal logic, a contradiction is the signal of defeat: but in the evolution of real knowledge it marks the first step in progress towards a victory.

ALFRED NORTH WHITEHEAD

L111
People who lean on logic and philosophy and rational exposition end by starving the best part of the mind.

J. B. YEATS

LONELINESS

L112
Men love because they are afraid of themselves, afraid of the loneliness that lives in them, and need someone in whom they can lose themselves as smoke loses itself in the sky.

V. F. CALVERTON

L113
There is none more lonely than the man who loves only himself.
ABRAHAM IBN ESRA

L114
At the innermost core of all loneliness is a deep and powerful yearning for union with one's lost self.
BRENDAN FRANCIS

L115
The deepest need of man is the need to overcome his separateness, to leave the prison of his aloneness.
ERICH FROMM

L116
It isn't the Devil in humanity that makes man a lonely creature, it's his Godlikeness. It's the fullness of the Good that can't get out or can't find its proper 'other place' that makes for loneliness.
FYNN

L117
We are born helpless. As soon as we are fully conscious we discover loneliness. We need others physically, emotionally, intellectually; we need them if we are to know anything, even ourselves.
C. S. LEWIS

L118
People are lonely because they build walls instead of bridges.
JOSEPH F. NEWTON

L119
Better be quarreling than lonesome.
IRISH PROVERB

L120
Language has created the word *loneliness* to express the pain of being alone, and the word *solitude* to express the glory of being alone.
PAUL TILLICH

L121
We all carry our own deep wound, which is the wound of our loneliness.
JEAN VANIER

L122
The soul hardly ever realises it, but whether he is a believer or not, his loneliness is really a homesickness for God.
HUBERT VAN ZELLER

L123
Loneliness, far from being a rare and curious phenomenon peculiar to myself and to a few other solitary men, is the central and inevitable fact of human existence.
THOMAS WOLFE

LORD'S PRAYER

L124
The prayer 'Thy Kingdom come', if we only knew it, is asking God to conduct a major operation.
GEORGE BUTTRICK

L125
What deep mysteries, my dearest brothers, are contained in the Lord's Prayer! How many and great they are! They are expressed in a few words but they are rich in spiritual power so that nothing is left out; every petition and prayer we have to make is included. It is a compendium of heavenly doctrine.
ST. CYPRIAN

L126
The 'Our Father' is a very personal prayer which nevertheless brings those praying closely together in the opening words. It is a very simple prayer of petition, but wholly concentrated on essentials, on God's cause which appears to be inextricably linked with man's cause.
HANS KUNG

L127
The Lord's Prayer is the prayer above all prayers. It is a prayer which the most high Master taught us, wherein are comprehended all spiritual and temporal blessings, and the strongest comforts in all trials, temptations and troubles, even in the hour of death.
MARTIN LUTHER

L128
The Lord's Prayer may be committed to memory quickly, but it is slowly learnt by heart.
FREDERICK D. MAURICE

L129
The Lord's Prayer contains the sum total of religion and morals.
ARTHUR WELLESLEY
(DUKE OF WELLINGTON)

LOVE

L130
Take away love and our earth is a tomb.
ROBERT BROWNING

L131
It is love which gives things their value. It makes sense of the difficulty of spending hours and hours on one's knees praying while so many men need looking after in the world.
CARLO CARRETTO

L132
Some day, after mastering the winds, the waves, the tides, and gravity, we shall harness for God the energies of love, and then, for the second time in the history of the world, man will have discovered fire.
P. TEILHARD DE CHARDIN

L133
Only love can bring individual beings to their perfect completion as individuals because only love takes possession of them and unites them by what lies deepest within them.
P. TEILHARD DE CHARDIN

L134
The love of a man and a woman gains immeasurably in power when placed under divine restraint.
ELISABETH ELLIOT

L135
To love is to admire with the heart; to admire is to love with the mind.
THEOPHILE GAUTIER

L136
To be loved for what one is, is the greatest exception. The great majority love in another only what they lend him, their own selves, their version of him.
JOHANN WOLFGANG VON GOETHE

L137
We are shaped and fashioned by what we love.
JOHANN WOLFGANG VON GOETHE

L138
In the evening of our lives we shall be examined in love.
ST. JOHN OF THE CROSS

L139
Only love lasts forever. Alone, it constructs the shape of eternity in the earthly and short-lived dimensions of the history of man on the earth.
POPE JOHN PAUL II

L140
I have decided to stick with love. Hate is too great a burden to bear.
MARTIN LUTHER KING JR

L141
Love is infallible; it has no errors, for all errors are the want of love.
WILLIAM LAW

L142
Love makes everything lovely; hate concentrates itself on the one thing hated.

GEORGE MACDONALD

L143
Love cures people – both the ones who give it and the ones who receive it.

CARL MENNINGER

L144
Love seeks one thing only: the good of the one loved. It leaves all the other secondary effects to take care of themselves. Love, therefore, is its own reward.

THOMAS MERTON

L145
Joy is love exalted; peace is love in repose; long-suffering is love enduring; gentleness is love in society; goodness is love in action; faith is love on the battlefield; meekness is love in school; and temperance is love in training.

DWIGHT L. MOODY

L146
Love does not consist in gazing at each other but in looking outward together in the same direction.

ANTOINE DE SAINT-EXUPÉRY

L147
Love is the only spiritual power that can overcome the self-centredness that is inherent in being alive. Love is the thing that makes life possible or, indeed, tolerable.

ARNOLD TOYNBEE

L148
Love is the greatest of all risks . . . the giving of myself. But dare I take this risk, diving into the swirling waters of loving fidelity?

JEAN VANIER

LOVE OF GOD
(See also GOD, LOVE and ONE GOD)

L149
To love God is something greater than to know him.

ST. THOMAS AQUINAS

L150
We should love God because he is God, and the measure of our love should be to love him without measure.

ST. BERNARD OF CLAIRVAUX

L151
Give me such love for God and men, as will blot out all hatred and bitterness.

DIETRICH BONHOEFFER

L152
He who loves his fellow man is loving God the best he can.

ALICE CARY

L153
The reason why God's servants love creatures so much is that they see how much Christ loves them, and it is one of the properties of love to love what is loved by the person we love.

ST. CATHERINE OF SIENA

L154
If God takes your lump of clay and remoulds it, it will be on the basis of love and not on the basis of power over you.

JAMES CONWAY

L155
Love is the movement, effusion and advancement of the heart toward the good.

ST. FRANCIS DE SALES

L156
When men are animated by the love of Christ they feel united, and the needs, sufferings and joys of

others are felt as their own.

POPE JOHN XXIII

L157
He is not to be gotten or holden by thought, but only by love.

JULIAN OF NORWICH

I 158
Human beings must be known to be loved, but divine things must be loved to be known.

BLAISE PASCAL

L159
It is the heart which experiences God and not the reason.

BLAISE PASCAL

L160
God does not love us because we are valuable. We are valuable because God loves us.

FULTON J. SHEEN

L161
Our love for God is tested by the question of whether we seek Him or His gifts.

RALPH W. SOCKMAN

L162
Love is the greatest thing that God can give us; for Himself is love: and it is the greatest thing we can give to God.

JEREMY TAYLOR

L163
Short arm needs man to reach to Heaven, so ready is Heaven to stoop to him.

FRANCIS THOMPSON

L164
It is always springtime in the heart that loves God.

JOHN VIANNEY

LOVE OF NEIGHBOUR
(See also CHARITY)

L165
He alone loves the Creator perfectly who manifests a pure love for his neighbour.

THE VENERABLE BEDE

L166
No man can be a friend of Jesus Christ who is not a friend to his neighbour.

ROBERT H. BENSON

L167
We make our friends; we make our enemies; but God makes our next door neighbour.

G. K. CHESTERTON

L168
We never love our neighbour so truly as when our love for him is prompted by the love of God.

FRANÇOIS FENELON

L169
To love our neighbour in charity is to love God in man.

ST. FRANCIS DE SALES

L170
We can live without our friends but not without our neighbours.

THOMAS FULLER

L171
Man becomes great exactly in the degree in which he works for the welfare of his fellow-men.

MOHANDAS GANDHI

L172
All is well with him who is beloved of his neighbours.

GEORGE HERBERT

L173
Your neighbour is the man who needs you.

ELBERT HUBBARD

L174
The good neighbour looks beyond the external accidents and discerns those inner qualities that make all men human and, therefore, brothers.

MARTIN LUTHER KING, JR.

L175
Next to the Blessed Sacrament itself, your neighbour is the holiest object presented to your senses. If he is your Christian neighbour, he is holy in almost the same way, for in him also Christ vere latitat – the glorified, Glory Himself, is truly hidden.

C. S. LEWIS

L176
The love of our neighbour is the only door out of the dungeon of self.

GEORGE MACDONALD

L177
Happy is the man who is able to love all men alike.

MAXIMUS THE CONFESSOR

L178
The camel never sees its own hump; but its neighbour's hump is ever before its eyes.

ARAB PROVERB

L179
No one is rich enough to do without a neighbour.

DANISH PROVERB

L180
He who prays for his neighbour will be loved for himself.

HEBREW PROVERB

L181
Love thy neighbour, even when he plays the trombone.

JEWISH PROVERB

L182
Love your neighbour, but don't pull down the hedge.

SWISS PROVERB

L183
Have a deaf ear for unkind remarks about others, and a blind eye to the trivial faults of your brethren.

SIR WALTER SCOTT

L184
Though we do not have our Lord with us in bodily presence, we have our neighbour, who, for the ends of love and loving service, is as good as our Lord himself.

ST. TERESA OF AVILA

L185
Man becomes a holy thing, a neighbour, only if we realise that he is the property of God and that Jesus Christ died for him.

HELMUT THIELECKE

LOYALTY
(See also PATRIOTISM)

L186
Loyalty means not that I *am* you, or that I *agree* with everything you say or that I believe you are always right. Loyalty means that I share a common ideal with you and that regardless of minor differences we fight for it, shoulder to shoulder, confident in one another's good faith, trust, constancy, and affection.

CARL MENNINGER

L187
It is better to be faithful than famous.

THEODORE ROOSEVELT

L188
Loyalty is the holiest good in the human heart.

SENECA

L189
Cursed be that loyalty which reaches so far as to go against the law of God.

ST. TERESA OF AVILA

LUXURY

L190
Comfort comes as a guest, lingers to become a host and stays to enslave.

LEE BICKMORE

L191
We act as though comfort and
luxury were the chief requirements
of life, when all that we need to
make us really happy is something
to be enthusiastic about.
CHARLES KINGSLEY

L192
Avarice and luxury, those pests
which have ever been the ruin of
every great state.
LIVY

L193
Luxury is the first, second, and
third cause of ruin of reputation. It
is the vampire which soothes us
into a fatal slumber while it sucks
the lifeblood of our veins.
HAMILTON MABIE

L194
Luxury makes a man so soft, that it
is hard to please him, and easy to
trouble him; so that his pleasures at
last become his burden. Luxury is a
nice master, hard to be pleased.
COMPTON MACKENZIE

L195
There has never yet been a man in
our history who led a life of ease
whose name is worth
remembering.
THEODORE ROOSEVELT

L196
Luxuries are what other people
buy.
DAVID WHITE

LYING
(See also DECEPTION)

L197
To hide a fault with a lie is to
replace a blot by a hole.
MARCUS AURELIUS

L198
It is a sovereign remedy against

lying to unsay the lie on the spot.
ST. FRANCIS DE SALES

L199
We lie loudest when we lie to
ourselves.
ERIC HOFFER

L200
He who permits himself to tell a lie
once finds it much easier to do it a
second and a third time till at
length it becomes habitual.
THOMAS JEFFERSON

L201
No man has a good enough
memory to make a successful liar.
ABRAHAM LINCOLN

L202
With lies you may go ahead in the
world – but you can never go back.
RUSSIAN PROVERB

L203
The cruellest lies are often told in
silence.
ROBERT LOUIS STEVENSON

L204
A lie can travel halfway around the
world while the truth is putting on
its shoes.
MARK TWAIN

MAN
(See also AGE and AGES OF
MAN, HUMAN CONDITION
and HUMANITY)

M1
European man strode into history
full of confidence in himself and his
creature powers. Today he leaves it
to pass into an unknown epoch,
discouraged, his faith in shreds.
NIKOLAI BERDYAEV

M2
Man will become better only when
you will make him see what he is
like.
ANTON CHEKHOV

M3
The more we really look at man as an animal, the less he will look.
G. K. CHESTERTON

M4
What a man is in the sight of God, so much he is and no more.
ST. FRANCIS OF ASSISI

M5
Whenever two people meet there are really six people present. There is each man as he sees himself, each man as the other person sees him, and each man as he really is.
WILLIAM JAMES

M6
Man lives a really human life thanks to culture.
POPE JOHN PAUL II

M7
Now man cannot live without some vision of himself. But still less can he live without a vision that is true to his inner experience and inner feeling.
D. H. LAWRENCE

M8
Man is but a reed, the most weak in nature, but he is a thinking reed.
BLAISE PASCAL

M9
Man is harder than rock, and more fragile than an egg.
YUGOSLAV PROVERB

M10
Made in God's image, man was made to be great, he was made to be beautiful and he was made to be creative in life and art. But his rebellion has led him into making himself into nothing but a machine.
FRANCIS A. SCHAEFFER

M11
The salvation of mankind lies only in making everything the concern of all.
ALEXANDER I. SOLZHENITSYN

M12
We must not reject man in favour of God, nor reject God in favour of man; for the glory of God is man alive, supremely in Christ.
LEON JOSEPH SUENENS

M13
Man is the only animal that blushes. Or needs to.
MARK TWAIN

M14
Man is a peculiar, puzzling paradox, groping for God and hoping to hide from Him at the selfsame time.
WILLIAM A. WARD

M15
Man is like nothing so much as a lump of muddy earth plunged into a very clear, pure brook.
ULRICH ZWINGLI

MANNERS
(See also BEHAVIOUR and COURTESY)

M16
Good manners are made up of petty sacrifices.
RALPH WALDO EMERSON

M17
Manners are the happy ways of doing things . . . if they are superficial, so are the dewdrops, which give such a depth to the morning meadow.
RALPH WALDO EMERSON

M18
It is superstitious to put one's faith in conventions; but it is arrogance not to submit to them.
BLAISE PASCAL

M19
Manners make the man.
ENGLISH PROVERB

MARRIAGE

M20
Marriage is our last, best chance to grow up.

JOSEPH BARTH

M21
Success in marriage is more than finding the right person: it is a matter of being the right person.

RABBI B. R. BRICKNER

M22
The desire to be instantly understood and accurately responded to remains with us through life and is one of the clearest expressions of closeness and love between people.

JACK DOMINIAN

M23
Marriage resembles a pair of shears, so joined that they cannot be separated, often moving in opposite directions yet always punishing anyone who comes between them.

P. FONTAINE

M24
The state of marriage is one that requires more virtue and constancy than any other; it is a perpetual exercise of mortification.

ST. FRANCIS DE SALES

M25
A successful marriage demands a divorce; a divorce from your own self-love.

PAUL FROST

M26
The sum which two married people owe to one another defies calculation. It is an infinite debt, which can only be discharged through all eternity.

JOHANN WOLFGANG VON GOETHE

M27
When men and women marry, the union should be made with the consent of the bishop, so that the marriage may be according to the Lord and not merely out of lust. Let all be done to the glory of God.

ST. IGNATIUS OF ANTIOCH

M28
A successful marriage is an edifice that must be rebuilt every day.

ANDRÉ MAUROIS

M29
There is no lonelier person than the one who lives with a spouse with whom he or she cannot communicate.

MARGARET MEAD

M30
Successful marriage is always a triangle: a man, a woman, and God.

CECIL MYERS

M31
Every man who is happily married is a successful man, even if he has failed in everything else.

WILLIAM LYON PHELPS

M32
A good husband should be deaf and a good wife blind.

FRENCH PROVERB

M33
Don't praise marriage on the third day, but after the third year.

RUSSIAN PROVERB

M34
A happy marriage is the union of two good forgivers.

ROBERT QUILLEN

M35
One of the great similarities between Christianity and marriage is that, for Christians, they both get better as we get older.

JEAN REES

M36
A good marriage is that in which each appoints the other guardian of his solitude.
RAINER MARIA RILKE

M37
Marriage is like twirling a baton, turning handsprings, or eating with chopsticks; it looks so easy till you try it.
HELEN ROWLAND

M38
And when will there be an end of marrying? I suppose, when there is an end of living.
QUINTUS TERTULLIAN

MARTYRDOM

M39
The martyrs were bound, imprisoned, scourged, racked, burnt, rent, butchered – and they multiplied.
ST. AUGUSTINE OF HIPPO

M40
A tear is an intellectual thing,
And a sigh is the sword of an Angel King,
And the bitter groan of the martyr's woe
Is an arrow from the Almighty's bow.
WILLIAM BLAKE

M41
Pain is superficial and therefore fear is. The torments of martyrdom are probably most keenly felt by the bystanders.
RALPH WALDO EMERSON

M42
Let others wear the martyr's crown; I am not worthy of this honour.
DESIDERIUS ERASMUS

M43
Fire and cross and battling with wild beasts, their clawing and tearing, the breaking of bones and mangling of members, the grinding of my whole body, the wicked torments of the devil – let them assail me, so long as I get to Jesus Christ.
ST. IGNATIUS OF ANTIOCH

M44
The only method by which religious truth can be established is by martyrdom.
SAMUEL JOHNSON

M45
No one is a martyr for a conclusion, no one is a martyr for an opinion; it is faith that makes martyrs.
JOHN HENRY NEWMAN

M46
It is not suffering but the cause which makes a martyr.
ENGLISH PROVERB

M47
Martyrdom has always been a proof of the intensity, never of the correctness of a belief.
ARTHUR SCHNITZLER

M48
We multiply whenever we are mown down by you; the blood of Christians is seed.
QUINTUS TERTULLIAN

M49
Love makes the whole difference between an execution and a martyrdom.
EVELYN UNDERHILL

MARY, MOTHER OF CHRIST

M50
In order that the body of Christ might be shown to be a real body, he was born of a woman: but in order that his Godhead might be

made clear he was born of a virgin.

ST. THOMAS AQUINAS

M51
If the Son is a King,the Mother who begot Him is rightly and truly considered a Queen and Sovereign.

ST. ATHANASIUS OF ALEXANDRIA

M52
Let us not imagine that we obscure the glory of the Son by the praise we lavish on the Mother; for the more she is honoured, the greater is the glory of her Son.

ST. BERNARD OF CLAIRVAUX

M53
'Behold thy mother' (Jn. 19:26). By these words, Mary, by reason of the love she bore them, became the Mother, not only of St. John, but of all men.

ST. BERNARDINE OF SIENA

M54
To work a wonder, God would have her shown, at once, a Bud, and yet a Rose full-blown.

ROBERT HERRICK

M55
Popular piety, normally, connected with devotion to Our Lady, certainly needs to be enlightened, guided, and purified. But as it is a devotion 'of the simple and poor', it generally expresses a certain 'thirst for God'. And then it is not necessarily a value sentiment, or an inferior form of religious expression. In fact it often contains a deep sense of God and his attributes, such as fatherhood, providence, loving presence, and mercy.

POPE JOHN PAUL II

M56
The feast we call *Annunciatio Mariae*, when the angel came to Mary and brought her the message from God, may be fitly called the Feast of Christ's Humanity, for then began our deliverance.

MARTIN LUTHER

M57
Since God has revealed very little to us about Mary, men who know nothing of who and what she was only reveal themselves when they try to add something to what God has told us about her.

THOMAS MERTON

M58
Mary's humble acceptance of the divine will is the starting point of the story of the redemption of the human race from sin.

ALAN RICHARDSON

M59
Our tainted nature's solitary boast.

WILLIAM WORDSWORTH

MATERIALISM
(See also POSSESSIONS and RICHES)

M60
Materialism is our great enemy. It is the chief 'ism' we have to combat and conquer. It is the mother of all the 'isms'.

FRANK BUCHMAN

M61
For every one hundred men who can stand adversity there is only one who can withstand prosperity.

THOMAS CARLYLE

M62
Lives based on having are less free than lives based either on doing or on being.

WILLIAM JAMES

M63
When money speaks, the truth is silent.

RUSSIAN PROVERB

M64

Theology must pay greater attention to the creational character and hence the high value of matter, of the material and sensible world.

MARCEL REDING

M65

Be sure, as long as worldly fancies you pursue, you are a hollow man – a pauper lives in you.

ANGELUS SILESIUS

M66

If you want to destroy a nation, give it too much – make it greedy, miserable and sick.

JOHN STEINBECK

M67

Unless our civilisation is redeemed spiritually, it cannot endure materially.

WOODROW WILSON

MATURITY
(See also CHARACTER)

M68

Most great men and women are not perfectly rounded in their personalities, but are instead people whose one driving enthusiasm is so great it makes their faults seem insignificant.

CHARLES A. CERAMI

M69

God instructs the heart, not by ideas, but by pains and contradictions.

JEAN PIERRE DE CAUSSADE

M70

The greater the difficulty, the more glory in surmounting it. Skilful pilots gain their reputation from storms and tempests.

EPICURUS

M71

God will not look you over for medals, degrees, or diplomas, but for scars.

ELBERT HUBBARD

M72

Spiritual maturity comes not by erudition, but by compliance with the known will of God.

D. W. LAMBERT

M73

If God sends us on stony paths, he will provide us with strong shoes.

ALEXANDER MACLAREN

M74

Maturity begins to grow when you can sense your concern for others outweighing your concern for yourself.

JOHN MACNAUGHTON

M75

Blisters are a painful experience, but if you get enough blisters in the same place, they will eventually produce a callus. That is what we call maturity.

HERBERT MILLER

M76

One of the marks of a mature person is the ability to dissent without creating dissension.

DON ROBINSON

M77

It takes a long time to bring excellence to maturity.

PUBLILIUS SYRUS

M78

Isn't it the greatest possible disaster, when you are wrestling with God, not to be beaten.

SIMONE WEIL

MEDIA

M79

Children who have been taught, or conditioned, to listen passively

159

most of the day to the warm verbal communications coming from the TV screen, to the deep emotional appeal of the so-called TV personality, are often unable to respond to real persons because they arouse so much less feeling than the skilled actor.

BRUNO BETTELHEIM

M80
If newspapers are useful in overthrowing tyrants, it is only to establish a tyranny of their own.

JAMES FENIMORE COOPER

M81
Parents generally pay vigilant attention to the type of friends with whom their children associate, but do not exercise a similar vigilance regarding the ideas which the radio, the television, records, papers and comics carry into the 'protected' and 'safe' intimacy of their homes.

POPE JOHN PAUL II

M82
Newspapers always excite curiosity. No one ever lays one down without a feeling of disappointment.

CHARLES LAMB

M83
We are drowning our youngsters in violence, cynicism and sadism piped into the living room and even the nursery. The grandchildren of the kids who used to weep because the Little Match Girl froze to death, now feel cheated if she isn't slugged, raped and thrown into a Bessemer converter.

JENKIN LLOYD JONES

M84
I find television very educating. Every time somebody turns on the set I go into the other room and read a book.

GROUCHO MARX

M85
I don't think that television has corrupted me. But I do think that man has invented it to flee from reality.

MALCOLM MUGGERIDGE

M86
Journalism is the ability to meet the challenge of filling space.

REBECCA WEST

MEDITATION
(See also CONTEMPLATION and PRAYER)

M87
To meditate on the life and sufferings of Jesus Christ I have called wisdom; in these I have placed the perfection of righteousness for me, the fulness of knowledge, the abundance of merits, the riches of salvation.

ST. BERNARD OF CLAIRVAUX

M88
Meditate daily on the words of your Creator. Learn the heart of God in the words of God, that your soul may be kindled with greater longings for heavenly joys.

POPE ST. GREGORY I

M89
Meditation is the attempt to provide the soul with a proper environment in which to grow and become.

MORTON T. KELSEY

M90
The all-important aim in Christian meditation is to allow God's mysterious and silent presence within us to become more and more not only a reality, but the reality in our lives; to let it become that reality which gives meaning and shape and purpose to everything we do; to everything we are.

JOHN MAIN

M91
Every man has a train of thought on which he rides when he is alone. The dignity and nobility of his life, as well as his happiness, depend upon the direction in which that train is going, the baggage it carries, and the scenery through which it travels.

JOSEPH FORT NEWTON

M92
The world is to the meditative man what the mulberry plant is to the silkworm.

ALEXANDER SMITH

M93
Proficiency in meditation lies not in thinking much, but in loving much. It is a way of seeking the divine companionship, the 'closer walk'. Thus it is that meditation has come to be called 'the mother of love'.

RICHARDSON WRIGHT

MEEKNESS
(See also GENTLENESS)

M94
Meekness is not weakness.

WILLIAM G. BENHAM

M95
Meekness takes injuries like pills, not chewing, but swallowing them down.

SIR THOMAS BROWNE

M96
Learn the blessedness of the unoffended in the face of the unexplainable.

AMY CARMICHAEL

M97
Meekness is love at school, at the school of Christ. It is the disciple learning to know, and fear, and distrust himself, and learning of him who is meek and lowly of heart, and so finding rest to his soul.

JAMES HAMILTON

M98
Meek endurance and meek obedience, the accepting of His dealings, of whatever complexion they are and however they may tear and desolate our hearts, without murmuring, without sulking, without rebellion or resistance, is the deepest conception of the meekness which Christ pronounced blessed.

ALEXANDER MACLAREN

MERCY

M99
Mercy, also, is a good thing, for it makes men perfect, in that it imitates the perfect Father. Nothing graces the Christian soul so much as mercy.

ST. AMBROSE

M100
The mercy of God may be found between the bridge and the stream.

ST. AUGUSTINE OF HIPPO

M101
Among the attributes of God, although they are all equal, mercy shines with even more brilliancy than justice.

MIGUEL DE CERVANTES

M102
For Mercy is a greater thing than right.

GEOFFREY CHAUCER

M103
Mercy imitates God and disappoints Satan.

ST. JOHN CHRYSOSTOM

M104
Reason to rule, but mercy to forgive: The first is law, the last prerogative.

JOHN DRYDEN

M105
We hand folks over to God's mercy, and show none ourselves.
GEORGE ELIOT

M106
Whoever falls from God's right hand is caught in his left.
EDWIN MARKHAM

M107
Teach me to feel another's woe, to hide the fault I see; that mercy I to others show, that mercy show to me.
ALEXANDER POPE

M108
Mercy is better than vengeance.
GREEK PROVERB

M109
As freely as the firmament embraces the world, so mercy must encircle friend and foe.
JOHANN C. F. VON SCHILLER

M110
If we refuse mercy here, we shall have justice in eternity.
JEREMY TAYLOR

MIND
(See also INTELLIGENCE)

M111
No mind, however loving, could bear to see plainly into all the recesses of another mind.
ARNOLD BENNETT

M112
I am incurably of the opinion that the object of opening the mind, as of opening the mouth, is to shut it again on something solid.
G. K. CHESTERTON

M113
There is no salvation save in truth, and the royal road of truth is by the mind.
MARTIN C. D'ARCY

M114
To the quiet mind all things are possible. What is the quiet mind? A quiet mind is one which nothing weighs on, nothing worries, which, free from ties and from all self-seeking, is wholly merged into the will of God and dead to its own.
MEISTER ECKHART

M115
The human mind is so constructed that it resists vigour and yields to gentleness.
ST. FRANCIS DE SALES

M116
An open scent bottle soon loses its scent. An open mind is often a vacant mind. There is something to be said for corks.
ARNOLD LUNN

M117
Our minds are like crows. They pick up everything that glitters, no matter how uncomfortable our nests get with all that metal in them.
THOMAS MERTON

M118
Almighty God influences us and works in us, through our minds, not without them or in spite of them.
JOHN HENRY NEWMAN

M119
If you keep your mind sufficiently open, people will throw a lot of rubbish into it.
WILLIAM A. ORTON

M120
No one would allow garbage at his table, but many allow it served into their minds.
FULTON J. SHEEN

M121
Untilled ground, however rich, will

bring forth thistles and thorns; so also the mind of man.

ST. TERESA OF AVILA

MINISTRY
(See also CLERGY and PRIESTHOOD)

M122
An upright minister asks, *what* recommends a man; a corrupt minister, *who*.

CHARLES CALEB COLTON

M123
The Lord opened unto me that being bred at Oxford or Cambridge was not enough to fit and qualify men to be ministers of Christ.

GEORGE FOX

M124
The life of a pious minister is visible rhetoric.

HERMAN HOOKER

M125
In God's house we must try to accept any job: cook or kitchen boy, waiter, stable boy, baker. If it pleases the king to call us into his private council, then we must go there, but without being too excited, for we know that our rewards depend not on the job itself but on the faithfulness with which we serve him.

POPE JOHN PAUL I

M126
The Lord did not promise a ministry free of trials. He simply assured us that he had overcome the forces of evil at work in man.

POPE JOHN PAUL II

M127
The Christian ministry is the worst of all trades, but the best of all professions.

JOSEPH FORT NEWTON

MIRACLES
(See also WONDER)

M128
I should not be a Christian but for the miracles.

ST. AUGUSTINE OF HIPPO

M129
It is only two years ago that the keeping of records was begun here in Hippo, and already, at this writing, we have nearly seventy attested miracles.

ST. AUGUSTINE OF HIPPO

M130
A miracle in the sense of the New Testament is not so much a breach of the laws of nature, but rather a remarkable or exceptional occurrence which brought an undeniable sense of the presence and power of God.

C. H. DODD

M131
All miracles are simply feeble lights like beacons on our way to the port where shines the light, the total light of the resurrection.

JACQUES ELLUL

M132
I cannot understand people having historical difficulties about miracles. For, once you grant that miracles can happen, all the historical evidence at our disposal bids us believe that sometimes they do.

RONALD A. KNOX

M133
The divine art of miracle is not an art of suspending the pattern to which events confirm, but of feeding new events into that pattern.

C. S. LEWIS

M134
Miracles are important, and are
only important because they
provide evidence of the fact that
the universe is not a closed system,
and that effects in the natural world
can be produced by the reactions of
non-human will.
ARNOLD LUNN

M135
The miracles of Jesus were the
ordinary works of his Father,
wrought small and swift that we
might take them in.
GEORGE MACDONALD

M136
Jesus was himself the one
convincing and permanent miracle.
IAN MACLAREN

M137
The Incarnation is the most
stupendous event which ever can
take place on earth; and after it and
henceforth, I do not see how we
can scruple at any miracle on the
mere ground of it being unlikely to
happen.
JOHN HENRY NEWMAN

M138
It would have approached nearer
to the idea of miracle if Jonah had
swallowed the whale.
THOMAS PAINE

M139
It is impossible on reasonable
grounds to disbelieve miracles.
BLAISE PASCAL

M140
Little saints also perform miracles.
DANISH PROVERB

M141
A miracle in the Biblical sense is an
event which happens in a manner
contrary to the regularly observed
processes of nature . . . It may
happen according to higher laws as
yet but dimly discerned by
scientists, and therefore must not
be thought of as an irrational
irruption of divine power into the
orderly realm of nature.
ALAN RICHARDSON

MISSION
(See also MISSIONARY)

M142
If people ask 'Why did he not
appear by means of other parts of
creation, and use some nobler
instrument, as the sun or moon or
stars or fire or air, instead of man
merely?' let them know that the
Lord came not to make a display,
but to teach and heal those who
were suffering.
ST. ATHANASIUS OF ALEXANDRIA

M143
Your love has a broken wing if it
cannot fly across the sea.
MALTBIE D. BABCOCK

M144
The Church exists by mission, as
fire exists by burning.
EMIL BRUNNER

M145
Our primary task is to create the
space for the word of God once
again to cut into our daily life
experience, in order to redeem and
liberate it.
THOMAS CULLINAN

M146
To practical people like Americans
there is no oral or written evidence
of the true religion so valid as the
spectacle of its power to change
bad men into good ones. Such a
people will not accept arguments
from history and from Scripture,
but those of a moral kind they
demand, they must see the theories
at work. A mission is a microcosm

of the Church as a moral force.
WALTER ELLIOTT

M147
The Spirit of Christ is the spirit of
missions, and the nearer we get to
him the more intensely missionary
we must become.
HENRY MARTYN

M148
The fact of the missions reveals the
Church's faith in herself as the
Catholic unity of mankind.
JOHN C. MURRAY

M149
Mission will not happen unless the
Church goes beyond its own life
out into active care in the local
neighbourhood.
DAVID SHEPPARD

MISSIONARY
(See also MISSION)

M150
We are the children of the converts
of foreign missionaries; and
fairness means that I must do to
others as men once did to me.
MALTBIE D. BABCOCK

M151
If God calls you to be a missionary,
don't stoop to be a king.
JORDON GROOMS

M152
The Bible is a missionary book.
Jesus Christ is the Father's
missionary to a lost world.
HAROLD LINDSELL

M153
God had an only Son, and he was a
missionary and a physician.
DAVID LIVINGSTONE

M154
The Spirit of Christ is the spirit of
missions, and the nearer we get to

Him the more intensely missionary
we must become.
HENRY MARTYN

MISTAKES
(See also ERROR)

M155
A man who has committed a
mistake and doesn't correct it is
committing another mistake.
CONFUCIUS

M156
The greatest mistake you can make
in this life is to be continually
fearing you will make one.
ELBERT HUBBARD

M157
An error no wider than a hair will
lead a hundred miles away from the
goal.
GERMAN PROVERB

M158
He is always right who suspects
that he makes mistakes.
SPANISH PROVERB

M159
The only man who never makes a
mistake is the man who never does
anything.
THEODORE ROOSEVELT

M160
More people would learn from
their mistakes if they weren't so
busy denying them.
HAROLD J. SMITH

MODESTY
(See also CHASTITY, PURITY
and VIRGINITY)

M161
Modesty is always the sign and
safeguard of a mystery. It is
explained by its
contrary – profanation.
HENRI FRÉDÉRIC AMIEL

M162
Guard your eyes, since they are the windows through which sin enters into the soul. Never look curiously on those things which are contrary to modesty, even slightly.
JOHN BOSCO

M163
Modesty is to merit what shade is to figures in a picture; it gives it strength and makes it stand out.
JEAN DE LA BRUYÈRE

M164
Modesty in human beings is praised because it is not a matter of nature, but of will.
LACTANTIUS

M165
To Christian modesty it is not enough to be so, but to seem so too.
QUINTUS TERTULLIAN

MONEY
(See also RICHES and WEALTH)

M166
Money is like muck, no good except it be spread.
FRANCIS BACON

M167
If you would know what the Lord God thinks of money, you have only to look at those to whom he gives it.
MAURICE BARING

M168
The golden age only comes to men when they have forgotten gold.
G. K. CHESTERTON

M169
If you make money your god, it will plague you like the devil.
HENRY FIELDING

M170
If a person gets his attitude toward money straight, it will help straighten out almost every other area in his life.
BILLY GRAHAM

M171
Money can buy the husk of many things, but not the kernel. It brings you food, but not appetite; medicine, but not health; acquaintances, but not friends; servants, but not faithfulness; days of joy, but not peace and happiness.
HENRIK IBSEN

M172
He who has money to spare has it always in his power to benefit others: and of such power a good man must always be desirous.
SAMUEL JOHNSON

M173
The real measure of our wealth is how much we'd be worth if we lost all our money.
JOHN HENRY JOWETT

M174
It cuts off from life, from vitality, from the alive sun and the alive earth, as *nothing* can. Nothing, not even the most fanatical dogmas of an iron-bound religion, can insulate us from the inrush of life and inspiration, as money can.
D. H. LAWRENCE

M175
If a man's religion does not affect his use of money, that man's religion is vain.
HUGH MARTIN

M176
Getting money is like digging with a needle; spending it is like water soaking into sand.
JAPANESE PROVERB

M177
Money really adds no more to the

wise than clothes can to the beautiful.

JEWISH PROVERB

M178
We can hardly respect money enough for the blood and toil it represents. Money is frightening. It can serve or destroy man.

MICHEL QUOIST

M179
Money has never yet made anyone rich.

SENECA

M180
Nothing that is God's is obtainable by money.

QUINTUS TERTULLIAN

M181
Make all you can, save all you can, give all you can.

JOHN WESLEY

MORALITY
(See also ETHICS)

M182
Love and *then* what you will, do.

ST. AUGUSTINE OF HIPPO

M183
The moral good is not a goal but an inner force which lights up man's life from within.

NIKOLAI BERDYAEV

M184
To deny the freedom of the will is to make morality impossible.

JAMES A. FROUDE

M185
All moral obligation resolves itself into the obligation of conformity to the will of God.

CHARLES HODGE

M186
Morality is not properly the doctrine of how we may make ourselves happy, but how we may

make ourselves worthy of happiness.

IMMANUEL KANT

M187
Strive we then to think aright: that is the first principle of moral life.

BLAISE PASCAL

M188
Right is right, even if everyone is against it; and wrong is wrong, even if everyone is for it.

WILLIAM PENN

MOTHERHOOD

M189
It was because my salvation was at stake that (my mother) loved Ambrose greatly and he loved her because of her fervent life of devotion, which took the form of good works and frequent churchgoing. Sometimes when he saw me he would break out in praise of her and congratulate me on having such a mother – not knowing what a son she had!

ST. AUGUSTINE OF HIPPO

M190
The God to whom little boys say their prayers has a face very like their mother's.

JAMES M. BARRIE

M191
I think it must somewhere be written, that the virtues of the mothers shall be visited on their children as well as the sins of the fathers.

CHARLES DICKENS

M192
The child, in the decisive first years of his life, has the experience of his mother, as an all-enveloping, protective, nourishing power. Mother is food; she is love; she is warmth; she is earth. To be loved

by her means to be alive, to be
rooted, to be at home.

ERICH FROMM

M193
The commonest fallacy among
women is that simply having
children makes one a
mother – which is as absurd as
believing that having a piano
makes one a musician.

SYDNEY HARRIS

M194
No man is poor who has had a
godly mother.

ABRAHAM LINCOLN

M195
God could not be everywhere, so
He made mothers.

JEWISH PROVERB

M196
In the eyes of its mother every
beetle is a gazelle.

MOROCCAN PROVERB

M197
An ounce of mother is worth a
pound of clergy.

SPANISH PROVERB

M198
Mother is the name of God in the
lips and hearts of little children.

WILLIAM MAKEPEACE THACKERAY

M199
The loveliest masterpiece of the
heart of God is the heart of a
mother.

ST. THÉRÈSE OF LISIEUX

MOTIVATION
(See also INTENTION)

M200
Lord, grant that I may always
desire more than I can accomplish.

MICHELANGELO BUONARROTI

M201
Pure motives will make a clear

flame. Impure motives are the
smoke that clogs the flame.

SIDNEY COOK

M202
The biggest gap in the world is the
gap between the justice of a cause
and the motives of the people
pushing it.

JOHN P. GRIER

M203
If no action is to be deemed
virtuous for which malice can
imagine a sinister motive, then
there never was a virtuous action.

THOMAS JEFFERSON

M204
Man sees your actions, but God
your motives.

THOMAS À KEMPIS

M205
If a man does not keep pace with
his companions, perhaps it is
because he hears a different
drummer.

HENRY DAVID THOREAU

MUSIC

M206
Music is a part of us, and either
ennobles or degrades our
behaviour.

AMICIUS M. S. BOETHIUS

M207
Take then, you, that smile on
strings,
those nobler sounds than mine,
The words that never lie, or brag,
or
flatter or malign.

G. K. CHESTERTON

M208
So is music an asylum. It takes us
out of the actual and whispers to us
dim secrets that startle our wonder

as to who we are, and for what,
whence, and whereto, all the great
interrogatories, like questioning
angels, float in on its waves of
sound.
RALPH WALDO EMERSON

M209
Next to theology I give to music the
highest place and honour. Music is
the art of the prophets, the only art
that can calm the agitations of the
soul; it is one of the most
magnificent and delightful presents
God has given us.
MARTIN LUTHER

M210
God save me from a bad neighbour
and a beginner on the fiddle.
ITALIAN PROVERB

M211
The thought of the eternal
efflorescence of music is a
comforting one, and comes like a
messenger of peace in the midst of
universal disturbance.
ROMAIN ROLLAND

M212
The only time that our blessed
Lord ever is recorded as having
sung is the night that He went out
to His death.
FULTON J. SHEEN

M213
A painter paints his pictures on
canvas. But musicians paint their
pictures on silence. We provide the
music and you provide the silence.
LEOPOLD STOKOWSKI

M214
Bach opens a vista to the universe.
After experiencing him, people
feel there is meaning to life after
all.
HELMUT WALCHA

MYSTERY

M215
We are hemmed round with
mystery, and the greatest mysteries
are contained in what we see and
do every day.
HENRI FRÉDÉRIC AMIEL

M216
The most beautiful experience we
can have is the mysterious. It is the
fundamental emotion which stands
at the cradle of true art and true
science.
ALBERT EINSTEIN

M217
The mysterious is always attractive.
People will always follow a veil.
BEDE JARRETT

M218
If the works of God were such as
might be easily comprehended by
human reason, they could not be
called wonderful or unspeakable.
THOMAS À KEMPIS

M219
A revelation is religious doctrine
viewed on its illuminated side; a
mystery is the selfsame doctrine
viewed on the side unilluminated.
JOHN HENRY NEWMAN

M220
The more unintelligent a man is,
the less mysterious existence seems
to him.
ARTHUR SCHOPENHAUER

MYSTICISM
(See also CONTEMPLATION)

M221
Only on the wings of mysticism can
the spirit soar to its full height.
ALEXIS CARREL

M222
For the mystic especially it is
important that theology should
flourish and good theologians

abound, for in the guidance which objective theology supplies lies the mystic's sole certainty of escaping self-delusion.

PHILIP HUGHES

M223
One of the greatest paradoxes of the mystical life is this: that a man cannot enter into the deepest centre of himself and pass through that centre into God, unless he is able to pass entirely out of himself and empty himself and give himself to other people in the purity of a selfless love.

THOMAS MERTON

M224
Any profound view of the world is mysticism, in that it brings men into a spiritual relation with the Infinite.

ALBERT SCHWEITZER

NAME

N1
Remember that man's name is to him the sweetest and most important sound in the English language.

DALE CARNEGIE

N2
A nickname is the hardest stone that the devil can throw at a man.

WILLIAM HAZLITT

N3
Thy name, O Lord, is for me oil poured out. For the grace of Thy visitation makes me fully understand the true meaning of Thy name, which is Jesus, Saviour.

WALTER HILTON

N4
Do not concern yourself with anxiety for the show of a great name.

THOMAS À KEMPIS

NATURE
(See also ECOLOGY)

N5
Nature knows nothing of rights. She knows only laws. Man, on the other hand, has ideals and aspirations.

JAMES TRUSLOW ADAMS

N6
Nature, the vicar of th' Almightie Lord.

GEOFFREY CHAUCER

N7
Nature is but a name for an effect whose cause is God.

WILLIAM COWPER

N8
Let us permit nature to have her way; she understands her business better than we do.

MICHEL DE MONTAIGNE

N9
Nature has some perfections, to show that she is the image of God; and some defects, to show that she is only his image.

BLAISE PASCAL

N10
All are but parts of one stupendous whole,
Whose body Nature is, and God the soul.

ALEXANDER POPE

N11
Nature does nothing in vain.

ENGLISH PROVERB

N12
It is through the natural that we encounter the supernatural, although the supernatural eludes the ability of the natural to exhaust its meaning.

MICHAEL RAMSEY

N13
The losing of Paradise is enacted over and over again by the children

of Adam and Eve. We clothe our souls with messages and doctrines and lose the touch of the great life in the naked breast of Nature.

RABINDRANATH TAGORE

OBEDIENCE

O1
The first degree of humility is obedience without delay.

ST. BENEDICT

O2
Thirty years of Our Lord's life are hidden in these words of the gospel: 'He was subject unto them.'

JACQUES B. BOSSUET

O3
How will you find good? It is not a thing of choices; it is a river that flows from the foot of the invisible throne, and flows by the path of obedience.

GEORGE ELIOT

O4
It is vain thought to flee from the work that God appoints us, for the sake of finding a greater blessing, instead of seeking it where alone it is to be found – in loving obedience.

GEORGE ELIOT

O5
We need only obey. There is guidance for each of us, and by lowly listening we shall hear the right word.

RALPH WALDO EMERSON

O6
Obedience to God is the most infallible evidence of sincere and supreme love to him.

NATHANAEL EMMONS

O7
Blessed are the obedient, for God will never suffer them to go astray.

ST. FRANCIS DE SALES

O8
Don't listen to friends when the Friend inside you says, 'Do this!'

MOHANDAS GANDHI

O9
No man securely commands but he who has learned to obey.

THOMAS À KEMPIS

O10
Every duty, even the least duty, involves the whole principle of obedience. And little duties make the will dutiful, that is supple and prompt to obey. Little obediences lead into great.

HENRY E. MANNING

O11
Obedience is all over the Gospels. The pliability of an obedient heart must be complete from the set of our wills right on through to our actions.

CATHERINE MARSHALL

O12
Justice is the insurance we have on our lives, and obedience is the premium we pay for it.

WILLIAM PENN

O13
Obedience is the mother of success, the wife of safety.

GREEK PROVERB

O14
No one can rule except one who can be ruled.

LATIN PROVERB

O15
Obedience is the fruit of faith; patience the bloom on the fruit.

CHRISTINA ROSSETTI

O16
We are born subjects, and to obey God is perfect liberty. He that does this shall be free, safe, and happy.
SENECA

O17
Every revelation of God is a demand, and the way to knowledge of God is by obedience.
WILLIAM TEMPLE

O18
Every great person has first learned how to obey, whom to obey, and when to obey.
WILLIAM A. WARD

OLD AGE
(See also AGE and MATURITY)

O19
To know how to grow old is the master work of wisdom, and one of the most difficult chapters in the great art of living.
HENRI FRÉDÉRIC AMIEL

O20
It is this very awareness that one is no longer an attractive object that makes life so unbearable for so many elderly people.
SIMONE DE BEAUVOIR

O21
The care of the old is a vocation as delicate and difficult as the care of the young.
JAMES DOUGLAS

O22
Life is a country that the old have seen, and lived in. Those who have to travel through it can only learn from them.
JOSEPH JOUBERT

O23
The older I grow the more I distrust the familiar doctrine that age brings wisdom.
HENRY L. MENCKEN

O24
To see a young couple loving each other is no wonder; but to see an old couple loving each other is the best sight of all.
WILLIAM MAKEPEACE THACKERAY

OMNIPOTENCE
(See also POWER)

O25
What is impossible to God? Not that which is difficult to His power, but that which is contrary to His nature.
ST. AMBROSE

O26
God is called omnipotent because He can do all things that are possible absolutely.
ST. THOMAS AQUINAS

O27
God is not in need of anything, but all things are in need of Him.
MARCIANUS ARISTIDES

O28
There is nothing that God cannot accomplish.
MARCUS TULLIUS CICERO

O29
God's omnipotence means power to do all that is intrinsically possible, not to do the intrinsically impossible. You may attribute miracles to him, but not nonsense.
C. S. LEWIS

O30
Calvary is the key to an omnipotence which works only and always through sacrificial love.
MICHAEL RAMSEY

OMNIPRESENCE
(See also GOD and
OMNISCIENCE)

O31
God is in all things; not, indeed, as
part of their essence, nor as an
accident; but as an agent is present
to that upon which it works.
ST. THOMAS AQUINAS

O32
It must therefore be acknowledged
that God is everywhere by the
presence of His Divinity but not
everywhere by the indwelling of
His grace.
ST. AUGUSTINE OF HIPPO

O33
A sense of Deity is inscribed on
every heart.
JOHN CALVIN

O34
Could we pierce the veil, and were
we vigilant and attentive, God
would reveal Himself continuously
to us and we should rejoice in His
actions in everything that
happened to us.
JEAN PIERRE DE CAUSSADE

O35
The remarkable thing about the
way in which people talk about
God, or about their relation to
God, is that it seems to escape
them completely that God hears
what they are saying.
SØREN KIERKEGAARD

O36
God is always with us, why should
we not always be with God?
WILLIAM ULLATHORNE

OMNISCIENCE
(See also KNOWLEDGE OF
GOD)

O37
God alone knows the depths and

the riches of His Godhead, and
divine wisdom alone can declare
His secrets.
ST. THOMAS AQUINAS

O38
What man is there who can
comprehend that wisdom by which
God knows all things, in such wise
that neither what we call things
past are past therein, nor what we
call things future are therein
looked for as coming, as though
they were absent; but both past and
future things together with those
actually present are all present.
ST. AUGUSTINE OF HIPPO

O39
We cannot too often think there is
a never-sleeping eye which reads
the heart and registers our
thoughts.
FRANCIS BACON

O40
If we consider the immensity and
singleness of God's wisdom, it is
one, simple, and indivisible; if the
great number of things with which
it has to do, it is manifold and
diverse.
JOHN OF SALISBURY

O41
There are three things that only
God knows: the beginning of
things, the cause of things, and the
end of things.
WELSH PROVERB

ONE GOD
(See also GOD and TRINITY)

O42
God has many names though he is
only one being.
ARISTOTLE

O43
God is an infinite circle whose

centre is everywhere and whose circumference is nowhere.

ST. AUGUSTINE OF HIPPO

O44
God is the Thou which by its very nature cannot become it.

MARTIN BUBER

O45
He who has gotten the whole world plus God has gotten no more than God by himself.

MEISTER ECKHART

O46
It has been the universal opinion of mankind from ancient times, from the earliest tradition of the protoplast, that there is one God, the Maker of heaven and earth . . . For nature reveals its Author, the work suggests the Artist, and the world manifests its Designer. But the whole Church throughout the world has received this tradition from the apostles.

ST. IRENAEUS

O47
One sole God; One sole ruler – his Law;
One sole interpreter of that Law – Humanity.

GIUSEPPE MAZZINI

O48
God is one; what He does, sees none.

YIDDISH PROVERB

O49
The name of this infinite and inexhaustible depth and ground of all being is God.

PAUL TILLICH

OPINION

O50
Opinion is that exercise of the human will which helps us to make a decision without information.

JOHN ERSKINE

O51
We are all of us, more or less, the slaves of opinion.

WILLIAM HAZLITT

O52
Rulers who prefer popular opinion to truth have as much power as robbers in the desert.

ST. JUSTIN MARTYR

O53
Opinion in good men is but knowledge in the making.

JOHN MILTON

OPPORTUNITY

O54
A wise man will make more opportunities than he finds.

FRANCIS BACON

O55
The secret of success in life is for a man to be ready for his opportunity when it comes.

BENJAMIN DISRAELI

O56
He who refuses to embrace an unique opportunity loses the prize as surely as if he had failed.

WILLIAM JAMES

O57
God often gives in one brief moment that which he has for a long time denied.

THOMAS À KEMPIS

O58
Dawn does not come twice to awaken a man.

ARAB PROVERB

O59
Opportunity makes the thief.

ENGLISH PROVERB

ORDER

O60
Good order is the foundation of all good things.
EDMUND BURKE

O61
Put things into their places, and they will put you in your place.
ARAB PROVERB

O62
Order is heaven's first law.
ENGLISH PROVERB

O63
The art of progress is to preserve order amid change, and to preserve change amid order. Life refuses to be embalmed alive.
ALFRED NORTH WHITEHEAD

ORIGINAL SIN
(see also FALL OF MAN)

O64
What history does is to uncover man's universal sin.
HERBERT BUTTERFIELD

O65
God has not been taken by surprise or forced to change his plans. He permitted original sin only because He had decided to remedy it by the wonderful gift of salvation.
CHARLES DAVIS

O66
Original sin is what results in us by reason of our birth into this condition of sin which precedes our own personal and conscious choices.
PETER DE ROSA

O67
All men find themselves born into an historical order where sin is there before them, dragging them down.
JOHN A. T. ROBINSON

ORTHODOXY
(See also DOGMA)

O68
Tradition by itself is not enough; it must be perpetually criticised and brought up to date under the supervision of what I call orthodoxy.
T. S. ELIOT

O69
By identifying the new learning with heresy we make orthodoxy synonymous with ignorance.
DESIDERIUS ERASMUS

O70
Orthodoxy is my doxy; heterodoxy is another man's doxy.
WILLIAM WARBURTON

O71
You may be as orthodox as the devil, and as wicked.
JOHN WESLEY

PAIN
(See also SUFFERING)

P1
Pain is no evil, unless it conquer us.
CHARLES KINGSLEY

P2
God whispers in our pleasures but shouts in our pain.
C. S. LEWIS

P3
When pain is to be borne, a little courage helps more than much knowledge, a little human sympathy more than much courage, and the least tincture of the love of God more than all.
C. S. LEWIS

P4
Pain and sorrow are the almost necessary medicines of the impetuosity of nature. Without these, men though men, are like

spoilt children; they act as if they considered everything must give way to their own wishes and conveniences.

JOHN HENRY NEWMAN

P5
Pain is the price that God putteth upon all things.

ENGLISH PROVERB

P6
Although today He prunes my twigs with pain,
Yet doth His blood nourish and warm my root:
Tomorrow I shall put forth buds again
And clothe myself with fruit.

CHRISTINA ROSSETTI

P7
The pain of the mind is worse than the pain of the body.

PUBLILIUS SYRUS

P8
Nothing begins, and nothing ends,
That is not paid with moan;
For we are born in other's pain,
And perish in our own.

FRANCIS THOMPSON

P9
Behind joy and laughter there may be a temperament, coarse, hard and callous. But behind sorrow there is always sorrow. Pain, unlike pleasure, wears no mask.

OSCAR WILDE

PARADISE
(See also HEAVEN)

P10
She is an all-pure soul who cannot love the paradise of God, but only the God of paradise.

ST. FRANCIS DE SALES

P11
He that will enter into Paradise must come with the right key.

THOMAS FULLER

P12
Can there be Paradise for any while there is Hell, conceived as unending torment, for some? Each supposedly damned soul was born into the world as a mother's child, and Paradise cannot be Paradise for her if her child is in such a Hell.

WILLIAM TEMPLE

P13
There is no expeditious road
To pack and label men for God,
And save them by the barrel-load.
Some may perchance, with strange surprise,
Have blundered into Paradise.

FRANCIS THOMPSON

PARDON
(See also FORGIVENESS and RECONCILIATION)

P14
The Lord is loving unto man, and swift to pardon, but slow to punish. Let no man therefore despair of his own salvation.

ST. CYRIL OF JERUSALEM

P15
Know all and you will pardon all.

THOMAS À KEMPIS

P16
One pardons in the degree that one loves.

FRANÇOIS DE LA ROCHEFOUCAULD

P17
Pardon, not wrath, is God's best attribute.

BAYARD TAYLOR

P18
How inconsistent it is to expect pardon of sins to be granted to a repentance which they have not fulfilled. This is to hold out your hand for merchandise, but not

produce the price. For repentance is the price at which the Lord has determined to award pardon.

QUINTUS TERTULLIAN

PARENTS
(See also FAMILY, FATHERHOOD and MOTHERHOOD)

P19
The religion of a child depends on what its mother and father are, and not on what they say.

HENRI FRÉDÉRIC AMIEL

P20
The joys of parents are secret; and so are their griefs and fears.

FRANCIS BACON

P21
We never know the love of the parent until we become parents ourselves.

HENRY WARD BEECHER

P22
Parents' influence is inevitable and continuous; they cannot be passive if they would. You cannot really *neglect* your children, you can *destroy* them.

FREDERICK W. FABER

P23
Parents have little time for children and a great vacuum has developed and into that vacuum is going to move some kind of ideology.

BILLY GRAHAM

P24
The most important thing a father can do for his children is to love their mother.

THEODORE M. HESBURGH

P25
Every word and deed of a parent is a fibre woven into the character of a child, which ultimately determines how that child fits into the fabric of society.

DAVID WILKERSON

PASSION
(See also EMOTION)

P26
A movement of the soul contrary to nature in the sense of disobedience to reason, that is what passions are.

ST. CLEMENT OF ALEXANDRIA

P27
Passions are vices or virtues in their highest powers.

JOHANN WOLFGANG VON GOETHE

P28
True quietness of heart is won by resisting our passions, not by obeying them.

THOMAS À KEMPIS

P29
We should employ our passions in the service of life, not spend life in the service of our passions.

RICHARD STEELE

P30
The happiness of a man in this life does not consist in the absence but in the mastery of his passions.

ALFRED, LORD TENNYSON

PATIENCE
(See also PERSEVERANCE)

P31
Patient endurance is the perfection of charity.

ST. AMBROSE

P32
Patience is the companion of wisdom.

ST. AUGUSTINE OF HIPPO

P33
Patience is not good, if when you

may be free you allow yourself to become a slave.

ST. BERNARD OF CLAIRVAUX

P34

Beware the fury of a patient man.

JOHN DRYDEN

P35

Possess your soul with patience.

JOHN DRYDEN

P36

We must wait for God, long, meekly, in the wind and wet, in the thunder and lightning, in the cold and the dark. Wait, and he will come. He never comes to those who do not wait.

FREDERICK W. FABER

P37

Be patient with every one, but above all with yourself. I mean, do not be disturbed because of your imperfections, and always rise up bravely from a fall.

ST. FRANCIS DE SALES

P38

The virtue of patience is the one which most assures us of perfection.

ST. FRANCIS DE SALES

P39

'Take your needle, my child, and work at your pattern; it will come out a rose by and by.' Life is like that; one stitch at a time taken patiently, and the pattern will come out all right like embroidery.

OLIVER WENDELL HOLMES

P40

All men commend patience, although few be willing to practise it.

THOMAS À KEMPIS

P41

Patience and diligence, like faith, remove mountains.

WILLIAM PENN

P42

One moment of patience may ward off great disaster, one moment of impatience may ruin a whole life.

CHINESE PROVERB

P43

Patience is power; with time and patience the mulberry leaf becomes silk.

CHINESE PROVERB

P44

Patience is a plaster for all sores.

ENGLISH PROVERB

P45

Patience is bitter, but its fruit is sweet.

JEAN JACQUES ROUSSEAU

P46

Patience is the ability to put up with people you'd like to put down.

ULRIKE RUFFERT

P47

It takes patience to appreciate domestic bliss; volatile spirits prefer unhappiness.

GEORGE SANTAYANA

P48

On every level of life from housework to heights of prayer, in all judgment and all efforts to get things done, hurry and impatience are sure marks of the amateur.

EVELYN UNDERHILL

P49

Patience with ourselves is a duty for Christians and the only humility. For it means patience with a growing creature whom God has taken in hand and whose completion he will effect in his own time and way.

EVELYN UNDERHILL

PATRIOTISM
(See also LOYALTY)

P50
Standing as I do in view of God and eternity, I realise that patriotism is not enough. I must have no hatred or bitterness for anyone.

EDITH CAVELL

P51
True patriotism does not exclude an understanding of the patriotism of others.

QUEEN ELIZABETH II

P52
Love for one's country which is not part of one's love for humanity is not love, but idolatrous worship.

ERICH FROMM

P53
Men and women who would shrink from doing anything dishonourable in the sphere of personal relationships are ready to lie and swindle, to steal, and even murder when they are representing their country.

ALDOUS HUXLEY

P54
Patriotism is the last refuge of a scoundrel.

SAMUEL JOHNSON

P55
Ask not what your country can do for you; ask what you can do for your country.

JOHN F. KENNEDY

P56
To me, it seems a dreadful indignity to have a soul controlled by geography.

GEORGE SANTAYANA

P57
Patriotism is your conviction that this country is superior to all other countries because you were born in it.

GEORGE BERNARD SHAW

P58
You'll never have a quiet world till you knock patriotism out of the human race.

GEORGE BERNARD SHAW

PEACE

P59
When Christ came into the world, peace was sung; and when He went out of the world, peace was bequeathed.

FRANCIS BACON

P60
Peace is liberty in tranquillity.

MARCUS TULLIUS CICERO

P61
If we will have peace without a worm in it, lay we the foundation of justice and good will.

OLIVER CROMWELL

P62
If the basis of peace is God, the secret of peace is trust.

J. B. FIGGIS

P63
My religion is based on truth and non-violence. Truth is my God and non-violence is the means to reach Him.

MOHANDAS GANDHI

P64
God takes life's pieces and gives us unbroken peace.

W. D. GOUGH

P65
Peace is such a precious jewel that I would give anything for it but truth.

MATTHEW HENRY

179

P66
Where there is peace, God is.
GEORGE HERBERT

P67
Peace is not made at the council tables, or by treaties, but in the hearts of men.
HERBERT HOOVER

P68
Only a world that is truly human can be a world that is peaceful and strong.
POPE JOHN PAUL II

P69
Thy peace shall be in much patience.
THOMAS À KEMPIS

P70
We should have much peace if we would not busy ourselves with the sayings and doing of others.
THOMAS À KEMPIS

P71
We have to make peace without limitations.
HAROLD LINDSELL

P72
The springs of human conflict cannot be eradicated through institutions, but only through the reform of the individual human being.
DOUGLAS MACARTHUR

P73
If we wish to have true peace, we must give it a soul. The soul of peace is love, which for us believers comes from the love of God and expresses itself in love for men.
POPE PAUL VI

P74
Peace within makes beauty without.
ENGLISH PROVERB

P75
Peace without truth is poison.
GERMAN PROVERB

P76
Peace is not an absence of war, it is a virtue, a state of mind, a disposition for benevolence, confidence, justice.
BARUCH DE SPINOZA

P77
Thinking about interior peace destroys interior peace. The patient who constantly feels his pulse is not getting any better.
HUBERT VAN ZELLER

PEOPLE

P78
The People, though we think of a great entity when we use the word, means nothing more than so many millions of individual men.
JAMES BRYCE

P79
The problems of the world reflect the people who live in it. Remake people and nations are remade.
FRANK BUCHMAN

P80
Men of integrity, by their very existence, rekindle the belief that as a people we can live above the level of moral squalor.
JOHN W. GARDNER

P81
God must love the common man; he made so many of them.
ABRAHAM LINCOLN

P82
Whatever you may be sure of, be sure of this, that you are dreadfully like other people.
JAMES RUSSELL LOWELL

P83
To try too hard to make people good is one way to make them

worse; the only way to make them good is to be good.

GEORGE MACDONALD

P84
The voice of the people, the voice of God.

LATIN PROVERB

P85
We must begin with people where they are, and not where we like them to be. They are not where our fathers were.

LORD SOPER

PERFECTION
(See also HOLINESS)

P86
Each and everything is said to be perfect in so far as it attains to its proper end; and this is its ultimate perfection.

ST. THOMAS AQUINAS

P87
No one is suddenly made perfect.

THE VENERABLE BEDE

P88
No man can advance three paces on the road to perfection unless Jesus Christ walks beside him.

ROBERT H. BENSON

P89
Perfection does not consist in lacerating or killing the body, but in killing our perverse self-will.

ST. CATHERINE OF SIENA

P90
Bachelors' wives and old maids' children are always perfect.

NICOLAS CHAMFORT

P91
It is only imperfection that complains of what is imperfect. The more perfect we are, the more gentle and quiet we become towards the defects of others.

FRANÇOIS FENELON

P92
Perfection does not lie in not seeing the world, but in not tasting or relishing it.

ST. FRANCIS DE SALES

P93
Wherever we find ourselves we not only may, but should seek perfection.

ST. FRANCIS DE SALES

P94
True perfection consists . . . in having but one fear, the loss of God's friendship.

ST. GREGORY OF NYSSA

P95
That soul is perfect which is guided habitually by the instinct of the Holy Spirit.

ISAAC HECKER

P96
He who would fully and feelingly understand the words of Christ, must study to make his whole life conformable to that of Christ.

THOMAS À KEMPIS

P97
It is right to be contented with what we have but never with what we are.

JAMES MACKINTOSH

P98
There are many people living in the midst of unattractive circumstances, amid hardships, toil, and disease, whose daily life breathes out most gentle music that blesses others about them.

J. F. MILLAR

P99
The diamond cannot be polished without friction, nor the man perfected without trials.

CHINESE PROVERB

P100
Perfection is being, not doing; it is
not to effect an act but to achieve a
character.
FULTON J. SHEEN

P101
If thou canst bear the whole yoke
of the Lord, thou wilt be perfect,
but if thou canst not, do what thou
canst.
TEACHING OF THE TWELVE APOSTLES

P102
What is Christian perfection?
Loving God with all our heart,
mind, soul and strength.
JOHN WESLEY

P103
The divine nature is perfection;
and to be nearest to the divine
nature is to be nearest to
perfection.
XENOPHON

PERSECUTION
(See also MARTYRDOM)

P104
To flee persecution implies no fault
in him who flees but in him who
persecutes.
ST. BERNARD OF CLAIRVAUX

P105
Religious persecution may shield
itself under the guise of a mistaken
and over-zealous piety.
EDMUND BURKE

P106
Opposition may become sweet to a
man when he has christened it
persecution.
GEORGE ELIOT

P107
Wherever you see persecution,
there is more than a probability
that truth is on the persecuted side.
HUGH LATIMER

PERSEVERANCE
(See also PATIENCE)

P108
We cannot command our final
perseverance, but must ask it from
God.
ST. THOMAS AQUINAS

P109
Genius, that power which dazzles
mortal eyes,
Is oft but perseverance in disguise.
HENRY AUSTIN

P110
Every noble work is at first
impossible.
THOMAS CARLYLE

P111
Never give in! Never give in!
Never, Never, Never, Never – in
anything great or small, large or
petty – never give in except to
convictions of honour and good
sense.
SIR WINSTON CHURCHILL

P112
Even the woodpecker owes his
success to the fact that he uses his
head and keeps pecking away until
he finishes the job he starts.
COLEMAN COX

P113
He greatly deceives himself who
thinks that prayer perfects one
without perseverance and
obedience.
ST. FRANCIS DE SALES

P114
Though perseverance does not
come from our power, yet it comes
within our power.
ST. FRANCIS DE SALES

P115
A tree is shown by its fruits, and in
the same way those who profess to
belong to Christ will be seen by
what they do. For what is needed is

not mere present profession, but perseverance to the end in the power of faith.

ST. IGNATIUS OF ANTIOCH

P116
Great works are performed not by strength but by perseverance.

SAMUEL JOHNSON

P117
He said not, 'Thou shalt not be tempested, thou shalt not be travailed, thou shalt not be afflicted,' but he said, 'Thou shalt not be overcome.'

JULIAN OF NORWICH

P118
The man who removed the mountain began by carrying away small stones.

CHINESE PROVERB

P119
The will to persevere is often the difference between failure and success.

DAVID SARNOFF

P120
By perseverance the snail reached the ark.

CHARLES H. SPURGEON

P121
'Tis known as perseverance in a good cause, and obstinacy in a bad one.

LAURENCE STERNE

PERSONALITY
(See also CHARACTER)

P122
Personality should reside in the will as in a castle, and issue orders to the passions and intellectual apprehensions, who, in their turn, should inform their master of external happenings and await his decision.

ROBERT H. BENSON

P123
Human personality and individuality written and signed by God on each human countenance . . . is something altogether sacred, something for the resurrection, for eternal life.

LEON BLOY

P124
Only when the Spirit of God takes possession of the 'old' man to transform him is the man made whole again. It is only when this threshold is crossed that personality takes on full meaning and significance.

ÉMILE CAILLIET

P125
Man's main task in life is to give birth to himself, to become what he potentially is. The most important product of his effort is his own personality.

ERICH FROMM

P126
It is a very significant fact that the idea of human personality, and also the practical recognition of the dignity of human personality, developed only during those centuries in which the dogmas of the Trinity and of the Incarnation were teaching Christendom the truths of divine personality.

JACQUES MARITAIN

P127
Personality is that being which has power over itself.

PAUL TILLICH

P128
Personality is born out of pain. It is the fire shut up in the flint.

J. B. YEATS

PHILOSOPHY

P129
Philosophy is merely thought that has been thought out. It is often a great bore. But man has no alternative, except between being influenced by thought that has been thought out and being influenced by thought that has not been thought out. The latter is what we commonly call culture and enlightenment.
G. K. CHESTERTON

P130
Is this not the task of philosophy to enquire about the divine?
ST. JUSTIN MARTYR

P131
Two things fill the mind with ever new and increasing wonder and awe – the starry heavens above me, and the moral law within me.
IMMANUEL KANT

P132
Philosophy does not seek to overthrow revelation; it seeks rather to defend it against assailants.
POPE LEO XIII

P133
Philosophy is the science of the limitations of the human mind. When you know philosophy, you know what you cannot know.
JOSEPH RICKABY

P134
Philosophy asks the simple question: What is it all about?
ALFRED NORTH WHITEHEAD

PIETY
(See also HOLINESS and PERFECTION)

P135
Genuine piety is the spring of peace of mind.
JEAN DE LA BRUYÈRE

P136
Do not, therefore, please yourself with thinking how piously you would act and submit to God in a plague, a famine, or persecution, but be intent upon the perfection of the present day, and be assured that the best way of showing a true zeal is to make little things the occasion of great piety.
WILLIAM LAW

P137
Piety requires us to renounce no ways of life where we can act reasonably and offer what we do to the glory of God.
WILLIAM LAW

P138
The moods and phrases of evangelical piety can substitute a kind of self-contemplation for the self-forgetful contemplation of God and obedience to him.
MICHAEL RAMSEY

P139
The consciousness that the human spirit is derived and responsible, that all its functions are heritages and trusts, involves a sentiment of gratitude and duty we may call piety.
GEORGE SANTAYANA

P140
He who is pious does not contend but teaches in love.
ULRICH ZWINGLI

PILGRIMAGE

P141
The pilgrim who spends all his time counting his steps will make little progress.
JEAN PIERRE CAMUS

P142
When the sweet showers of April fall and shoot
Down through the drought of

March to pierce the root,
Then people long to go on
pilgrimages
And palmers long to seek the
stranger strands
Of far-off saints, hallowed in
sundry lands,
And specially, from every shire's
end
In England, down to Canterbury
they wend
To seek the holy blissful martyr,
quick
In giving help to them when they
were sick.

GEOFFREY CHAUCER

P143
God knows well which are the best
pilgrims.

ENGLISH PROVERB

P144
God made the moon as well as the
sun: and when he does not see fit to
grant us the sunlight, he means us
to guide our steps as well as we can
by moonlight.

RICHARD WHATELY

PITY
(See also SYMPATHY)

P145
Justice seeks out the merits of the
case, but pity only regards the
need.

ST. BERNARD OF CLAIRVAUX

P146
Pity melts the mind to love.

JOHN DRYDEN

P147
He that pities another remembers
himself.

GEORGE HERBERT

P148
To pity the unhappy is not contrary
to selfish desire; on the other hand,
we are glad of the occasion to thus

testify friendship and attract to
ourselves the reputation of
tenderness, without giving
anything.

BLAISE PASCAL

P149
Pity is akin to love.

ENGLISH PROVERB

P150
For pity, more than any other
feeling, is a 'learned' emotion; a
child will have it least of all.

THOMAS WOLFE

PLEASURE
(See also LEISURE)

P151
It is nonsense to speak of 'higher'
and 'lower' pleasures. To a hungry
man it is, rightly, more important
that he eats than that he
philosophise.

W. H. AUDEN

P152
In diving to the bottom of pleasure
we bring up more gravel than
pearls.

HONORÉ DE BALZAC

P153
We must be able to find pleasure in
ourselves when alone, and in our
neighbour when in his company.

JEAN PIERRE CAMUS

P154
There is something self-defeating
in the too conscious pursuit of
pleasure.

MAX EASTMAN

P155
The inward pleasure of imparting
pleasure, that is the choicest of all.

NATHANIEL HAWTHORNE

P156
No display of virtue gives an act

distinction if its origin is rooted in pleasure.

JOHN OF SALISBURY

P157
Pleasure-seeking is a barren business; happiness is never found till we have the grace to stop looking for it, and to give our attention to persons and matters external to ourselves.

J. I. PACKER

P158
Pleasure is frail like a dewdrop, while it laughs it dies.

RABINDRANATH TAGORE

POLITICS
(See also DEMOCRACY and GOVERNMENT)

P159
Political life neither provides our final end nor contains the happiness we seek for ourselves or others . . . The purpose of temporal tranquillity, which well-ordered policies establish and maintain, is to give opportunities for contemplating truth.

ST. THOMAS AQUINAS

P160
The good of man must be the end of the science of politics.

ARISTOTLE

P161
Nothing doth more hurt in a state than that cunning men pass for wise.

FRANCIS BACON

P162
All the politics-as-usual of today seems so terribly antiquated; it lags so sadly behind the actual situation of man – and behind even our present knowledge of man.

WILLIAM BARRETT

P163
Politics, and the fate of mankind, are shaped by men without ideals and without greatness. Men who have greatness within them don't go in for politics.

ALBERT CAMUS

P164
Since a politician never believes what he says, he is always astonished when others do.

CHARLES DE GAULLE

P165
He who shall introduce into public affairs the principles of primitive Christianity will revolutionise the world.

BENJAMIN FRANKLIN

P166
We know that separation of State and Church is a source of strength, but the conscience of our nation does not call for separation between men of State and faith in the Supreme Being.

LYNDON B. JOHNSON

P167
Christian political action does not mean waiting for the orders of the bishop or campaigning under the banner of the Church; rather, it means bringing to politics a sense of Christian responsibility.

FRANZISKUS KOENIG

P168
Politics are a part of morals.

HENRY E. MANNING

P169
Nothing is politically right which is morally wrong.

DANIEL O'CONNELL

P170
The penalty that good men pay for not being interested in politics is to

be governed by men worse than themselves.

PLATO

P171
Bishops and Christians generally should beware of simply following politicians. A politician has an excuse for compromising, but it seems to me a Christian bishop has not.

T. D. ROBERTS

POOR IN SPIRIT
(See also BEATITUDES)

P172
If any person, because of his state of life, cannot do without wealth and position, let him at least keep his heart empty of love of them.

ST. ANGELA

P173
The man who is poor in spirit is the man who has realised that things mean nothing, and that God means everything.

WILLIAM BARCLAY

P174
He is rich in spirit who has his riches in his spirit or his spirit in his riches; he is poor in spirit who has no riches in his spirit, nor his spirit in his riches.

ST. FRANCIS DE SALES

P175
He is rich enough who is poor with Christ.

ST. JEROME

P176
'Poor in spirit' refers, not precisely to humility, but to an attitude of dependence on God and detachment from earthly supports.

RONALD KNOX

P177
He is not poor that hath little, but he that desireth much.

ENGLISH PROVERB

P178
The poor man, rich in faith, who toils for the love of God and is generous of the little fruit of his labours, is much nearer to Heaven than the rich man who spends a fortune in good works from no higher motive than his natural inclination to benevolence.

WILLIAM ULLATHORNE

POSSESSIONS
(See also MATERIALISM, RICHES and WEALTH)

P179
It is easier to renounce worldly possessions than it is to renounce the love of them.

WALTER HILTON

P180
Let temporal things serve thy use, but the eternal be the object of thy desire.

THOMAS À KEMPIS

P181
To pretend to satisfy one's desires by possession is like using straw to put out a fire.

CHINESE PROVERB

P182
All that we possess is qualified by what we are.

JOHN LANCASTER SPALDING

POVERTY
(See also HUNGER)

P183
Poverty is an anomaly to rich people; it is difficult to make out why people who want dinner do not ring the bell.

WALTER BAGEHOT

P184
A poor man with nothing in his belly needs hope and illusion, more than bread.
GEORGE BERNANOS

P185
No man should praise poverty but he who is poor.
ST. BERNARD OF CLAIRVAUX

P186
The conspicuously wealthy turn up urging the character-building value of privation for the poor.
JOHN K. GALBRAITH

P187
Man is God's image; but a poor man is Christ's stamp to boot.
GEORGE HERBERT

P188
If a free society cannot help the many who are poor, it cannot save the few who are rich.
JOHN F. KENNEDY

P189
The rich will do everything for the poor but get off their backs.
KARL MARX

P190
Satan now is wiser than of yore,
And tempts by making rich,
not making poor.
ALEXANDER POPE

P191
Whoso stoppeth his ear at the poor shall cry himself and not be heard.
HEBREW PROVERB

P192
Poverty is a blessing hated by all men.
ITALIAN PROVERB

P193
It is no disgrace to be poor – which is the only good thing you can say about it.
JEWISH PROVERB

P194
Not he who has little, but he who wishes for more, is poor.
LATIN PROVERB

P195
Must the hunger become anger and the anger fury before anything will be done?
JOHN STEINBECK

POWER
(See also OMNIPOTENCE)

P196
Power is not revealed by striking hard or often, but by striking true.
HONORÉ DE BALZAC

P197
We are the wire, God is the current. Our only power is to let the current pass through us.
CARLO CARRETTO

P198
I have never been able to conceive how any rational being could propose happiness to himself from the exercise of power over others.
THOMAS JEFFERSON

P199
There is one source of power that is stronger than every disappointment, bitterness or ingrained mistrust, and that power is Jesus Christ, who brought forgiveness and reconciliation to the world.
POPE JOHN PAUL II

P200
Real power in prayer flows only when man's spirit touches God's spirit.
CATHERINE MARSHALL

P201
No man can do the work of God until he has the Holy Spirit and is endued with power. It is impossible

to preach the Gospel save in the power of the Spirit.

G. CAMPBELL MORGAN

P202
The same power that brought Christ back from the dead is operative within those who are Christ's. The resurrection is an ongoing thing.

LEON MORRIS

P203
Power undirected by high purpose spells calamity; and high purpose by itself is utterly useless if the power to put it into effect is lacking.

THEODORE ROOSEVELT

P204
Next to power without honour, the most dangerous thing in the world is power without humour.

ERIC SEVAREID

P205
In order to obtain and hold power a man must love it. Thus the effort to get it is not likely to be coupled with goodness, but with the opposite qualities of pride, craft, and cruelty.

COUNT LEO TOLSTOY

PRAISE
(See also WORSHIP)

P206
Modesty is the only sure bait when you angle for praise.

G. K. CHESTERTON

P207
You don't have to be afraid of praising God too much; unlike humans He never gets a big head.

PAUL DIBBLE

P208
Praise makes good men better and bad men worse.

THOMAS FULLER

P209
Neither praise or dispraise thyself, thy actions serve the turn.

GEORGE HERBERT

P210
Praise I call the product of the singing heart. It is the inner man responding – the moment you begin to delight in beauty, your heart and mind are raised.

BASIL HUME

P211
The trouble with most of us is that we would rather be ruined by praise than saved by criticism.

NORMAN VINCENT PEALE

P212
Let every man praise the bridge he goes over.

ENGLISH PROVERB

P213
If one man praises you, a thousand will repeat the praise.

JAPANESE PROVERB

P214
It is a sure sign of mediocrity to be niggardly with praise.

MARQUIS DE VAUVENARGUES

PRAYER
(See also CONTEMPLATION and MEDITATION)

P215
He prays best who does not know that he is praying.

ST. ANTHONY OF PADUA

P216
Do not let us fail one another in interest, care and practical help; but supremely we must not fail one another in prayer.

MICHAEL BAUGHEN

P217
If you are swept off your feet, it's time to get on your knees.

FREDERICK BECK

Prayer

P218
A prayer in its simplest definition is merely a wish turned Godward.

PHILLIPS BROOKS

P219
In prayer it is better to have a heart without words, than words without a heart.

JOHN BUNYAN

P220
Prayer is a shield to the soul, a sacrifice to God, and a scourge to Satan.

JOHN BUNYAN

P221
Prayer is and remains always a native and deep impulse of the soul of man.

THOMAS CARLYLE

P222
The degree of our faith is the degree of our prayer.
The strength of our hope is the strength of our prayer.
The warmth of our charity is the warmth of our prayer.

CARLO CARRETTO

P223
Pray as you can and do not try to pray as you can't.

JOHN CHAPMAN

P224
The biggest problem in prayer is how to 'let go and let God'.

GLENN CLARK

P225
Prayer is conversation with God.

ST. CLEMENT OF ALEXANDRIA

P226
Really to pray is to stand to attention in the presence of the King and to be prepared to take orders from Him.

DONALD COGGAN

P227
Keep praying, but be thankful that God's answers are wiser than your prayers!

WILLIAM CULBERTSON

P228
When we have learned to offer up every duty connected with our situation in life as a sacrifice to God, a settled employment becomes just a settled habit of prayer.

THOMAS ERSKINE

P229
Talk to him in prayer of all your wants, your troubles, even of the weariness you feel in serving him. You cannot speak too freely, too trustfully, to him.

FRANÇOIS FENELON

P230
A good prayer, though often used, is still fresh and fair in the eyes and ears of heaven.

THOMAS FULLER

P231
He causes his prayers to be of more avail to himself, who offers them also for others.

POPE ST. GREGORY I

P232
Prayer is the breath of the new-born soul, and there can be no Christian life without it.

ROWLAND HILL

P233
Certain thoughts are prayers. There are moments when, whatever be the attitude of the body, the soul is on its knees.

VICTOR HUGO

P234
Perfume all your actions with the life-giving breath of prayer.

POPE JOHN XXIII

P235
God loves us to pray to him, and he very much dislikes our making prayer an excuse for neglecting the effort of doing good works.

POPE JOHN PAUL I

P236
He who has learned to pray has learned the greatest secret of a holy and a happy life.

WILLIAM LAW

P237
You need not cry very loud; he is nearer to us than we think.

BROTHER LAWRENCE

P238
Prayer is the most important thing in my life. If I should neglect prayer for a single day, I should lose a great deal of the fire of faith.

MARTIN LUTHER

P239
God insists that we ask, not because *He* needs to know our situation, but because *we* need the spiritual discipline of asking.

CATHERINE MARSHALL

P240
The purpose of all prayer is to find God's will and to make that will our prayer.

CATHERINE MARSHALL

P241
In a single day I have prayed as many as a hundred times, and in the night almost as often.

ST. PATRICK

P242
Prayer is the pillow of religion.

ARAB PROVERB

P243
Pray to God in the storm – but keep on rowing.

DANISH PROVERB

P244
Pray as though no work would help, and work as though no prayer would help.

GERMAN PROVERB

P245
If you pray for another, you will be helped yourself.

YIDDISH PROVERB

P246
What's important is that God is so much part and parcel of life that spontaneous mental chat becomes second nature.

CLIFF RICHARD

P247
The man of prayer finds his happiness in continually creating, searching, being with Christ.

ROGER SCHUTZ

P248
Whether we like it or not, asking is the rule of the Kingdom.

CHARLES H. SPURGEON

P249
Prayer if it is real is an acknowledgment of our finitude, our need, our openness to be changed, our readiness to be surprised, yes astonished by the 'beams of love'.

DOUGLAS STEERE

P250
Prayer enlarges the heart until it is capable of containing God's gift of himself.

MOTHER TERESA

P251
All that should be sought for in the exercise of prayer is conformity of our will and the divine will, in which consists the highest perfection.

ST. TERESA OF AVILA

P252
We are always in the presence of God, yet it seems to me that those

who pray are in his presence in a very different sense.

ST. TERESA OF AVILA

P253
If your prayer is selfish, the answer will be something that will rebuke your selfishness. You may not recognise it as having come at all, but it is sure to be there.

WILLIAM TEMPLE

P254
I have so much to do that I must spend several hours in prayer before I am able to do it.

JOHN WESLEY

PREACHING
(See also MINISTRY)

P255
Preaching is truth through personality.

PHILLIPS BROOKS

P256
To love to preach is one thing – to love those to whom we preach, quite another.

RICHARD CECIL

P257
No man has a right so to preach as to send his hearers away on flat tyres. A discouraged man is not an asset but a liability.

CLOVIS G. CHAPPELL

P258
The authority of those who preach is often an obstacle to those who wish to learn.

MARCUS TULLIUS CICERO

P259
The expertise of the pulpit can only be learned slowly and, it may well be, with a strange mixture of pain and joy.

DONALD COGGAN

P260
Avoid showing, if you can help it, any sign of displeasure when you are preaching, or at least anger, as I did one day when they rang the bell before I had finished.

ST. FRANCIS DE SALES

P261
It is no use walking anywhere to preach unless we preach as we walk.

ST. FRANCIS OF ASSISI

P262
The test of a preacher is that his congregation goes away saying, not 'What a lovely sermon!' but 'I will do something.'

ST. FRANCIS DE SALES

P263
Wherever the Gospel is preached, no matter how crudely, there are bound to be results.

BILLY GRAHAM

P264
When I preach I regard neither doctors nor magistrates, of whom I have above forty in my congregation; I have all my eyes on the servant maids and on the children. And if the learned men are not well pleased with what they hear, well, the door is open.

MARTIN LUTHER

P265
It is very important to live your faith by confessing it, and one of the best ways to confess it is to preach it.

THOMAS MERTON

P266
My grand point in preaching is to break the hard heart and to heal the broken one.

JOHN NEWTON

P267
The half-baked sermon causes spiritual indigestion.
AUSTIN O'MALLEY

P268
A sermon is a proclamation of the generous love of God in Christ, or it is not a Christian sermon.
NORMAN PITTENGER

P269
Those having torches will pass them on to others.
GREEK PROVERB

P270
The teacher is like the candle, which lights others in consuming itself.
ITALIAN PROVERB

P271
When you preach the Gospel, beware of preaching it as the religion which explains everything.
ALBERT SCHWEITZER

P272
Give me one hundred preachers who fear nothing but sin and desire nothing but God, and I care not a straw whether they be clergymen or laymen, such alone will shake the gates of hell and set up the Kingdom of God upon earth.
JOHN WESLEY

PREDESTINATION
(See also DESTINY)

P273
The reason for the predestination of some, and reprobation of others, must be sought for in the goodness of God.
ST. THOMAS AQUINAS

P274
God chose us in Christ before the foundation of the world, predestinating us to the adoption of children, not because we were going to be ourselves holy and immaculate, but He chose and predestinated us that we might be so.
ST. AUGUSTINE OF HIPPO

P275
God has an exasperating habit of laying his hands on the wrong man.
JOSEPH D. BLINCO

P276
It must be borne in mind that God foreknows but does not predetermine everything, since He foreknows all that is in us, but does not predetermine it all.
ST. JOHN OF DAMASCUS

P277
God is preparing his heroes; and when the opportunity comes, he can fit them into their places in a moment, and the world will wonder where they came from.
A. B. SIMPSON

PREJUDICE
(See also BIGOTRY)

P278
Prejudgments become prejudices only if they are not reversible when exposed to new knowledge.
GORDON W. ALLPORT

P279
A prejudice is a vagrant opinion without visible means of support.
AMBROSE BIERCE

P280
The man who never alters his opinion is like standing water, and breeds reptiles of the mind.
WILLIAM BLAKE

P281
The chief cause of human errors is to be found in the prejudices picked up in childhood.
RENE DESCARTES

Pride

P282
Ignorance is less remote from the truth than prejudice.
DENIS DIDEROT

P283
She spoke of heaven and an angelic host;
She spoke of God and the Holy Ghost;
She spoke of Christ's teachings of man's brotherhood;
Yet when she had to sit beside a negro once – she stood.
ELIZABETH HART

P284
Prejudice is never easy unless it can pass itself off for reason.
WILLIAM HAZLITT

P285
Prejudice is the child of ignorance.
WILLIAM HAZLITT

P286
Dogs bark at every one they do not know.
HERACLITUS

P287
A great many people think they are thinking when they are merely rearranging their prejudices.
WILLIAM JAMES

P288
Prejudice, not being founded on reason, cannot be removed by argument.
SAMUEL JOHNSON

P289
Nothing is so firmly believed as that which is least known.
MICHEL DE MONTAIGNE

P290
It is with narrow-minded people as with narrow-necked bottles; the less they have in them, the more noise they make in pouring it out.
ALEXANDER POPE

P291
Drive out prejudices by the door, they will come back by the window.
FRENCH PROVERB

P292
No physician can cure the blind in mind.
JEWISH PROVERB

P293
Very few people take the trouble to use their brains as long as their prejudices are in working condition.
ROY L. SMITH

P294
Never try to reason the prejudice out of a man. It was not reasoned into him and cannot be reasoned out.
SYDNEY SMITH

P295
It is never too late to give up your prejudices.
HENRY DAVID THOREAU

P296
Prejudices are what rule the vulgar crowd.
FRANÇOIS MARIE VOLTAIRE

PRIDE
(See also VANITY)

P297
Pride strives for perverse excellence, a very special sin when God is despised, but also present whenever our neighbour is despised.
ST. THOMAS AQUINAS

P298
Pride is the ground in which all the other sins grow, and the parent from which all the other sins come.
WILLIAM BARCLAY

P299
The just estimate of ourselves at the moment of triumph is the most

eminent renunciation of pride.
WILLIAM ELLERY CHANNING

P300
Pride and grace dwell never in one place.
THOMAS FULLER

P301
You can have no greater sign of a confirmed pride than when you think you are humble enough.
WILLIAM LAW

P302
A proud man is always looking down on things and people; and, of course, as long as you're looking down, you can't see something that's above you.
C. S. LEWIS

P303
God sends no one away empty except those who are full of themselves.
DWIGHT L. MOODY

P304
Pride is at the bottom of all great mistakes.
JOHN RUSKIN

P305
Pride is an established conviction of one's own paramount worth in some particular respect; while vanity is the desire of rousing such a conviction in others.
ARTHUR SCHOPENHAUER

P306
Be not proud of race, face, place or grace.
CHARLES H. SPURGEON

PRIESTHOOD
(See also MINISTRY and CLERGY)

P307
I always like to associate with a lot of priests because it makes me understand anti-clerical things so well.
HILAIRE BELLOC

P308
The priesthood requires a great soul; for the priest has many harassing troubles of his own, and has need of innumerable eyes on all sides.
ST. JOHN CHRYSOSTOM

P309
He cannot have the ordination of the Church who does not hold the unity of the Church.
ST. CYPRIAN

P310
But now I see well the old proverb is true:
That parish priest forgetteth that ever he was clerk!
JOHN HEYWOOD

P311
The priesthood is the spiritual power conferred on the ministers of the Church by Christ for the purpose of dispensing the sacraments to the faithful.
JOHN OF PARIS

P312
A constant danger with priests, even zealous priests, is that they become so immersed in the work of the Lord that they neglect the Lord of the work.
POPE JOHN PAUL II

P313
A blot upon a layman's coat is little seen; a spot upon an alb cannot be hid.
HENRY E. MANNING

P314
A priest ought to be no place where his Master would not go, nor employ in anything which his Master would not do.
HENRY E. MANNING

PRINCIPLES

P315
It is easier to fight for one's
principles than to live up to them.
ALFRED ADLER

P316
Nothing can bring you peace but
the triumph of principle.
RALPH WALDO EMERSON

P317
One cannot found a religion by
putting together principles.
ERICH FROMM

P318
Principles always become a matter
of vehement discussion when
practice is at ebb.
GEORGE GISSING

P319
In matters of principle, stand like a
rock; in matters of taste, swim with
the current.
THOMAS JEFFERSON

PROCRASTINATION

P320
The effect of my procrastination is
that, always busy with the
preliminaries and antecedents, I
am never able to begin to produce.
HENRI FRÉDÉRIC AMIEL

P321
I could give no reply except a lazy
and drowsy, 'Yes, Lord, yes. I'll
get to it right away; just don't
bother me for a little while.' But
'right away' didn't happen right
away; and 'a little while' turned out
to be a very long while.
ST. AUGUSTINE OF HIPPO

P322
Procrastination is the art of
keeping up with yesterday.
DON MARQUIS

P323
Tomorrow is often the busiest day
of the week.
SPANISH PROVERB

P324
Procrastination is the thief of time.
EDWARD YOUNG

PROGRESS

P325
What we call progress is the
exchange of one nuisance for
another nuisance.
GEORGE ELIOT

P326
All that is human must retrograde
if it does not advance.
EDWARD GIBBON

P327
I consider that the way of life in
urbanised, rich countries, as it
exists today, and as it is likely to go
on developing, is probably the
most degraded and unillumined
ever to come to pass on earth.
MALCOLM MUGGERIDGE

P328
Progress may have been all right
once, but it's gone on too long.
OGDEN NASH

P329
The test of our progress is not
whether we add more to the
abundance of those who have
much; it is whether we provide
enough for those who have too
little.
FRANKLIN D. ROOSEVELT

P330
Those who speak most of progress
measure it by quantity and not by
quality.
GEORGE SANTAYANA

PROMISE

P331
Promises may get friends, but it is performance that must nurse and keep them.
OWEN FELTHAM

P332
God's promises are like the stars; the darker the night the brighter they shine.
DAVID NICHOLAS

P333
From the promise to the deed is a day's journey.
BULGARIAN PROVERB

P334
He that promises too much means nothing.
ENGLISH PROVERB

P335
He who is slow in making a promise is most likely to be faithful in the performance of it.
JEAN JACQUES ROUSSEAU

P336
God is the God of promise. He keeps His word, even when that seems impossible; even when the circumstances seem to point to the opposite.
COLIN URQUHART

PROOF

P337
The proof of the pudding is the eating.
MIGUEL DE CERVANTES

P338
A Christianity which does not prove its worth in practice degenerates into dry scholasticism and idle talk.
ABRAHAM KUYPER

P339
Confidence in the goodness of another is good proof of one's own goodness.
MICHEL DE MONTAIGNE

P340
For when one's proofs are aptly chosen,
Four are as valid as four dozen.
MATTHEW PRIOR

PROPHECY
(See also REVELATION)

P341
Every honest man is a prophet; he utters his opinion both of private and public matters. Thus, if you go on so, the result is so. He never says, such a thing will happen let you do what you will. A prophet is a seer, not an arbitrary dictator.
WILLIAM BLAKE

P342
The task of prophecy has been to 'discern the signs of the times,' to see what God is bringing to pass as the history of peoples and societies unfolds, to point to the judgment he brings upon all institutions.
JOHN B. COBURN

P343
If we do not listen to the prophets we shall have to listen to Providence.
A. C. CRAIG

P344
The prophet is to be no mere announcer, he is rather God's agent who by the 'word' accomplishes what he foretells, whether good or bad.
FLEMING JAMES

P345
Prophets were twice stoned – first in anger, then, after their death, with a handsome slab in the graveyard.
CHRISTOPHER MORLEY

P346
Not everyone who speaks in the spirit is a prophet, but only if he follows the conduct of the Lord.
TEACHING OF THE TWELVE APOSTLES

P347
The prophet is primarily the man, not to whom God has communicated certain thoughts, but whose mind is illuminated by the divine spirit to interpret aright the divine acts; and the act is primary.
WILLIAM TEMPLE

PROVIDENCE
(See also ABANDONMENT and WILL OF GOD)

P348
Trust the past to the mercy of God, the present to his love, and the future to his Providence.
ST. AUGUSTINE OF HIPPO

P349
Men must pursue things which are just in present, and leave the future to the divine Providence.
FRANCIS BACON

P350
Behind the frowning Providence He hides a smiling face.
WILLIAM COWPER

P351
Accept the place the Divine Providence has found for you, the society of your contemporaries, the connection of events.
RALPH WALDO EMERSON

P352
We sleep in peace in the arms of God,
when we yield ourselves up to his Providence.
FRANÇOIS FENELON

P353
Providence is the care God takes of all existing things.
JOHN OF DAMASCUS

P354
God wishes each of us to work as hard as we can, holding nothing back but giving ourselves to the utmost, and when we can do no more, then is the moment when the hand of Divine Providence is stretched out to us and takes over.
DON ORIONE

P355
What God sends is better than what men ask for.
CROATIAN PROVERB

P356
Providence assists not the idle.
LATIN PROVERB

P357
God builds the nest of the blind bird.
TURKISH PROVERB

P358
He who gives us teeth will give us bread.
YIDDISH PROVERB

P359
There's a divinity that shapes our ends,
Rough-hew them how we will.
WILLIAM SHAKESPEARE

P360
God tempers the wind to the shorn lamb.
LAURENCE STERNE

P361
In all created things discern the Providence and wisdom of God, and in all things give Him thanks.
ST. TERESA OF AVILA

P362
Providence has at all times been my only dependence, for all other

resources seem to have failed us.
GEORGE WASHINGTON

P363
I firmly believe in Divine
Providence.
Without it, I think I should go
crazy.
Without God the world would be a
maze without a clue.
WOODROW WILSON

PRUDENCE
(See also WISDOM)

P364
No man is prudent who is ignorant
of God.
ST. AMBROSE

P365
Few pay attention to prudence
because few possess it.
ST. BERNARD OF CLAIRVAUX

P366
The man who would truly love, and
know to the full what it means, will
beware of that timid limping thing
which sometimes parades, and
hides its littleness, under the name
of prudence.
ALBAN GOODIER

P367
Whose house is glass must not
throw stones at another.
GEORGE HERBERT

P368
We must not trust every word of
others or feeling within ourselves,
but cautiously and patiently try the
matter, whether it be of God.
THOMAS À KEMPIS

P369
Better is to bow than break.
ENGLISH PROVERB

P370
Always wise men go back to leap
the further.
FRENCH PROVERB

PURITY
(See also CHASTITY and
MODESTY)

P371
Purity means that we put on the
likeness of God, as far as is
humanly possible.
ST. JOHN CLIMACUS

P372
Still to the lowly soul
He doth Himself impart,
And for His cradle and His throne
Chooseth the pure in heart.
JOHN KEBLE

P373
A pure heart penetrates Heaven
and Hell.
THOMAS À KEMPIS

P374
The impure then cannot love God;
and those who are without love of
God cannot really be pure. Purity
prepares the soul for love, and love
confirms the soul in purity.
JOHN HENRY NEWMAN

P375
The stream is always purer at its
source.
BLAISE PASCAL

P376
The pure soul is a beautiful rose,
and the Three Divine Persons
descend from Heaven to inhale its
fragrance.
JOHN VIANNEY

P377
Purity is the power to contemplate
defilement.
SIMONE WEIL

PURPOSE
(See also INTENTION)

P378
A good archer is not known by his
arrows but his aim.
THOMAS FULLER

P379
Purpose is what gives life a meaning.
C. H. PARKHURST

P380
Continuity of purpose is one of the most essential ingredients of happiness in the long run, and for most men this comes chiefly through their work.
BERTRAND RUSSELL

P381
Man, made in the image of God, has a purpose – to be in relationship to God, who is there. Man forgets his purpose and thus he forgets who he is and what life means.
FRANCIS A. SCHAEFFER

P382
Every life should have a purpose to which it can give the energies of its mind and the enthusiasms of its heart. That life without a purpose will be prey to the perverted ways waiting for the uncommitted life.
NEIL C. STRAIT

QUIETNESS
(See also SILENCE and SOLITUDE)

Q1
If we have not quiet in our minds, outward comfort will do no more for us than a golden slipper on a gouty foot.
JOHN BUNYAN

Q2
O God, make us children of quietness, and heirs of peace.
ST. CLEMENT OF ALEXANDRIA

Q3
A little with quiet
Is the only diet.
GEORGE HERBERT

Q4
Happiness is the harvest of a quiet eye.
AUSTIN O'MALLEY

Q5
All the troubles of life come upon us because we refuse to sit quietly for a while each day in our rooms.
BLAISE PASCAL

Q6
It is difficult to be quiet if you have nothing to do.
ARTHUR SCHOPENHAUER

Q7
God is a tranquil Being, and abides in a tranquil eternity. So must thy spirit become a tranquil and clear little pool, wherein the serene light of God can be mirrored.
GERHARD TERSTEEGEN

RACE

R1
The easiest idea to sell anyone is that he is better than someone else. The appeal of the Ku Klux Klan and racist agitators rests on this type of salesmanship.
GORDON W. ALLPORT

R2
Skin colour does not matter to God, for he is looking upon the heart . . . When men are standing at the foot of the cross there are no racial barriers.
BILLY GRAHAM

R3
Racism is man's gravest threat to man – the maximum of hatred for a minimum of reason.
ABRAHAM JOSHUA HESCHEL

R4
We must recognise that the motives and forces behind racism are the

Anti-Christ, denying that man is
made in the divine image.
TREVOR HUDDLESTON

R5
Even though human beings differ
from one another by virtue of their
ethnic peculiarities, they all possess
certain common elements and are
inclined by nature to meet each
other in the world of spiritual
values.
POPE JOHN XXIII

R6
After all, there is but one
race – humanity.
GEORGE MOORE

R7
A heavy guilt rests upon us for
what the whites of all nations have
done to the coloured peoples.
When we do good to them, it is not
benevolence – it is atonement.
ALBERT SCHWEITZER

R8
There is no more evil thing in this
world than race prejudice . . . It
justifies and holds together more
baseness, cruelty, and abomination
than any other sort of error in the
world.
H. G. WELLS

REALITY

R9
Make the application of
Christianity to present-day life a
reality, and none will support it
with more zeal than the workers.
KEIR HARDIE

R10
Facts call us to reflect, even as the
tossings of a capsizing vessel cause
the crew to rush on deck and to
climb the masts.
ALBERT SCHWEITZER

R11
Christ moves among the pots and
pans.
ST. TERESA OF AVILA

R12
A test of what is real is that it is
hard and rough. Joys are found in
it, not pleasure. What is pleasant
belongs to dreams.
SIMONE WEIL

REASON
(See also PHILOSOPHY)

R13
Reason in man is rather like God in
the world.
ST. THOMAS AQUINAS

R14
Reason is a light that God has
kindled in the soul.
ARISTOTLE

R15
Natural reason is a good tree which
God has planted in us; the fruits
which spring from it cannot but be
good.
ST. FRANCIS DE SALES

R16
Your own reason is the only oracle
given you by heaven, and you are
answerable for, not the rightness,
but the uprightness of the decision.
THOMAS JEFFERSON

R17
Reason, or the exercise of reason,
is a living spontaneous energy
within, not an art.
JOHN HENRY NEWMAN

RECONCILIATION
(See also FORGIVENESS and
REPENTANCE)

R18
'Forgiving' as well as 'giving' is
painful, penitential; perhaps if the
Church can be seen as a forgiving

and reconciling community, it will be possible to persuade people of the need for penitence.

JAMES D. CRICHTON

R19
It takes two sides to make a lasting peace, but it only takes one to make the first step.

EDWARD M. KENNEDY

R20
Reconciliation sounds a large theological term, but it simply means coming to ourselves and arising and going to our Father.

JOHN OMAN

R21
A love of reconciliation is not weakness or cowardice. It demands courage, nobility, generosity, sometimes heroism, an overcoming of oneself rather than of one's adversary. At times it may even seem like dishonour, but it never offends against true justice or denies the rights of the poor. In reality, it is the patient, wise art of peace, of loving, of living with one's fellows, after the example of Christ, with a strength of heart and mind modelled on his.

POPE PAUL VI

REDEMPTION
(See also ATONEMENT and SALVATION)

R22
For no one is redeemed except through unmerited mercy, and no one is condemned except through merited judgment.

ST. AUGUSTINE OF HIPPO

R23
And now without redemption all mankind
Must have been lost, adjudge'd to

Death and Hell
By doom severe.

JOHN MILTON

R24
Redemption does not only look back to Calvary. It looks forward to the freedom in which the redeemed stand. Precisely because they have been redeemed at such a cost, believers must be God's men.

LEON MORRIS

R25
People will never take evil seriously nor even see much need to tap the resources of God until they join in with the costly redemptive purposes of love.

J. B. PHILLIPS

REFORM
(See also REFORMATION and REVOLUTION)

R26
All zeal for a reform, that gives offence
To peace and charity, is mere pretence.

WILLIAM COWPER

R27
Every reform movement has a lunatic fringe.

THEODORE ROOSEVELT

R28
The best reformers the world has ever seen are those who commence on themselves.

GEORGE BERNARD SHAW

R29
All reformers, however strict their social conscience, live in houses just as big as they can pay for.

LOGAN PEARSALL SMITH

REFORMATION

R30
It cannot be denied that corruption of morals prevailed in the sixteenth

century to such an extent as to call for a sweeping reformation, and that laxity of discipline invaded even the sanctuary.

JAMES GIBBONS

R31
The question most disputed at the time of the Reformation, namely justification by faith alone, now leaves people in the Protestant Churches just as cold as those in the Catholic Church.

HANS KUNG

R32
The authors and protagonists saw the Reformation as the recovery of the pure revelation of primitive Christianity, the 'word of God undefiled', while the Catholic Church of the time saw it mainly as a rejection of Christian truth.

JOSEPH LORTZ

R33
To make a crooked stick straight, we bend it the contrary way.

MICHEL DE MONTAIGNE

R34
Every reformation must have its victims.
You can't expect the fatted calf to share
the enthusiasm of the angels over the prodigal's return.

H. H. MUNRO

R35
Every generation needs re-generation.

CHARLES H. SPURGEON

R36
Every church should be engaged in continuous self-reformation, scrutinising its traditions in the light of Scripture and where necessary modifying them.

JOHN R. W. STOTT

RELATIONSHIPS
(See also FRIENDSHIP, LOVE, and LOVE OF NEIGHBOUR)

R37
Nothing is a greater impediment to being on good terms with others than being ill at ease with yourself.

HONORÉ DE BALZAC

R38
Have a heart that never hardens, and a temper that never tires, and a touch that never hurts.

CHARLES DICKENS

R39
I think people ought to fulfil sacredly their desires. And this means fulfilling the deepest desire, which is a desire to live unhampered by things that are extraneous, a desire for pure relationships and living truth.

D. H. LAWRENCE

R40
Once the realisation is accepted that even between the closest human beings infinite distances continue to exist, a wonderful living side by side can grow up, if they succeed in loving the distance between them which makes it possible for each to see the other whole against the sky.

RAINER MARIA RILKE

R41
Christianity is not a religion, it is a relationship.

DR. THIEME

R42
It is better to be alone than in bad company.

GEORGE WASHINGTON

R43
Kissing is a means of getting two people so close together that they can't see anything wrong with each other.

GENE YASENAK

RELIGION

R44
For true religion is that by which
the soul is united to God so that it
binds itself again by reconciliation
to Him from Whom it had broken
off, as it were, by sin.

ST. AUGUSTINE OF HIPPO

R45
A religion that is small enough for
our understanding is not great
enough for our need.

ARTHUR JAMES BALFOUR

R46
Religion is excellent stuff for
keeping common people quiet.

NAPOLEON BONAPARTE

R47
It is the root of all religion that a
man knows that he is nothing in
order to thank God that he is
something.

G. K. CHESTERTON

R48
Let your religion be less of a theory
and more of a love affair.

G. K. CHESTERTON

R49
Religion has its origins in the
depths of the soul and it can be
understood only by those who are
prepared to take the plunge.

CHRISTOPHER DAWSON

R50
Science without religion is lame,
religion without science is blind.

ALBERT EINSTEIN

R51
Religions are man's search for
God; the Gospel is God's search
for man. There are many religions,
but one Gospel.

E. STANLEY JONES

R52
The heart of religion lies in its
personal pronouns.

MARTIN LUTHER

R53
We have been dosing our people
with religion when what they need
is not that but the living God.

FREDERICK D. MAURICE

R54
A man who is religious, is religious
morning, noon, and night; his
religion is a certain character, a
mould in which his thoughts,
words, and actions are cast, all
forming parts of one and the same
whole.

JOHN HENRY NEWMAN

R55
What a travesty to think religion
means saving my little soul through
my little good deeds and the rest of
the world go hang.

GERALD VANN

R56
How poor and thin a thing is all
purely personal religion. Religion
to be deep and rich must be
historical.

FRIEDRICH VON HUGEL

R57
Some people have just enough
religion to make them
uncomfortable.

JOHN WESLEY

REPENTANCE
(See also FORGIVENESS)

R58
To him who still remains in this
world no repentance is too late.
The approach to God's mercy is
open, and the access is easy to
those who seek and apprehend the
truth.

ST. CYPRIAN

R59
Sleep with clean hands, either kept clean all day by integrity or washed clean at night by repentance.

JOHN DONNE

R60
When thou attackest the roots of sin, fix thy thought upon the God whom thou desirest rather than upon the sin which thou abhorrest.

WALTER HILTON

R61
For right as by the courtesy of God He forgets our sins when we repent, right so will He that we forget our sin, and all our heaviness, and all our doubtful dreads.

JULIAN OF NORWICH

R62
To do so no more is the truest repentance.

MARTIN LUTHER

R63
It is never too late to repent.

ENGLISH PROVERB

R64
Our repentance is not so much regret for the ill we have done as fear of the ill that may happen to us in consequence.

FRANÇOIS DE LA ROCHEFOUCAULD

R65
The world, as we live in it, is like a shop window into which some mischievous person has got overnight, and shifted all the price-labels so that the cheap things have the high price-labels on them, and the really precious things are priced low. We let ourselves be taken in. Repentance means getting those price-labels back in the right place.

WILLIAM TEMPLE

R66
Repentance must be something more than mere remorse for sins: it comprehends a change of nature befitting heavens.

LEW WALLACE

R67
It can take less than a minute to commit a sin. It takes not as long to obtain God's forgiveness. Penitence and amendment should take a lifetime.

HUBERT VAN ZELLER

REPUTATION
(See also CHARACTER)

R68
A good name is better than great riches.

MIGUEL DE CERVANTES

R69
Excessive fear of losing a good name indicates a great distrust of its foundation, which is the truth of a good life.

ST. FRANCIS DE SALES

R70
Reputation is but a signboard to show where virtue lodges.

ST. FRANCIS DE SALES

R71
Glass, china, and reputation, are easily cracked and never well mended.

BENJAMIN FRANKLIN

R72
What people say behind your back is your standing in the community.

EDGAR W. HOWE

R73
Many a man's reputation would not know his character if they met on the street.

ELBERT HUBBARD

R74
Good will, like a good name, is got by many actions, and lost by one.
FRANCIS JEFFREY

R75
The reputation of a man is like his shadow; it sometimes follows and sometimes precedes him; it is sometimes longer and sometimes shorter than his natural size.
FRENCH PROVERB

RESPONSIBILITY
(See also DUTY)

R76
Our main business is not to see what lies dimly at a distance, but to do what lies clearly at hand.
THOMAS CARLYLE

R77
When you have saved a boy from the possibility of making any mistake, you have also prevented him from developing initiative.
JOHN ERSKINE

R78
To let oneself be bound by a duty from the moment you see it approaching is part of the integrity that alone justifies responsibility.
DAG HAMMARSKJOLD

R79
To be a man is, precisely, to be responsible.
ANTOINE DE SAINT-EXUPÉRY

R80
Man must cease attributing his problems to his environment, and learn again to exercise his will – his personal responsibility in the realm of faith and morals.
ALBERT SCHWEITZER

R81
Few things help an individual more than to place responsibility upon him, and to let him know that you trust him.
BOOKER T. WASHINGTON

R82
The most important thought I ever had was that of my individual responsibility to God.
DANIEL WEBSTER

RESURRECTION
(See also EASTER)

R83
I know of no one fact in the history of mankind which is proved by better evidence of every sort, to the understanding of a fair enquirer, than the great sign which God has given us that Christ died and rose again from the dead.
THOMAS ARNOLD

R84
Christ has turned all our sunsets into dawns.
ST. CLEMENT OF ALEXANDRIA

R85
Let us consider, beloved, how the Lord is continually revealing to us the resurrection that is to be. Of this He has constituted the Lord Jesus Christ the first-fruits, by raising Him from the dead.
POPE ST. CLEMENT II

R86
By virtue of the Resurrection, nothing any longer kills inevitably but everything is capable of becoming the blessed touch of the divine hands, the blessed influence of the will of God upon our lives.
P. TEILHARD DE CHARDIN

R87
The entire New Testament is witness that the real presence of Christ was not withdrawn when the Resurrection 'appearances' ceased. The unique and evanescent

meetings with the risen Lord triggered off a new kind of relation which proved permanent.

C. H. DODD

R88
Our Lord has written the promise of the Resurrection, not in books alone, but in every leaf in springtime.

MARTIN LUTHER

R89
The birth and rapid rise of the Christian Church therefore remain an unsolved enigma for any historian who refuses to take seriously the only explanation offered by the Church itself.

C. F. D. MOULE

R90
To renounce all is to gain all; to descend is to rise; to die is to live.

KARL RAHNER

R91
Christianity is a religion of miracle, and the miracle of Christ's Resurrection is the living centre and object of Christian faith.

ALAN RICHARDSON

R92
Christian theology has never suggested that the 'fact' of Christ's Resurrection could be known apart from faith.

ALAN RICHARDSON

R93
Every parting gives a foretaste of death; every coming together again a foretaste of the Resurrection.

ARTHUR SCHOPENHAUER

R94
Christianity is in its very essence a resurrection religion. The concept of resurrection lies at its heart. If you remove it, Christianity is destroyed.

JOHN R. W. STOTT

R95
If Christ be not risen, the dreadful consequence is not that death ends life, but that we are still in our sins.

G. A. STUDDERT-KENNEDY

R96
Fellowship with Christ is participation in the divine life which finds its fullest expression in triumph over death. Life is a larger word than Resurrection; but Resurrection is, so to speak, the crucial quality of life.

WILLIAM TEMPLE

R97
The Gospels do not explain the Resurrection; the Resurrection explains the Gospels. Belief in the Resurrection is not an appendage to the Christian faith, it *is* the Christian faith.

JOHN S. WHALE

R98
The background of resurrection is always impossibility. And with impossibility staring us in the face, the prelude to resurrection is invariably doubt, confusion, strife, and the cynical smile which is our defence against them. Resurrection is always the defiance of the absurd.

H. A. WILLIAMS

REVELATION

R99
Human salvation demands the divine disclosure of truths surpassing reason.

ST. THOMAS AQUINAS

R100
To see a World in a Grain of Sand,
  And a Heaven in a Wild Flower,
Hold Infinity in the palm of your hand,
  And Eternity in an hour.

WILLIAM BLAKE

Revelation

R101

The first and most important thing we know about God is that we know nothing about him except what he himself makes known.

EMIL BRUNNER

R102

Man cannot cover what God would reveal.

THOMAS CAMPBELL

R103

A Christian cannot live by philosophy. Only the light of Christian revelation gives the end as well as the means of life. It is the same for you as for me and the man in the street. If one has more learning, another has more grace, it is all one.

JOHN CHAPMAN

R104

Every revelation of truth felt with interior savour and spiritual joy is a secret whispering of God in the ear of a pure soul.

WALTER HILTON

R105

Revelation is the act of communicating divine knowledge by the Spirit to the mind. Inspiration is the act of the same Spirit, controlling those who make the truth known.

CHARLES HODGE

R106

Knowing all things, therefore, and providing for what is profitable for each one, He revealed that which it was to our profit to know; but what we were unable to bear He kept secret.

ST. JOHN OF DAMASCUS

R107

Revelation consists of the initiative of God, who personally came to meet man, in order to open with him a dialogue of salvation. It was God who began the talk, and it is God who carries it forward.

POPE JOHN PAUL II

R108

The core of Christian revelation is that Jesus Christ is the sole legitimate Lord of all human lives.

H. KRAEMER

R109

Every act formed by charity is a revelation of God. Every word of truth and love, every hand extended in kindness, echoes the inner life of the Trinity.

GABRIEL MORAN

R110

We do not believe that God has added, or ever will add, anything to His revelation in His Son. But we can now see many things in that revelation which could not be seen by those who first received it. Each generation of Christians, and each people to which the Christian Gospel is preached, makes its own contribution to the understanding of the riches of Jesus Christ.

C. B. MOSS

R111

As prayer is the voice of man to God, so revelation is the voice of God to man.

JOHN HENRY NEWMAN

R112

In revelation, God is the agent as well as the object. It is not just that men speak about God, or for God; God speaks for Himself, and talks to us in person.

J. I. PACKER

R113

Man is the revelation of the Infinite, and it does not become finite in him. It remains the Infinite.

MARK RUTHERFORD

R114
Only because the Word, as love, has already been spoken and understood, can man give a loving answer, an answer which simply means making 'free passage' for the Word.
HANS URS VON BALTHASAR

REVENGE

R115
The noblest vengeance is to forgive.
HENRY G. BOHN

R116
Revenge is the abject pleasure of an abject mind.
DECIMUS JUVENAL

R117
Perhaps because our passions are less strong, perhaps even because the teaching of Christ has at last penetrated our thick heads, we look upon revenge as discreditable.
W. SOMERSET MAUGHAM

R118
Revenge is a dish that should be eaten cold.
ENGLISH PROVERB

R119
The smallest revenge will poison the soul.
JEWISH PROVERB

REVERENCE

R120
A deep reverence for human life is worth more than a thousand executions for the prevention of murder; and is, in fact, the great security of human life. The law of capital punishment, whilst pretending to support this reverence, does in fact tend to destroy it.
JOHN BRIGHT

R121
Lambs have the grace to kneel while nursing.
CHINESE PROVERB

R122
The first mark of a Christian is a deep reverence for persons as destined for eternity with God.
MICHAEL RAMSEY

R123
Reverence is the attitude which can be designated as the mother of all moral life, for in it man first takes a position toward the world which opens his spiritual eyes and enables him to grasp values.
DIETRICH VON HILDEBRAND

REVOLUTION
(See also REFORM and REFORMATION)

R124
Every revolutionary ends by becoming either an oppressor or a heretic.
ALBERT CAMUS

R125
The great revolution of the future will be nature's revolt against man.
HOLBROOK JACKSON

R126
Those who make peaceful revolution impossible will make violent revolution inevitable.
JOHN F. KENNEDY

R127
If omnipotent love did truly transform our hearts, the exterior work of reform would already be half done.
JACQUES MARITAIN

R128
Revolutions are not made with rosewater.
ENGLISH PROVERB

R129
Every revolution by force only puts more violent means of enslavement into the hands of the person in power.

COUNT LEO TOLSTOY

R130
Every successful revolution puts on, in time, the robes of the tyrant it has deposed.

BARBARA TUCHMAN

RICHES
(See also MATERIALISM and WEALTH)

R131
I cannot call riches better than the baggage of virtue; for as the baggage is to an army, so is riches to virtue, it cannot be spared nor left behind, but it hindereth the march.

FRANCIS BACON

R132
Theirs is an endless road, a hopeless maze, who seek for goods before they seek for God.

ST. BERNARD OF CLAIRVAUX

R133
Riches are not forbidden, but the pride of them is.

ST. JOHN CHRYSOSTOM

R134
Many speak the truth when they say that they despise riches, but they mean the riches possessed by other men.

CHARLES CALEB COLTON

R135
The rich in this world cannot be made useful for the Lord, unless their riches have been cut out of them.

SHEPHERD OF HERMAS

R136
The accumulation of vast wealth while so many are languishing in misery is a grave transgression of God's law, with the consequence that the greedy, avaricious man is never at ease in his mind: he is in fact a most unhappy creature.

POPE JOHN XXIII

R137
Riches serve a wise man but command a fool.

ENGLISH PROVERB

R138
Riches are like salt water, the more you drink the more you thirst.

ROMAN PROVERB

RIGHT

R139
One may go wrong in many different ways, but right only in one.

ARISTOTLE

R140
Never claim as a right what you can ask as a favour.

JOHN CHURTON COLLINS

R141
Let us have faith that right makes might, and in that faith let us to the end dare to do our duty as we understand it.

ABRAHAM LINCOLN

R142
Right is right, even if everyone is against it; and wrong is wrong, even if everyone is for it.

WILLIAM PENN

R143
Being in the right does not depend on having a loud voice.

CHINESE PROVERB

R144
There is only one way of seeing things rightly, and that is seeing the whole of them.

JOHN RUSKIN

R145
To be right with God has often meant to be in trouble with men.
A. W. TOZER

R146
Always do right. This will gratify some people and astonish the rest.
MARK TWAIN

RIGHTEOUSNESS
(See also REDEMPTION and SALVATION)

R147
Christ came to reveal what righteousness really is, for nothing will do except righteousness, and no other conception of righteousness will do except Christ's conception of it – his method and secret.
MATTHEW ARNOLD

R148
What is all righteousness that men devise?
What – but a sordid bargain for the skies?
WILLIAM COWPER

R149
If there be ground for you to trust in your own righteousness, then all that Christ did to purchase salvation, and all that God did to prepare the way for it, is in vain.
JONATHAN EDWARDS

R150
Righteousness is obedience to law, observance of duty, and fidelity to conscience.
J. P. HOPPS

R151
The righteousness of Jesus is the righteousness of a Godward relationship of trust, dependence, receptivity.
MICHAEL RAMSEY

SACRAMENTS

S1
The symbolic actions of former and present times, which because of their pertaining to divine things are called sacraments.
ST. AUGUSTINE OF HIPPO

S2
All the sacraments appear as vital acts of the Church in the process of its self-realisation as the primordial sacrament. In these acts the Church gives concrete form to its own essence, which is to be the eschatological, historical and social presence of God's self-communication to the world for the sake of individuals in the moments essential to their salvation.
KARL RAHNER

S3
For mankind there are two unique sacraments which disclose the meaning and convey the experience of reality: they are the created universe and the person of Jesus Christ.
CHARLES E. RAVEN

S4
The meaning of each sacrament is derived from two things: its reference to the paschal mystery and the particular situation of the individual or community upon whom the sacramental celebration focuses.
MARK SEARLE

S5
Each sacrament is the personal saving act of the risen Christ himself, but realised in the visible form of an official act of the Church.
E. SCHILLEBEECKX

211

S6
In the sacraments nature participates in the process of salvation. Bread and wine, water and light, and all the great elements of nature become the bearers of spiritual meaning and saving power. Natural and spiritual powers are united – reunited – in the sacrament.

PAUL TILLICH

SACRIFICE

S7
The sacrifice most acceptable to God is complete renunciation of the body and its passions. This is the only real piety.

ST. CLEMENT OF ALEXANDRIA

S8
Come, let us offer Christ the great, universal sacrifice of our love, and pour out before him our richest hymns and prayers. For he offered his cross to God as a sacrifice in order to make us all rich.

ST. EPHREM

S9
Man's strongest instinct is to self-preservation; grace's highest call is to self-sacrifice.

PAUL FROST

S10
Without sacrifice there is no resurrection. Nothing grows and blooms save by giving. All you try to save in yourself wastes and perishes.

ANDRÉ GIDE

S11
Was anything real ever gained without sacrifice of some kind?

ARTHUR HELPS

S12
I offer my life as a sacrifice for the successful outcome of the Ecumenical Council and for peace among men.

POPE JOHN XXIII

S13
It is only through the mystery of self-sacrifice that a man may find himself anew.

CARL GUSTAV JUNG

S14
The principle of sacrifice is that we choose to do or to suffer what apart from our love we should not choose to do or to suffer.

WILLIAM TEMPLE

SADNESS

(See also GRIEF and SORROW)

S15
There is only one sadness, the sadness of not being a saint.

LEON BLOY

S16
I have taken life on the sad side, and it has helped me to understand many, many failures, many utter ruins.

ABBÉ HUVELIN

S17
I love everything in life, even to be sad.

ARTUR RUBINSTEIN

SAINTS

(See also HOLINESS and PERFECTION)

S18
It is said that a saint is one who always chooses the better of the two courses open to him at every step.

ROBERT H. BENSON

S19
A saint is never consciously a saint;

a saint is consciously dependent on God.

OSWALD CHAMBERS

S20
The great painter boasted that he mixed all his colours with brains, and the great saint may be said to mix all his thoughts with thanks.

G. K. CHESTERTON

S21
And Satan trembles when he sees,
The weakest saint upon his knees.

WILLIAM COWPER

S22
The saints are God's jewels, highly esteemed by and dear to him; they are a royal diadem in his hand.

MATTHEW HENRY

S23
Many of the insights of the saint stem from his experience as a sinner.

ERIC HOFFER

S24
A saint is one who makes goodness attractive.

LAURENCE HOUSEMAN

S25
The way of the world is to praise dead saints and to persecute living ones.

NATHANIEL HOWE

S26
What saint has ever won his crown without first contending for it?

ST. JEROME

S27
God creates out of nothing. Wonderful, you say. Yes, to be sure, but He does what is still more wonderful: He makes saints out of sinners.

SØREN KIERKEGAARD

S28
Nature requires the saint since he alone knows the miracle of transfiguration; growth and development, the very highest and most sustained incarnation, never weary him.

FRIEDRICH NIETZSCHE

S29
Grace is indeed required to turn a man into a saint; and he who doubts this does not know what either a man or a saint is.

BLAISE PASCAL

S30
The power of the soul for good is in proportion to the strength of its passions. Sanctity is not the negation of passion but its order. Hence great saints have often been great sinners.

COVENTRY PATMORE

S31
The saint does everything that any other decent person does, only somewhat better and with a totally different motive.

COVENTRY PATMORE

S32
A saint abroad and a devil at home.

ENGLISH PROVERB

S33
Saint cannot, if God will not.

FRENCH PROVERB

S34
It is easier to make a saint out of a libertine than out of a prig.

GEORGE SANTAYANA

S35
Saints are persons who make it easier for others to believe in God.

NATHAN SÖDERBLOM

S36
The saint is saint, not because he is 'good' but because he is transparent for something that is more than he himself is.

PAUL TILLICH

SALVATION
(See also REDEMPTION,
RIGHTEOUSNESS and
SAVIOUR)

S37
Divine care supplies everybody
with the means necessary for
salvation, so long as he on his part
does not put up obstacles.
St. Thomas Aquinas

S38
Salvation is seeing that the universe
is good, and becoming a part of
that goodness.
Arthur G. Clutton-Brock

S39
The knowledge of sin is the
beginning of salvation.
Epicurus

S40
No man has the right to abandon
the care of his salvation to another.
Thomas Jefferson

S41
The salvation of a single soul is
more important than the
production or preservation of all
the epics and tragedies in the
world.
C. S. Lewis

S42
The way to be saved is not to delay,
but to come and take.
Dwight L. Moody

S43
Salvation is from God only.
Latin Proverb

S44
God has shewn forth his saving
righteousness in the sacrificial
death of Christ, and the sole
requirement of those who would
avail themselves of this salvation is
that they should believe and be
baptised in the faith of Jesus
Messiah.
Alan Richardson

S45
The terms for 'salvation' in many
languages are derived from roots
like salvus, saos, whole, heil, which
all designate health, the opposite of
disintegration and disruption.
Salvation is healing in the ultimate
sense; it is final cosmic and
individual healing.
Paul Tillich

SATAN
(See also DEVIL)

S46
Satan deals with confusion and lies.
Put the truth in front of him and he
is gone.
Paul Mattock

S47
Anyone who obeys Christ by
making Christ's submission to God
the basis of one's own life will be
saved from bondage to Satan and
from fear of death.
Mark Searle

S48
Satan finds some mischief still
For idle hands to do.
Isaac Watts

SAVIOUR
(See also JESUS CHRIST and
SALVATION)

S49
While the Saviour does not reject
the willing, He does not constrain
the unwilling; while He does not
deny Himself to whose who seek
Him, He does not strive with those
who cast Him out.
St. Ambrose

S50
To follow the Saviour is to participate in salvation; to follow the light is to perceive the light.
ST. IRENAEUS

S51
The Saviour leaves his imprint on every single act of charity.
POPE JOHN PAUL II

S52
If we really know Christ as our Saviour our hearts are broken and cannot be hard, and we cannot refuse forgiveness.
MARTYN LLOYD-JONES

S53
To know Christ is not to speculate about the mode of his incarnation, but to know his saving benefits.
PHILIP MELANCHTON

S54
Verbally in Scripture, visually in sacrament, Jesus Christ is set forth as the only Saviour of sinners.
JOHN R. W. STOTT

SCANDAL
(See also GOSSIP)

S55
Scandal will rub out like dirt when it is dry.
THOMAS FULLER

S56
Everything in turn, except scandal, whose turn is always.
ENGLISH PROVERB

S57
Scandal is gossip made tedious by morality.
OSCAR WILDE

SCIENCE

S58
We have too many men of science, too few men of God. We have grasped the mystery of the atom, and rejected the Sermon on the Mount. The world has achieved brilliance without wisdom, power without conscience.
OMAR BRADLEY

S59
There is something in man which your science cannot satisfy.
THOMAS CARLYLE

S60
Science without religion is lame, religion without science is blind.
ALBERT EINSTEIN

S61
Science is not to be regarded merely as a store-house of facts to be used for material purposes, but as one of the great human endeavours to be ranked with arts and religion as the guide and expression of man's fearless quest for truth.
RICHARD GREGORY

S62
In everything that relates to science, I am a whole encyclopaedia behind the rest of the world.
CHARLES LAMB

S63
There is one thing even more vital to science than intelligent methods; and that is, the sincere desire to find out the truth, whatever it may be.
CHARLES SANDERS PEIRCE

SCRIPTURE
(See also BIBLE)

S64
As in Paradise, God walks in the Holy Scriptures, seeking man.
ST. AMBROSE

215

S65
Divine Scripture is the feast of wisdom, and the single books are the various dishes.

ST. AMBROSE

S66
The whole series of the divine Scriptures is interpreted in a fourfold way. In all holy books one should ascertain what everlasting truths are therein intimated, what deeds are narrated, what future events are foretold, and what commands or counsels are there contained.

THE VENERABLE BEDE

S67
It is a great thing, this reading of the Scriptures! For it is not possible ever to exhaust the mind of the Scriptures. It is a well that has no bottom.

ST. JOHN CHRYSOSTOM

S68
Explain the Scriptures by the Scriptures.

ST. CLEMENT OF ALEXANDRIA

S69
In the Scriptures be the fat pastures of the soul; therein is no venomous meat, no unwholesome thing; they be the very dainty and pure feeding. He that is ignorant, shall find there what he should learn.

THOMAS CRANMER

S70
These writings bring back to you the living image of that most holy mind, the very Christ himself speaking, healing, dying, rising, in fact so entirely present, that you would see less of him if you beheld him with your eyes.

DESIDERIUS ERASMUS

S71
Holy Scripture is a stream of running water, where alike the elephant may swim, and the lamb walk without losing its feet.

POPE ST. GREGORY I

S72
There is only one real inevitability: It is necessary that the Scripture be fulfilled.

CARL F. HENRY

S73
The book of books, the storehouse and magazine of life and comfort, the holy Scriptures.

GEORGE HERBERT

S74
To be ignorant of the Scripture is not to know Christ.

ST. JEROME

S75
Every Christian must refer 'always and everywhere' to the Scriptures for all his choices, becoming 'like a child' before it, seeking in it the most effective remedy against all his various weaknesses, and not daring to take a step without being illuminated by the divine rays of those words.

POPE JOHN PAUL II

S76
The way to understand the Scriptures and all theology is to become holy. It is to be under the authority of the Spirit.

MARTYN LLOYD-JONES

S77
God the Father is the giver of Holy Scripture; God the Son is the theme of Holy Scriptures; and God the Spirit is the author, authenticator, and interpreter, of Holy Scripture.

J. I. PACKER

S78
Scripture is full of Christ. From Genesis to Revelation everything breathes of Him, not every letter of

every sentence, but the spirit of every chapter.

FREDERICK W. ROBERTSON

S79
If we value the Scriptures very highly, this is not for themselves, but because they are the Father's testimony to Christ.

JOHN R. W. STOTT

S80
The Scriptures of God, whether belonging to Christian or Jew, are much more ancient than any secular literature.

QUINTUS TERTULLIAN

S81
Most people are bothered by those passages in Scripture which they cannot understand; but as for me, I always noticed that the passages in Scripture which trouble me most are those that I do understand.

MARK TWAIN

SECOND COMING
(See also JUDGMENT)

S82
There are three distinct comings of the Lord of which I know; His coming to men; His coming into men; and His coming against men.

ST. BERNARD OF CLAIRVAUX

S83
We are not a post-war generation; but a pre-peace generation. Jesus is coming.

CORRIE TEN BOOM

S84
Whatever resistance we see today offered by almost all the world to the progress of the truth, we must not doubt that our Lord will come at last to break through all the undertakings of men and make a passage for his word.

JOHN CALVIN

S85
When Christ appears in the clouds he will simply be manifesting a metamorphosis that has been slowly accomplished under his influence in the heart of the mass of mankind.

P. TEILHARD DE CHARDIN

S86
Christ designed that the day of his coming should be hid from us, that being in suspense, we might be as it were upon the watch.

MARTIN LUTHER

S87
We are beginning to realise that the Parousia or Second Coming is not a once-and-for-all event in the historical future, whether near or remote, but part of a myth designed to clarify what it means – as well as what it will mean – to see all things 'new' in the Kingdom of God.

JOHN A. T. ROBINSON

SEEKING GOD
(See also KNOWLEDGE OF GOD)

S88
It is in silence that God is known, and through mysteries that He declares Himself.

ROBERT H. BENSON

S89
I hurry wherever I am beckoned, in search of what can bring men together in the name of the essential.

HELDER CAMARA

S90
He is to be seen in the light of a cottage window as well as in the sun or the stars.

ARTHUR G. CLUTTON-BROCK

S91

We must wait for God, long, meekly, in the wind and wet, in the thunder and lightning, in the cold and the dark. Wait, and he will come. He never comes to those who do not wait. He does not go their road. When he comes, go with him, but go slowly, fall a little behind; when he quickens his pace, be sure of it before you quicken yours. But when he slackens, slacken at once; and do not be slow only, but silent, very silent, for he is God.

FREDERICK W. FABER

S92

Each conception of spiritual beauty is a glimpse of God.

MOSES MENDELSSOHN

S93

Whosoever walks towards God one cubit, God runs towards him twain.

JEWISH PROVERB

S94

Many millions search for God and find Him in their hearts.

SIKH PROVERB

S95

To have found God is not an end in itself but a beginning.

FRANZ ROSENZWEIG

SELF
(See also SELFISHNESS and SELF-LOVE)

S96

We are all serving a life sentence in the dungeon of self.

CYRIL CONNOLLY

S97

The true value of a human being is determined primarily by the measure and the sense in which he has attained liberation from the self.

ALBERT EINSTEIN

S98

The living self has one purpose only: to come into its own fullness of being, as a tree comes into full blossom, or a bird into spring beauty, or a tiger into lustre.

D. H. LAWRENCE

S99

A man needs self-acceptance or he can't live with himself; he needs self-criticism or others can't live with him.

JAMES A. PIKE

S100

What other people think of me is becoming less and less important; what they think of Jesus because of me is critical.

CLIFF RICHARD

S101

Nothing seems to me of the smallest value except what one gets out of oneself.

OSCAR WILDE

SELF-DENIAL
(See also UNSELFISHNESS)

S102

Inwardness, mildness, and self-renouncement do make for man's happiness.

MATTHEW ARNOLD

S103

Self-admiration is the death of the soul. To admire ourselves as we are is to have no wish to change. And with those who don't want to change, the soul is dead.

WILLIAM BARCLAY

S104

All great virtues bear the imprint of self-denial.

WILLIAM ELLERY CHANNING

S105

The most satisfying thing in life is to have been able to give a large part of oneself to others.

P. TEILHARD DE CHARDIN

S106

The true value of a human being is determined primarily by the measure and the sense in which he has attained liberation from the self.

ALBERT EINSTEIN

S107

You give but little when you give of your possessions. It is when you give of yourself that you truly give.

KAHLIL GIBRAN

S108

All along the Christian course, there must be set up altars to God on which you sacrifice yourself, or you will never advance a step.

ALEXANDER MACLAREN

S109

They that deny themselves for Christ shall enjoy themselves in Christ.

JOHN MASON

S110

One secret act of self-denial, one sacrifice of inclination to duty, is worth all the mere good thoughts, warm feelings, passionate prayers in which idle people indulge themselves.

JOHN HENRY NEWMAN

S111

The cross that Jesus tells us to carry is the one that we willingly take up ourselves – the cross of self-denial in order that we might live for the glory of the Father.

COLIN URQUHART

SELF-DISCIPLINE
(See also SELF-DENIAL)

S112

We must be anchored in self-discipline if we are to venture successfully in freedom.

HAROLD E. KOHN

S113

There is endless room for rebellion against ourselves.

GEORGE MACDONALD

S114

Self-discipline never means giving up anything, for giving up is a loss. Our Lord did not ask us to give up the things of earth, but to exchange them for better things.

FULTON J. SHEEN

S115

He that commands others is not so much as free, if he doth not govern himself. The greatest performance in the life of man is the government of his spirit.

BENJAMIN WHICHCOTE

SELFISHNESS
(See also SELF and SELF-LOVE)

S116

Living in our selfishness means stopping at human limits and preventing our transformation into Divine Love.

CARLO CARRETTO

S117

No indulgence of passion destroys the spiritual nature so much as respectable selfishness.

GEORGE MACDONALD

S118

Nine-tenths of our unhappiness is selfishness, and is an insult cast in the face of God.

G. H. MORRISON

S119

The man who lives by himself and for himself is apt to be corrupted by the company he keeps.

CHARLES H. PARKHURST

Self-knowledge

S120
When a man is wrapped up in himself he makes a pretty small package.

JOHN RUSKIN

S121
Selfishness is the only real atheism.

ISRAEL ZANGWILL

SELF-KNOWLEDGE

S122
What use do I put my soul to? It is a very serviceable question this, and should frequently be put.

MARCUS AURELIUS

S123
He who knows himself best esteems himself least.

HENRY G. BOHN

S124
Nothing is so easy as to deceive one's self.

DEMOSTHENES

S125
A man has many skins in himself, covering the depths of his heart. Man knows so many things; he does not know himself. Why, thirty or forty skins or hides, just like an ox's or a bear's, so thick and hard, cover the soul. Go into your own ground and learn to know yourself there.

MEISTER ECKHART

S126
A humble knowledge of yourself is a surer way to God than a deep search after learning.

THOMAS À KEMPIS

S127
The highest and most profitable reading is the true knowledge and consideration of ourselves.

THOMAS À KEMPIS

S128
Know yourself, and your neighbour will not mistake you.

SCOTTISH PROVERB

S129
Other men's sins are before our eyes; our own are behind our backs.

SENECA

S130
Most of us do not like to look inside ourselves for the same reason we don't like to open a letter that has bad news.

FULTON J. SHEEN

S131
It is a great grace of God to practise self-examination; but too much is as bad as too little.

ST. TERESA OF AVILA

SELF-LOVE

S132
We would worry less about what others think of us if we realised how seldom they do.

ETHEL BARRETT

S133
It is our self-importance, not our misery, that gets in His way.

DANIEL CONSIDINE

S134
Self-love is cunning, it pushes and insinuates itself into everything, while making us believe it is not there at all.

ST. FRANCIS DE SALES

S135
You have an ego – a consciousness of being an individual. But that doesn't mean that you are to worship yourself, to think constantly of yourself, and to live entirely for self.

BILLY GRAHAM

S136
Your life is without a foundation, if

in any matter, you choose on your own behalf.

DAG HAMMARSKJOLD

S137
Self-love is a mote in every man's eye.

ENGLISH PROVERB

S138
He who lives to benefit himself confers on the world a benefit when he dies.

QUINTUS TERTULLIAN

S139
Self-centredness completely vitiates communication – with either God or man.

HUBERT VAN ZELLER

SELF-RESPECT
(See also PRIDE)

S140
Never esteem anything as of advantage to thee that shall make thee break thy word or lose thy self-respect.

MARCUS AURELIUS

S141
First learn to love yourself, and then you can love me.

ST. BERNARD OF CLAIRVAUX

S142
If you want to be respected by others the great thing is to respect yourself.

FEODOR DOSTOEVSKI

S143
Self-respect and honour cannot be protected by others. They are for each individual himself or herself to guard.

MOHANDAS GANDHI

S144
He who makes a beast of himself gets rid of the pain of being a man.

SAMUEL JOHNSON

S145
No one can make you feel inferior without your consent.

ELEANOR ROOSEVELT

S146
Self-respect is the noblest garment with which a man may clothe himself, the most elevating feeling with which the mind can be inspired.

SAMUEL SMILES

S147
Take yourself as you are, and do not try to live by one part alone and starve the other.

JANET ERSKINE STUART

SENTIMENT
(See also EMOTION)

S148
Sentiment is the main opponent of spirituality.

ART GLASSER

S149
Trust not to thy feeling, for whatever it be now, it will quickly be changed into another thing.

THOMAS À KEMPIS

S150
Seeing's believing but feeling is God's own truth.

IRISH PROVERB

S151
Analysis, synthesis, reasoning, abstraction, and experience, wishing to take counsel together, begin by banishing sentiment, which carries away the light when it departs, and leaves them in darkness.

JOSEPH ROUX

S152
Never trust a sentimentalist. They are all alike, pretenders to virtue, at heart selfish frauds and sensualists.

J. B. YEATS

SERMONS
(See also PREACHING)

S153
Every man is a priest, even involuntarily; his conduct is an unspoken sermon, which is for ever preaching to others.

HENRI FRÉDÉRIC AMIEL

S154
The sermons I like best are those that have more love for one's neighbour than indignation against him.

ST. FRANCIS DE SALES

S155
It requires great listening as well as great preaching to make a great sermon.

JOHN ANDREW HOLMES

S156
He that has but one word of God before him, and out of that word cannot make a sermon, can never be a preacher.

MARTIN LUTHER

S157
The half-baked sermon causes spiritual indigestion.

AUSTIN O'MALLEY

S158
A sermon is a proclamation of the generous love of God in Christ, or it is not a Christian sermon.

NORMAN PITTENGER

S159
Some clergy prepare their sermons; others prepare themselves.

SAMUEL WILBERFORCE

SERVICE

S160
Ready service, according to our ability, even in very small things and even if rendered by women, is acceptable to God.

ST. BASIL

S161
In Jesus the service of God and the service of the least of the brethren were one.

DIETRICH BONHOEFFER

S162
No one gives himself freely and willingly to God's service unless, having tasted his Fatherly love, he is drawn to love and worship him in return.

JOHN CALVIN

S163
If one were in a rapture like St. Paul, and there was a sick man needing help, I think it would be best to throw off the rapture and show love by service to the needy.

MEISTER ECKHART

S164
The service we render for others is really the rent we pay for our room on this earth.

WILFRED GRENFELL

S165
You have not done enough, you have never done enough, so long as it is still possible that you have something to contribute.

DAG HAMMARSKJOLD

S166
Service is God's way of releasing the individual, whereas slavery is man's way of destroying him.

MICHAEL HARPER

S167
The service that counts is the service that costs.

HOWARD HENDRICKS

S168
He that serves God for money will serve the Devil for better wages.

ENGLISH PROVERB

S169
He who serves is preserved.

LATIN PROVERB

S170

There is no higher religion than human service. To work for the common good is the greatest creed.

ALBERT SCHWEITZER

S171

If she (Martha) had been like the Magdalene, rapt in contemplation, there would have been no one to give to eat to this divine Guest.

ST. TERESA OF AVILA

SEX

S172

About sex especially men are born unbalanced; we might almost say men are born mad. They scarcely reach sanity till they reach sanctity.

G. K. CHESTERTON

S173

Whenever Christ was confronted by people in sexual disarray, he took good care to safeguard sexuality by reminding them that they had to avoid sin; that is to say to use their sexuality in a fully human way.

JACK DOMINIAN

S174

Love may or may not include sexual attraction. It may express itself in sexual desire. But sexual desire is not love. Desire is quite compatible with personal hatred, or contempt, or indifference.

JOHN MACMURRAY

S175

Sexuality throws no light upon love, but only through love can we learn to understand sexuality.

EUGEN ROSENSTOCK-HUESSY

S176

Sex has become one of the most discussed subjects of modern times. The Victorians pretended it did not exist; the moderns pretend that nothing else exists.

FULTON J. SHEEN

S177

A person who despises or undervalues or neglects the opposite sex will soon need humanising.

CHARLES SIMMONS

S178

I lose my respect for the man who can make the mystery of sex the subject of a coarse jest, yet, when you speak earnestly and seriously on the subject, is silent.

HENRY DAVID THOREAU

SHAME

S179

It is a shame not to be shameless.

ST. AUGUSTINE OF HIPPO

S180

He that has no shame has no conscience.

THOMAS FULLER

S181

Where there is yet shame, there may in time be virtue.

SAMUEL JOHNSON

S182

None but the shamefaced lose.

FRENCH PROVERB

S183

I never wonder to see men wicked, but I often wonder to see them not ashamed.

JONATHAN SWIFT

S184

I have known all evils; virtue can surmount them, but what generous heart can endure shame?

FRANÇOIS MARIE VOLTAIRE

SICKNESS

S185
Before all things and above all things, care must be taken of the sick, so that they may be served in very deed as Christ himself . . . But let the sick on their part consider that they are being served for the honour of God, and not provoke their brethren who are serving them by their unreasonable demands. Yet they should be patiently borne with, because from such as these is gained a more abundant reward.

ST. BENEDICT

S186
The best prayers have often more groans than words.

JOHN BUNYAN

S187
Long illnesses are good schools of mercy for those who tend the sick, and of loving patience for those who suffer.

JEAN PIERRE CAMUS

S188
Make sickness itself a prayer.

ST. FRANCIS DE SALES

S189
The sick are to realise that they are sons of God by the very fact that the scourge of discipline chastises them. For unless it were his plan to give them an inheritance after their chastisements, he would not trouble to school them in afflictions.

POPE ST. GREGORY I

S190
Jesus came to save persons, not just souls. He came to help the suffering in whatever way they were suffering. Sickness of the body was part of the kingdom of Satan he had come to destroy.

FRANCIS MACNUTT

S191
Disease makes men more physical; it leaves them nothing but body.

THOMAS MANN

S192
Sickness is every man's master.

DANISH PROVERB

S193
Sickness shows us what we are.

LATIN PROVERB

S194
I enjoy convalescence. It is the part that makes the illness worthwhile.

GEORGE BERNARD SHAW

SILENCE
(See also QUIETNESS and SOLITUDE)

S195
To forbear replying to an unjust reproach, and overlook it with a generous or, if possible, with an entire neglect of it, is one of the most heroic acts of a great mind.

JOSEPH ADDISON

S196
It is in silence that God is known, and through mysteries that He declares Himself.

ROBERT H. BENSON

S197
Mere silence is not wisdom, for wisdom consists in knowing when and how to speak and when and where to keep silent.

JEAN PIERRE CAMUS

S198
The very best and utmost of attainment in this life is to remain still and let God act and speak in thee.

MEISTER ECKHART

S199
Christ is the still point of the turning world.

T. S. ELIOT

S200

How can you expect God to speak in that gentle and inward voice which melts the soul, when you are making so much noise with your rapid reflections? Be silent, and God will speak again.

FRANÇOIS FENELON

S201

The Father uttered one Word; that Word is his Son, and he utters him for ever in everlasting silence; and in silence the soul has to hear it.

ST. JOHN OF THE CROSS

S202

Better to remain silent and be thought a fool than to speak and to remove all doubt.

ABRAHAM LINCOLN

S203

'Rest in the Lord; wait patiently for Him.' In Hebrew, 'be silent to God and let Him mould thee.' Keep still, and He will mould thee to the right shape.

MARTIN LUTHER

S204

With silence one irritates the Devil.

BULGARIAN PROVERB

S205

Be silent about great things; let them grow inside you. Never discuss them: discussion is so limiting and distracting. It makes things grow smaller. You think you swallow things when they ought to swallow you. Before all greatness, be silent – in art, in music, in religion: silence.

FRIEDRICH VON HUGEL

S206

The greatest ideas, the most profound thoughts, and the most beautiful poetry are born from the womb of silence.

WILLIAM A. WARD

SIMPLICITY

S207

One can acquire 'simplicity', but 'simpleness' is innate. Education and culture may bring 'simplicity' – indeed, it ought to be one of their essential aims – but simpleness is a gift.

DIETRICH BONHOEFFER

S208

All great things are simple, and many can be expressed in a single word: freedom; justice; honour; duty; mercy; hope.

SIR WINSTON CHURCHILL

S209

Simple and sincere minds are never more than half mistaken.

JOSEPH JOUBERT

S210

Blissful are the simple, for they shall have much peace.

THOMAS À KEMPIS

SIN

S211

Everyone who commits sin is the slave of sin.

ST. AMBROSE

S212

To sin is nothing else than not to render to God his due.

ST. ANSELM

S213

Sin is not a monster to be mused on, but an impotence to be got rid of.

MATTHEW ARNOLD

S214

The greatest fault is to be conscious of none.

THOMAS CARLYLE

S215

To sin is human, but to persist in sin is devilish.

ST. CATHERINE OF SIENA

S216
Keep yourself from opportunity and God will keep you from sins.

JACOB CATS

S217
God loves us *in* our sin, and *through* our sin, and goes on loving us, looking for a response.

DONALD COGGAN

S218
Sin is a power in our life: let us fairly understand that it can only be met by another power.

HENRY DRUMMOND

S219
Can any sin be called light, since every sin involves some contempt of God.

EUCHERIUS

S220
Sin is not hurtful because it is forbidden, but sin is forbidden because it is hurtful.

BENJAMIN FRANKLIN

S221
Beware the pious fool, and the wise sinner.

IBN GABIROL

S222
I see no fault that I might not have committed myself.

JOHANN WOLFGANG VON GOETHE

S223
Let it be assured that to do no wrong is really superhuman, and belongs to God alone.

GREGORY NAZIANZEN

S224
When thou attackest the roots of sin, fix thy thought more upon the God whom thou desirest than upon the sin which thou abhorrest.

WALTER HILTON

S225
Sin is always a squandering of our humanity, a squandering of our most precious values.

POPE JOHN PAUL II

S226
As long as we be meddling with any part of sin, we shall never see clearly the blissful countenance of our Lord.

JULIAN OF NORWICH

S227
All the old primitive sins are not dead, but are crouching in the dark corners of our modern hearts.

CARL GUSTAV JUNG

S228
Sin is essentially a departure from God.

MARTIN LUTHER

S229
The ultimate proof of the sinner is that he does not know his own sin.

MARTIN LUTHER

S230
The most serious sin is one of thought, the sin of pride.

POPE PAUL VI

S231
Every sin brings its punishment with it.

ENGLISH PROVERB

S232
Sin can be well guarded, but cannot be free from anxiety.

LATIN PROVERB

S233
Almost all our faults are more pardonable than the methods we think up to hide them.

FRANÇOIS DE LA ROCHEFOUCAULD

S234
The first step towards the soul's recovery is the knowledge of the sin committed.

SENECA

S235
No sin is small. No grain of sand is small in the mechanism of a watch.
JEREMY TAYLOR

S236
For the religious man to do wrong is to defy his King; for the Christian, it is to wound his Friend.
WILLIAM TEMPLE

S237
Be ashamed of nothing but sin: not of fetching wood, or drawing water, if time permit; not of cleaning your own shoes or your neighbour's.
JOHN WESLEY

SINCERITY
(See also INTEGRITY)

S238
Be what thou seemest! Live thy creed!
HORATIUS BONAR

S239
Sincerity is never ludicrous; it is always respectable.
CHARLOTTE BRONTË

S240
The sincere alone can recognise sincerity.
THOMAS CARLYLE

S241
The Devil is sincere, but he is sincerely wrong.
BILLY GRAHAM

S242
If you take heed what you are within, you shall not reckon what men say of you. Man looks on the visage and God on the heart. Man considers the deeds and God praises the thoughts.
THOMAS À KEMPIS

S243
Be suspicious of your sincerity when you are the advocate of that upon which your livelihood depends.
JOHN LANCASTER SPALDING

SLANDER

S244
Too often do we call the truths which offend us by the name of slander.
JEAN PIERRE CAMUS

S245
Slander flings stones at itself.
THOMAS FULLER

S246
Whispered insinuations are the rhetoric of the Devil.
JOHANN WOLFGANG VON GOETHE

S247
If slander be a snake, it is winged one – it flies as well as creeps.
DOUGLAS JERROLD

S248
Slander is a shipwreck by a dry tempest.
ENGLISH PROVERB

S249
What is slander: A verdict of 'guilty' pronounced in the absence of the accused, with closed doors, without defence or appeal, by an interested and prejudiced judge.
JOSEPH ROUX

S250
The slanderous tongue kills three: the slandered, the slanderer, and him who listens to the slander.
THE TALMUD

SLAVERY

S251
The peculiar characteristic of slavery is to be always in fear.
ST. AMBROSE

S252
Whether slaves or freemen, we are

227

all one in Christ, and have to serve alike in the army of the same Lord.

ST. BENEDICT

S253
In Africa, as elsewhere, it was the practice of primitive tribes to war against one another and, when victorious, to massacre or enslave the conquered. From the latter process arose the practice of trading in and transporting slaves.

ARTHUR BRYANT

S254
Excessive liberty leads both nations and individuals into excessive slavery.

MARCUS TULLIUS CICERO

S255
Slavery still exists in some thirty countries and is likely to survive in many of them for a long time to come.

NOËL MOSTERT

S256
But do you, who are slaves, be subject to your master, as to God's representative, in reverence and fear.

TEACHING OF THE TWELVE APOSTLES

SLEEP

S257
For what else is sleep but a daily death which does not completely remove man hence nor detain him too long? And what else is death, but a very long and very deep sleep from which God arouses man?

ST. AUGUSTINE OF HIPPO

S258
Lying in bed would be an altogether perfect and supreme experience if only one had a coloured pencil long enough to draw on the ceiling.

G. K. CHESTERTON

S259
Don't count sheep if you can't sleep. Talk to the shepherd.

PAUL FROST

S260
Sleep is, in fine, so like death I dare not trust it without my prayers.

THOMAS FULLER

S261
Sleep that knits up the ravell'd sleave of care.

WILLIAM SHAKESPEARE

S262
The death of each day's life, sore Labour's bath,
Balm of hurt minds, great nature's second course,
Chief nourisher in life's feast.

WILLIAM SHAKESPEARE

SOCIAL JUSTICE

S263
Through love the supreme norm remains the will of God, who wants man's total well-being; what helps man, our neighbour or our neighbours, is right.

HANS KUNG

S264
The aim and purpose of socialist doctrine is the promotion on earth of human equality and social justice. This – with different emphasis – is also part of the doctrine of Christianity.

JULIUS K. NYERERE

S265
It is impossible to be just if one is not generous.

JOSEPH ROUX

S266
Disbelief in Christianity is not so much to be dreaded as its acceptance with a complete denial of it in society and politics.

MARK RUTHERFORD

S267
Society must be made to rest upon justice and love, without which it is but organised wrong.
JOHN LANCASTER SPALDING

S268
If the Christian tries to spread the good news of salvation through Jesus Christ, he should also join in the fight against social injustice and political oppression.
JOHN R. W. STOTT

S269
The preaching of the Gospel and its acceptance imply a social revolution whereby the hungry are fed and justice becomes the right of all.
LEON JOSEPH SUENENS

SOCIETY

S270
What is not good for the hive is not good for the bees.
MARCUS AURELIUS

S271
Human beings and human societies are not structures that are built or machines that are forged. They are plants that grow and must be tended as such.
SIR WINSTON CHURCHILL

S272
To seek the society of others and to shun it are two blameworthy extremes in the devotion of those who live in the world.
ST. FRANCIS DE SALES

S273
Civil society was renovated in every part by the teachings of Christianity. In the strength of that renewal the human race was lifted up to better things. Nay, it was brought back from death to life.
POPE LEO XIII

S274
Society has always seemed to demand a little more from human beings than it will get in practice.
GEORGE ORWELL

S275
The final decision as to what the future of a society shall be depends not on how near its organisation is to perfection, but on the degree of worthiness in its individual members.
ALBERT SCHWEITZER

S276
There is no structural organisation of society which can bring about the coming of the Kingdom of God on earth, since all systems can be perverted by the selfishness of man.
WILLIAM TEMPLE

SOLITUDE
(See also QUIETNESS and SILENCE)

S277
Enter into the inner chamber of your mind. Shut out all things save God and whatever may aid you in seeking God; and having barred the door of your chamber, seek him.
ST. ANSELM OF CANTERBURY

S278
This great misfortune – to be incapable of solitude.
JEAN DE LA BRUYÉRE

S279
It is known to many that we need solitude to find ourselves. Perhaps it is not so well known that we need solitude to find our fellows. Even the Saviour is described as reaching mankind through the wilderness.
HAVELOCK ELLIS

S280
It is easy in the world to live after the world's opinion; it is easy in solitude to live after your own; but the great man is he who in the midst of the crowd keeps with perfect sweetness the independence of solitude.
RALPH WALDO EMERSON

S281
Solitude is a wonderful thing when one is at peace with oneself and when there is a definite task to be accomplished.
JOHANN WOLFGANG VON GOETHE

S282
There is no true solitude except interior solitude.
THOMAS MERTON

S283
He who does not enjoy solitude will not love freedom.
ARTHUR SCHOPENHAUER

S284
A wise man is never less alone than when he is alone.
JONATHAN SWIFT

S285
I never found the companion that was so companionable as solitude.
HENRY DAVID THOREAU

S286
To go up alone into the mountain and come back as an ambassador to the world, has ever been the method of humanity's best friends.
EVELYN UNDERHILL

S287
Practise the art of 'aloneness' and you will discover the treasure of tranquillity. Develop the art of solitude and you will unearth the gift of serenity.
WILLIAM A. WARD

SORROW
(See also GRIEF)

S288
Sorrow is given us on purpose to cure us of sin.
ST. JOHN CHRYSOSTOM

S289
Sorrow makes us all children again – destroys all differences of intellect. The wisest know nothing.
RALPH WALDO EMERSON

S290
Nothing but sin should sadden us, and to this sorrow for sin it is necessary that holy joy should be attached.
ST. FRANCIS DE SALES

S291
Sorrow is a fruit; God does not make it grow on limbs too weak to bear it.
VICTOR HUGO

S292
Sorrow you can hold, however desolating, if nobody speaks to you. If they speak, you break down.
BEDE JARRETT

S293
Sorrow, like rain, makes roses and mud.
AUSTIN O'MALLEY

S294
Sorrow makes silence her best orator.
ENGLISH PROVERB

S295
Where there is sorrow, there is holy ground.
OSCAR WILDE

SPIRITUAL LIFE

S296
Every advance in spiritual life has its corresponding dangers; every

step that we rise nearer God increases the depths of the gulf into which we may fall.

ROBERT H. BENSON

S297
He who believes himself to be far advanced in the spiritual life has not even made a good beginning.

JEAN PIERRE CAMUS

S298
It is right that you should begin again every day. There is no better way to finish the spiritual life than to be ever beginning it over again, and never to think that you have done enough.

ST. FRANCIS DE SALES

S299
Spiritual rose bushes are not like natural rose bushes; with these latter the thorns remain but the roses pass, with the former the thorns pass and the roses remain.

ST. FRANCIS DE SALES

S300
Every man has two journeys to make through life. There is the outer journey, with its various incidents and the milestones . . . There is also an inner journey, a spiritual Odyssey, with a secret history of its own.

WILLIAM R. INGE

S301
The more a man is united within himself, and interiorly simple, the more and higher things doth he understand without labour; because he receiveth the light of understanding from above.

THOMAS À KEMPIS

S302
Spirituality really means 'Holy Spirit at work', a profound action of the Holy Spirit in his Church,

renewing that Church from the inside.

LEON JOSEPH SUENENS

S303
Interior growth is only possible when we commit ourselves with and to others.

JEAN VANIER

STATE
(See also GOVERNMENT)

S304
What is a state but a multitude of men, brought together into some bond of agreement.

ST. AUGUSTINE OF HIPPO

S305
A state is an association of families and their common affairs, governed by a supreme power and by reason.

JEAN BODIN

S306
A state without the means of some change is without the means of its conservation.

EDMUND BURKE

S307
The office of government is not to confer happiness but to give men opportunity to work out happiness for themselves.

WILLIAM ELLERY CHANNING

STEWARDSHIP

S308
Stewardship is what a man does after he says, 'I believe'.'

W. H. GREEVER

S309
The two things which, of all others, most want to be under a strict rule, and which are the greatest blessings to ourselves and to others, when they are rightly used, are our time and our money.

WILLIAM LAW

S310

Stewardship is the acceptance from God of personal responsibility for all of life and life's affairs.

ROSWELL C. LONG

STRENGTH

S311

When You are our strength, it is strength indeed, but when our strength is our own it is only weakness.

ST. AUGUSTINE OF HIPPO

S312

It is a sign of strength, not of weakness, to admit that you don't know all the answers.

JOHN P. LOUGHRANE

S313

When God wants to move a mountain, he does not take a bar of iron, but he takes a little worm. The fact is, we have too much strength. We are not weak enough. It is not our strength that we want. One drop of God's strength is worth more than all the world.

DWIGHT L. MOODY

S314

When we feel us too bold, remember our own feebleness. When we feel us too faint, remember Christ's strength.

SIR THOMAS MORE

S315

One has always strength enough to bear the misfortunes of one's friends.

ENGLISH PROVERB

S316

Strenuousness is the open foe of attainment. The strength that wins is calm and has an exhaustless source in its passive depths.

RABINDRANATH TAGORE

SUCCESS

S317

The figure of the Crucified invalidates all thought which takes success for its standard.

DIETRICH BONHOEFFER

S318

Try not to become a man of success but rather try to become a man of value.

ALBERT EINSTEIN

S319

The religious man is the only successful man.

FREDERICK W. FABER

S320

Since modern man experiences himself both as the seller and as the commodity to be sold on the market, his self-esteem depends on conditions beyond his control. If he is 'successful', he is valuable; if he is not, he is worthless.

ERICH FROMM

S321

Real success is not in having climbed the heights but in having maintained a foothold there.

PAUL FROST

S322

Success consists of getting up just one more time than you fall.

OLIVER GOLDSMITH

S323

Let us work as if success depended upon ourselves alone; but with heartfelt conviction that we are doing nothing and God everything.

ST. IGNATIUS LOYOLA

S324

Success makes a fool seem wise.

ENGLISH PROVERB

S325

Success, which is something so simple in the end, is made up of

thousands of things, we never fully know what.
RAINER MARIA RILKE

SUFFERING
(See also PAIN)

S326
A Christian is someone who shares the sufferings of God in the world.
DIETRICH BONHOEFFER

S327
One ounce of patient suffering is worth far more than a pound of action.
JEAN PIERRE CAMUS

S328
When one is in very great pain and fear it is extremely difficult to pray coherently, and I could only raise my mind in anguish to God and ask for strength to hold on.
SHEILA CASSIDY

S329
The strangest truth of the Gospel is that redemption comes through suffering.
MILO L. CHAPMAN

S330
Jesus did not come to explain away suffering or remove it. He came to fill it with His Presence.
PAUL CLAUDEL

S331
Take the cross he sends, as it is, and not as you imagine it to be.
CORNELIA CONNELLY

S332
The only cure for suffering is to face it head on, grasp it round the neck, and use it.
MARY CRAIG

S333
The hardest heart and grossest ignorance must disappear before the fire of suffering without anger and malice.
MOHANDAS GANDHI

S334
The chief pang of most trials is not so much the actual suffering itself as our own spirit of resistance to it.
JEAN NICHOLAS GROU

S335
The purest suffering hears and carries in its train the purest understanding.
ST. JOHN OF THE CROSS

S336
He who knoweth how to suffer will enjoy much peace. Such a one is a conqueror of himself and lord of the world, a friend of Christ, and an heir of Heaven.
THOMAS À KEMPIS

S337
Unearned suffering is redemptive.
MARTIN LUTHER KING JR.

S338
Know how sublime a thing it is to suffer and be strong.
HENRY WORDSWORTH LONGFELLOW

S339
Our suffering is not worthy the name of suffering. When I consider my crosses, tribulations, and temptations, I shame myself almost to death, thinking what are they in comparison of the sufferings of my blessed Saviour Christ Jesus.
MARTIN LUTHER

S340
It is a glorious thing to be indifferent to suffering, but only to one's own suffering.
ROBERT LYND

S341
The greatness of our God must be tested by the desire we have of suffering for his sake.
PHILIP NERI

S342

We all suffer for each other, and gain by each other's suffering; for man never stands alone here, though he will stand by himself one day hereafter; but here he is a social being, and goes forward to his longed for home as one of a large company.

JOHN HENRY NEWMAN

S343

He who suffers much will know much.

GREEK PROVERB

S344

Torture us, rack us, condemn us, crush us; your cruelty only proves our innocence. That is why God suffers us to suffer all this.

QUINTUS TERTULLIAN

S345

Suffering is the very best gift He has to give us. He gives it only to his chosen friends.

ST. THÉRÈSE OF LISIEUX

S346

It is by those who have suffered that the world has been advanced.

COUNT LEO TOLSTOY

S347

Suffering is the money with which one buys heaven.

THEOPHANE VÉNARD

SUNDAY

S348

Sunday clears away the rust of the whole week.

JOSEPH ADDISON

S349

God ended all the world's array,
And rested on the seventh day:
His holy voice proclaimed it blest,
And named it for the sabbath rest.

THE VENERABLE BEDE

S350

There are many persons who look on Sunday as a sponge to wipe out the sins of the week.

HENRY WARD BEECHER

S351

The Lord's Day is so called, because on that day, the joy of our Lord's resurrection is celebrated. This day the Jews did not observe, but it was declared by the Christians in honour of the Lord's resurrection, and the celebration began from that time.

ST. ISIDORE

S352

Sunday, indeed, is the day on which we hold our common assembly because it is the first day on which God, transforming the darkness and matter, created the world; and our Saviour, Jesus Christ, arose from the dead on the same day. For they crucified Him on the day before, that of Saturn, and on the day after, Sunday, He appeared to His apostles and disciples, and taught them the things which we have passed on to you also for consideration.

ST. JUSTIN MARTYR

S353

Everything has its weekday side and its Sunday side.

G. C. LICHTENBERG

S354

The Sabbath is the golden clasp that binds together the volume of the week.

J. C. MACAULEY

S355

Come day, go day, God send Sunday.

ENGLISH PROVERB

S356

If you want to kill Christianity, you

must abolish Sunday.
FRANÇOIS MARIE VOLTAIRE

SUPERSTITION

S357
There is a superstition in avoiding superstition.
FRANCIS BACON

S358
Superstition is a religion of feeble minds.
EDMUND BURKE

S359
The Devil divides the world between atheism and superstition.
GEORGE HERBERT

S360
Superstition is the cruellest thing in the world. Faith is to live in the sun. Superstition is to sit in darkness.
KATHERINE T. HINKSON

SYMPATHY

S361
Next to love, sympathy is the dimmest passion of the human heart.
EDMUND BURKE

S362
Harmony of aim, and identity of conclusion, is the secret of the sympathetic life.
RALPH WALDO EMERSON

S363
Nothing is more salutary for those who are in affliction than to become consolers.
MAURICE HULST

TACT

T1
Silence is not always tact, and it is tact that is golden – not silence.
SAMUEL BUTLER

T2
Mention not a halter in the house of him that was hanged.
GEORGE HERBERT

T3
Tact is the ability to describe others as they see themselves.
ABRAHAM LINCOLN

TALENT
(See also GENIUS)

T4
Doing easily what others find difficult is talent; doing what is impossible is genius.
HENRI FRÉDÉRIC AMIEL

T5
Talents are distributed unevenly, it is true: to one ten, and to another five; but each has one pound, all alike.
ROBERT H. BENSON

T6
If people knew how hard I have to work to gain my mastery, it would not seem wonderful at all.
MICHELANGELO BUONARROTI

T7
Iron rusts from disuse; stagnant water loses its purity, and in cold weather becomes frozen; even so does inaction sap the vigours of the mind.
LEONARDO DA VINCI

T8
There is a great deal of unmapped country within us.
GEORGE ELIOT

T9
No one respects a talent that is concealed.
DESIDERIUS ERASMUS

T10
Talent is the capacity of doing anything that depends on application and industry; it is

voluntary power, while genius is involuntary.

WILLIAM HAZLITT

T11
Alas for those who never sing, but die with all their music in them.

OLIVER WENDELL HOLMES

T12
Talent is God-given; be thankful. Conceit is self-given, be careful.

THOMAS LA MANCE

T13
Nobody don't never get nothing for nothing nowhere, no time, no how.

AMERICAN PROVERB

T14
Often the greatest talents lie unseen.

LATIN PROVERB

T15
Nature has concealed at the bottom of our minds talents and abilities of which we are not aware.

FRANÇOIS DE LA ROCHEFOUCAULD

T16
No talent can survive the blight of neglect.

EDGAR A. WHITNEY

T17
The real tragedy of life is not in being limited to one talent, but in the failure to use the one talent.

EDGAR W. WORK

TALK
(See also COMMUNICATION, CONVERSATION and WORDS)

T18
Speaking without thinking is shooting without aiming.

WILLIAM G. BENHAM

T19
Speak when you are angry and you will make the best speech you will ever regret.

AMBROSE BIERCE

T20
I suspect that the real reason that an Englishman does not talk is that he cannot leave off talking. I suspect that my solitary countrymen, hiding in separate railway compartments, are not so much retiring as a race of Trappists escaping from a race of talkers.

G. K. CHESTERTON

T21
If you don't say anything, you won't be called on to repeat it.

CALVIN COOLIDGE

T22
Insinuations are the rhetoric of the Devil.

JOHANN WOLFGANG VON GOETHE

T23
The wise hand does not all that the foolish mouth speaks.

GEORGE HERBERT

T24
Think twice before you speak and then say it to yourself.

ELBERT HUBBARD

T25
Don't say all you'd like to say lest you hear something you wouldn't like to hear.

SEUMAS MACMANUS

T26
A word rashly spoken cannot be brought back by a chariot and four horses.

CHINESE PROVERB

T27
The greatest talkers are always the least doers.

ENGLISH PROVERB

T28
Man is caught by his tongue, and an ox by his horns.

RUSSIAN PROVERB

T29
He who talks much is sometimes right.

SPANISH PROVERB

TEMPERANCE
(See also SELF-DENIAL)

T30
Temperance is the moderating of one's desires in obedience to reason.

MARCUS TULLIUS CICERO

T31
Temperance is to the body what religion is to the soul – the foundation of health, strength and peace.

TYRON EDWARDS

T32
Temperance is the control of all the functions of our bodies. The man who refuses liquor, goes in for apple pie, and develops a paunch, is no ethical leader for me.

JOHN ERSKINE

T33
If we give more to the flesh than we ought, we nourish our enemy; if we give not to her necessity what we ought, we destroy a citizen.

POPE ST. GREGORY I

T34
Temperance is corporal piety; it is the preservation of divine order in the body.

THEODORE PARKER

T35
To go beyond the bounds of moderation is to outrage humanity.

BLAISE PASCAL

T36
Temperate temperance is best; intemperate temperance injures the cause of temperance.

MARK TWAIN

TEMPTATION

T37
He who with his whole heart draws near unto God must of necessity be proved by temptation and trial.

ST. ALBERT THE GREAT

T38
The Devil tempts that he may ruin; God tempts that He may crown.

ST. AMBROSE

T39
It is good to be without vices, but it is not good to be without temptations.

WALTER BAGEHOT

T40
Temptations, when we first meet them, are as the lion that roared upon Samson; but if we overcome them, the next time we see them we shall find a nest of honey within them.

JOHN BUNYAN

T41
No man is matriculated to the art of life till he has been well tempted.

GEORGE ELIOT

T42
As the Sandwich-Islander believes that the strength and valour of the enemy he kills passes into himself, so we gain the strength of the temptations we resist.

RALPH WALDO EMERSON

T43
Every moment of resistance to temptation is a victory.

FREDERICK W. FABER

T44
To realise God's presence is the one sovereign remedy against temptation.

FRANÇOIS FENELON

T45
If it takes temptation and sin to

show God in his true colours and
Satan in his, something has been
saved from the wreck.
MICHAEL GREEN

T46
No man is so perfect and holy as
not to have sometimes
temptations; and we cannot be
wholly without them.
THOMAS À KEMPIS

T47
There is no order so holy, nor place
so retired, where there are not
temptations and adversities.
THOMAS À KEMPIS

T48
God chooses that men should be
tried, but let a man beware of
tempting his neighbour.
GEORGE MACDONALD

T49
The heron's a saint when there are
no fish in sight.
BENGALESE PROVERB

T50
God promises a safe landing but
not a calm passage.
BULGARIAN PROVERB

T51
To pray against temptations, and
yet to rush into occasions, is to
thrust your fingers into the fire, and
then pray they might not be burnt.
THOMAS SECKER

T52
You are not tempted because you
are evil; you are tempted because
you are human.
FULTON J. SHEEN

T53
Some temptations come to the
industrious, but all temptations
attack the idle.
CHARLES H. SPURGEON

T54
The greatest of all evils is not to be
tempted, because there are then
grounds for believing that the Devil
looks upon us as his property.
JOHN VIANNEY

THANKSGIVING
(See also GRATITUDE)

T55
No duty is more urgent than that of
returning thanks.
ST. AMBROSE

T56
Pride slays thanksgiving, but an
humble mind is the soil out of
which thanks naturally grows. A
proud man is seldom a grateful
man, for he never thinks he gets as
much as he deserves.
HENRY WARD BEECHER

T57
We should spend as much time in
thanking God for His benefits as
we do in asking Him for them.
ST. VINCENT DE PAUL

T58
Awake with a winged heart, and
give thanks for another day of
loving!
KAHLIL GIBRAN

T59
Joy untouched by thankfulness is
always suspect.
THEODOR HAECKER

T60
One act of thanksgiving when
things go wrong with us is worth a
thousand thanks when things are
agreeable to our inclination.
JOHN OF AVILA

T61
Give thanks frequently to God for
all the benefits he has conferred on

you, that you may be worthy to receive more.

ST. LOUIS IX

T62

The thankful heart is the only door that opens to God.

JOE ORTON

T63

Who does not thank for little will not thank for much.

ESTONIAN PROVERB

T64

Three things for which thanks are due: an invitation, a gift and a warning.

WELSH PROVERB

T65

Were there no God, we would be in this glorious world with grateful hearts: and no one to thank.

CHRISTINA ROSSETTI

THEOLOGY

T66

Theology deserves to be called the highest wisdom, for everything is viewed in the light of the first cause.

ST. THOMAS AQUINAS

T67

Theology is but our ideas of truth classified and arranged.

HENRY WARD BEECHER

T68

Theology is only articulate religion.

G. K. CHESTERTON

T69

The broad ethics of Jesus were quickly narrowed to village theologies.

RALPH WALDO EMERSON

T70

Love is the abridgement of all theology.

ST. FRANCIS DE SALES

T71

Your theology is what you are when the talking stops and the action starts.

COLIN MORRIS

T72

The publican stood afar off and beat his breast and said, 'God be merciful to me, a sinner.' I tell you that man had the finest theology of any man in all England.

CHARLES H. SPURGEON

T73

Theology, like gold, is where you find it.

BRUCE VAWTER

THOUGHT
(See also MIND)

T74

Thought is a kind of sight of the mind.

ST. AUGUSTINE OF HIPPO

T75

When evil thoughts come into your heart, dash them at once on the rock of Christ.

ST. BENEDICT

T76

Men have the power of thinking that they may avoid sin.

ST. JOHN CHRYSOSTOM

T77

When the first spark of thought appeared on the earth, life found it had brought into the world a power capable of criticising it and judging it.

P. TEILHARD DE CHARDIN

T78

There is no expedient to which a man will not go to avoid the real labour of thinking.

THOMAS EDISON

T79

It isn't what people think that is important, but the reason they think what they think.

EUGENE IONESCO

T80

Where all think alike, no one thinks very much.

WALTER LIPPMANN

T81

Occupy your minds with good thoughts, or the enemy will fill them with bad ones: unoccupied they cannot be.

SIR THOMAS MORE

T82

By space the universe embraces me and swallows me up like an atom, by thought I embrace the universe.

BLAISE PASCAL

T83

Men fear thought as they fear nothing else on earth – more than ruin, more even than death.

BERTRAND RUSSELL

TIME

T84

It is the wisest who grieve most at loss of time.

DANTE ALIGHIERI

T85

Time is a three-fold present: the present as we experience it, the past as a present memory, and the future as a present expectation.

ST. AUGUSTINE OF HIPPO

T86

He who kills time commits suicide.

FREDERICK BECK

T87

Time must always ultimately teach.

HILAIRE BELLOC

T88

If a man has no time or only a short time for seeing people, you can be fairly sure that he is neither very important nor very busy.

JOHN S. CHURCHILL

T89

The voice of Time cries to man, 'Advance'. Time is for his advancement and improvement, for his greater worth, his greater happiness, his better life.

CHARLES DICKENS

T90

Time deals gently with those who take it gently.

ANATOLE FRANCE

T91

Dost thou love life? Then do not squander Time, for that's the stuff Life is made of.

BENJAMIN FRANKLIN

T92

One always has time enough if one will apply it.

JOHANN WOLFGANG VON GOETHE

T93

Time is a circus, always packing up and moving away.

BEN HECHT

T94

Do not walk through time without leaving worthy evidence of your passage.

POPE JOHN XXIII

T95

The great rule of moral conduct is, next to God, to respect time.

JOHANN K. LAVATER

T96

Next to grace time is the most precious gift of God. Yet how much of both we waste. We say that time does many things. It teaches us many lessons, weans us from many follies, strengthens us in good resolves, and heals many wounds. And yet it does none of these things. Time does nothing. But time is the condition of all these things which God does in time. Time is full of eternity. As we use it so shall we be. Every day has its opportunities, every hour its offer of grace.

HENRY E. MANNING

T97
Throughout the whole (New Testament) there runs the conviction that the time looked forward to by the prophets has in fact arrived in history with the advent of Jesus Christ . . . The time of Jesus is *kairos* – a time of opportunity. To embrace the opportunity means salvation; to neglect it, disaster. There is no third course.

JOHN MARSH

T98
Time and tide wait for no man.

ENGLISH PROVERB

T99
There is no mortar that time will not loose.

FRENCH PROVERB

T100
The moment passed is no longer; the future may never be; the present is all of which man is the master.

JEAN JACQUES ROUSSEAU

T101
He who neglects the present moment throws away all he has.

JOHANN C. F. VON SCHILLER

T102
Come what, come may, time and the hour run through the roughest day.

WILLIAM SHAKESPEARE

T103
Time is the deposit each one has in the bank of God and no one knows the balance.

RALPH W. SOCKMAN

TOLERANCE

T104
I have seen gross intolerance shown in support of tolerance.

SAMUEL TAYLOR COLERIDGE

T105
Tolerance is the posture and cordial effort to understand another's beliefs, practices, and habits without necessarily sharing or accepting them.

JOSHUA LIEBMAN

T106
The modern theory that you should always treat the religious convictions of other people with profound respect finds no support in the Gospels. Mutual tolerance of religious views is the product not of faith, but of doubt.

ARNOLD LUNN

TORTURE
(See also SUFFERING)

T107
To shelter or give medical aid to a man on the run, from a police force which will torture and perhaps kill him, is an act of Christian love demanded by Christ in the Gospel and is no more a political act than giving first aid and a cup of tea to a Member of Parliament who has a car smash outside your door.

SHEILA CASSIDY

T108
Wild animals never kill for sport. Man is the only one to whom the torture and death of his fellow-creatures is amusing in itself.

JAMES A. FROUDE

T109
Civilised mankind has of will
ceased to torture, but in our
process of being civilised we have
won, I suspect, intensified capacity
to suffer.

S. WEIR MITCHELL

TRADITION

T110
Scripture has been God's way of
fixing tradition, and rendering it
trustworthy at any distance of time.

HENRY ALFORD

T111
Since it has been shown that the
Church's traditions are subsequent
to the Church, it follows that the
Church does not derive its
authority from the traditions but
that the traditions derive their
authority from the Church.

DANTE ALIGHIERI

T112
There is a difference between
apostolic tradition and
ecclesiastical tradition, the former
being the foundation of the latter.
They cannot therefore be
coordinated.

OSCAR CULLMANN

T113
So that the river of tradition may
come down to us we must
continually dredge its bed.

HENRI DE LUBAC

T114
Tradition is a guide and not a
gaoler.

W. SOMERSET MAUGHAM

T115
Tradition and conscience are the
two wings given to the human soul
to reach the truth.

GIUSEPPE MAZZINI

T116
Tradition has its legitimate place
and its true source. By tradition is
meant, what has ever been held, as
far as we know, though we do not
know how it came to be held, and
for that very reason think it true,
because else it would not be held.

JOHN HENRY NEWMAN

T117
Tradition is the living faith of the
dead; traditionalism is the dead
faith of the living.

JAROSLAV PELIKAN

T118
Tradition will be our guide to the
interpretation of the Bible through
the appeal to the total life and
experience of the Church from the
ancient Fathers onwards.

MICHAEL RAMSEY

T119
The Spirit who interprets the
Scriptures is none other than the
Risen Lord himself; the tradition of
the Church is actually shaped and
guided by the Spirit of the Risen
Christ.

ALAN RICHARDSON

T120
Ultimate authority is in Scripture,
in God speaking through Scripture,
for whereas tradition is oral, open
and often self-contradictory,
Scripture is written, fixed and
always self-consistent.

JOHN R. W. STOTT

TRINITY
(See also GOD)

T121
The divine nature is really and
entirely identical with each of the
three persons, all of whom can
therefore be called one: I and the
Father are one.

ST. THOMAS AQUINAS

T122
How can plurality consist with unity, or unity with plurality? To examine the fact closely is rashness, to believe it is piety, to know it is life, and life eternal.
ST. BERNARD OF CLAIRVAUX

T123
The distinction of persons is true only for our knowledge of God, not for his inner Being, which we cannot know.
MILLAR BURROWS

T124
The unity of Father, Son and Spirit is a unity of operation and revelation in which they are involved as three very diverse factors, to be described at best in analogical terms.
HANS KUNG

T125
In God there can be no selfishness, because the three selves of God are three subsistent relations of selflessness, overflowing and superabounding in joy in the perfection of their gift of their one life to one another.
THOMAS MERTON

T126
Without belief in God's revelation the Trinity cannot be known at all; and even for believers it is incomprehensible in an exceptionally high degree, indeed, in the highest degree. There it is a mystery in the truest, highest, most beautiful sense of the word.
M. J. SCHEEBEN

T127
God dwells in our heart by faith, and Christ by his Spirit, and the Holy Spirit by his purities; so that we are also cabinets of the mysterious Trinity; and what is this short of Heaven itself, but as infancy is short of manhood, and letters of words?
JEREMY TAYLOR

TROUBLE

T128
He that seeks trouble never misses.
GEORGE HERBERT

T129
If pleasures are greatest in anticipation, just remember that this is also true of trouble.
ELBERT HUBBARD

T130
There is no man in the world without some trouble or affliction, though he be a king or a pope.
THOMAS À KEMPIS

T131
Trouble will rain on those who are already wet.
SPANISH PROVERB

T132
Trouble is a marvellous mortifier of pride and an effectual restrainer of self-will.
W. MORLEY PUNSHON

T133
There were no troubles in my own life, except the troubles inseparable from being a spirit living in the flesh.
GEORGE SANTAYANA

TRUST
(See also CONFIDENCE and FAITH)

T134
He who trusts in himself is lost. He who trusts in God can do all things.
ST. ALPHONSUS LIGUORI

T135
The greatest trust between man and man is the trust of giving counsel.
FRANCIS BACON

T136
Put your trust in God, but keep
your powder dry.

OLIVER CROMWELL

T137
Those who trust us educate us.

GEORGE ELIOT

T138
What is more elevating and
transporting, than the generosity of
heart which risks everything on
God's word?

JOHN HENRY NEWMAN

T139
Trust in God, but mind your
business.

RUSSIAN PROVERB

T140
The more we depend on God the
more dependable we find He is.

CLIFF RICHARD

T141
God is faithful, and if we serve him
faithfully, he will provide for our
needs.

ST. RICHARD OF CHICHESTER

T142
Consider seriously how quickly
people change, and how little trust
is to be had in them; and cleave fast
unto God, Who changeth not.

ST. TERESA OF AVILA

T143
God is full of compassion, and
never fails those who are afflicted
and despised, if they trust in him
alone.

ST. TERESA OF AVILA

T144
Trust is a treasured item and
relationship. Once it is tarnished, it
is hard to restore it to its original
glow.

WILLIAM A. WARD

TRUTH

T145
Truth is not only violated by
falsehood; it may be equally
outraged by silence.

HENRI FRÉDÉRIC AMIEL

T146
Every truth without
exception – and whoever may utter
it – is from the Holy Ghost.

ST. THOMAS AQUINAS

T147
If it is not right, do not do it; if it is
not true, do not say it.

MARCUS AURELIUS

T148
Truth which is merely told is quick
to be forgotten; truth which is
discovered lasts a lifetime.

WILLIAM BARCLAY

T149
Truth exists, only falsehood has to
be invented.

GEORGE BRAQUE

T150
I thirst for truth, but shall not reach
it till I reach the source.

ROBERT BROWNING

T151
Truth is incontrovertible. Panic
may resent it; ignorance may
deride it; malice may distort it; but
there it is.

SIR WINSTON CHURCHILL

T152
The greatest friend of truth is
Time, her greatest enemy is
Prejudice, and her constant
companion is Humility.

CHARLES CALEB COLTON

T153
Truth is the foundation of all
knowledge and the cement of all
societies.

JOHN DRYDEN

T154
If God were able to backslide from truth, I would fain cling to truth and let God go.

MEISTER ECKHART

T155
If you tell the truth, you have infinite power supporting you; but if not, you have infinite power against you.

CHARLES GORDON

T156
Truth does not allow us to despair of our opponents. The man of peace inspired by truth does not equate his opponent with the error into which he sees him fall.

POPE JOHN PAUL II

T157
No truth can really exist external to Christianity.

JOHN HENRY NEWMAN

T158
He who does not bellow the truth when he knows the truth makes himself the accomplice of liars and forgers.

CHARLES PÉGUY

T159
Seven years of silent enquiry are needful for a man to learn the truth, but fourteen in order to learn how to make it known to his fellow men.

PLATO

T160
The grave of one who dies for the truth is holy ground.

GERMAN PROVERB

T161
Tell the truth and run.

JUGOSLAV PROVERB

T162
Time discovers truth.

LATIN PROVERB

T163
Truth is God's daughter.

SPANISH PROVERB

T164
The truth is cruel, but it can be loved, and it makes free those who have loved it.

GEORGE SANTAYANA

T165
Let us rejoice in the Truth, wherever we find its lamp burning.

ALBERT SCHWEITZER

T166
No generation can claim to have plumbed to the depths the unfathomable riches of Christ. The Holy Spirit has promised to lead us step by step into the fullness of truth.

LEON JOSEPH SUENENS

T167
Any human being can penetrate to the kingdom of truth, if only he longs for truth and perpetually concentrates all his attention upon its attainment.

SIMONE WEIL

TYRANNY

T168
Of all the tyrants that the world affords,
Our own affections are the fiercest lords.

WILLIAM ALEXANDER

T169
Justice without force is powerless; force without justice is tyrannical.

BLAISE PASCAL

T170
Men must be governed by God or they will be ruled by tyrants.

WILLIAM PENN

T171
Nothing is more abhorrent to the

tyrant than the service of Christ.
GIROLAMO SAVONAROLA

T172
The tyrant is nothing but a slave
turned inside out.
HERBERT SPENCER

UNBELIEF
(See also ATHEISM)

U1
No man is an unbeliever, but
because he will be so; and every
man is not an unbeliever, because
the grace of God conquers some,
changes their wills, and binds them
to Christ.
STEPHEN CHARNOCK

U2
He who proselytises in the cause of
unbelief is basically a man in need
of belief.
ERIC HOFFER

U3
Unbelief is blind.
JOHN MILTON

U4
He who does not believe that God
is above all is either a fool or has no
experience of life.
CAECILIUS STATIUS

UNDERSTANDING

U5
Don't try to reach God with your
understanding; that is impossible.
Reach him in love; that is possible.
CARLO CARRETTO

U6
Of course, understanding of our
fellow beings is important. But this
understanding becomes fruitful
only when it is sustained by
sympathetic feeling in joy and
sorrow.
ALBERT EINSTEIN

U7
Understanding a person does not
mean condoning: it only means
that one does not accuse him as if
one were God or a judge placed
above him.
ERICH FROMM

U8
What we do not understand we do
not possess.
JOHANN WOLFGANG VON GOETHE

U9
What is most necessary for
understanding divine things is
prayer.
ORIGEN

U10
Understanding is the wealth of
wealth.
ARAB PROVERB

UNIVERSE
(See also CREATION and
WORLD)

U11
The more we learn about the
wonders of our universe, the more
clearly we are going to perceive the
hand of God.
FRANK BORMANN

U12
The universe is but one vast symbol
of God.
THOMAS CARLYLE

U13
The celestial order and beauty of
the universe compel me to admit
that there is some excellent and
eternal Being, who deserves the
respect and homage of men.
MARCUS TULLIUS CICERO

U14
You will hardly find one among the
profounder sort of scientific minds,
without peculiar religious feelings
of his own . . . His religious feeling

takes the form of rapturous amazement at the harmony of the natural law.

ALBERT EINSTEIN

U15

I believe there is life on other planets with principalities and sovereignties, perhaps different from us, but all a part of God's universe.

BILLY GRAHAM

U16

God showed me a little thing the size of a hazelnut in the palm of my hand, and it was as round as a ball. I thought, 'What may this be?' and was answered thus: 'It is the universe.'

JULIAN OF NORWICH

U17

These are thy glorious works, Parent of good.

JOHN MILTON

U18

The universe is a thought of God.

JOHANN C. F. VON SCHILLER

U19

That the universe was formed by a fortuitous concourse of atoms, I will no more believe than that the accidental jumbling of the alphabet would fall into a most ingenious treatise of philosophy.

JONATHAN SWIFT

UNSELFISHNESS
(See also GENEROSITY and SELF-DENIAL)

U20

The secret of being loved is in being lovely; and the secret of being lovely is in being unselfish.

JOSIAH HOLLAND

U21

I find life an exciting business, and most exciting when it is lived for others.

HELEN KELLER

U22

If people knew how much ill-feeling unselfishness occasions, it would not be so often recommended from the pulpit!

C. S. LEWIS

U23

Neighbours praise unselfishness because they profit by it.

FRIEDRICH NIETZSCHE

U24

Real unselfishness consists in sharing the interests of others.

GEORGE SANTAYANA

VANITY
(See also PRIDE)

V1

Vanity is the pride of nature.

WILLIAM G. BENHAM

V2

And the name of that town is Vanity: and at the town there is a fair kept, called Vanity Fair.

JOHN BUNYAN

V3

At all times, but especially now, it is pertinent to say, 'Vanity of vanities, all is vanity.'

ST. JOHN CHRYSOSTOM

V4

A vain man can never be utterly ruthless; he wants to win applause and therefore he accommodates himself to others.

JOHANN WOLFGANG VON GOETHE

V5

The greatest magnifying glasses in the world are a man's own eyes when they look upon his own person.

ALEXANDER POPE

V6

Vain-glory blossoms but never bears.

ENGLISH PROVERB

V7

An ounce of vanity spoils a hundred weight of merit.

FRENCH PROVERB

V8

Most of us would be far enough from vanity if we heard all the things that are said of us.

JOSEPH RICKABY

V9

Provided a man is not mad, he can be cured of every folly but vanity.

JEAN JACQUES ROUSSEAU

VICE

V10

We make a ladder of our vices, if we trample those same vices underfoot.

ST. AUGUSTINE OF HIPPO

V11

This is the definition of vice: the wrong use, in violation of the Lord's command, of what has been given us by God for a good purpose.

ST. BASIL

V12

In other living creatures the ignorance of themselves is nature, but in men it is vice.

AMICIUS M. S. BOETHIUS

V13

Men wish to be saved from the mischiefs of their vices, but not from their vices.

RALPH WALDO EMERSON

V14

There is a capacity of virtue in us, and there is a capacity of vice to make your blood creep.

RALPH WALDO EMERSON

V15

If every year we rooted out one vice, we should soon become perfect.

THOMAS À KEMPIS

V16

Vice is often clothed in virtue's habit.

ENGLISH PROVERB

V17

Vices creep into our hearts under the name of virtues.

SENECA

VICTORY

V18

If Christ is with us, who is against us? You can fight with confidence where you are sure of victory. With Christ and for Christ victory is certain.

ST. BERNARD OF CLAIRVAUX

V19

The first step on the way to victory is to recognise the enemy.

CORRIE TEN BOOM

V20

Unless the battle has preceded, there cannot be a victory . . . for the helmsman is recognised in the tempest; the soldier is proven in warfare.

ST. CYPRIAN

V21

Even victors are by victory undone.

JOHN DRYDEN

V22

The way to get the most out of a victory is to follow it up with another which makes it look small.

HENRY S. HASKINS

V23

It is a great victory that comes without blood.

GEORGE HERBERT

V24
He conquers twice who upon victory overcomes himself.
PUBLILIUS SYRUS

VIOLENCE
V25
In some cases non-violence requires more militancy than violence.
CÉSAR CHÁVEZ

V26
Violence is always an offence, an insult to man, both to the one who perpetrates it and to the one who suffers it.
POPE JOHN PAUL II

V27
It is well known that firearms go off by themselves if only enough of them are together.
CARL GUSTAV JUNG

V28
Returning violence for violence multiplies violence, adding deeper darkness to a night already devoid of stars.
MARTIN LUTHER KING JR.

V29
The modern choice is between non-violence or non-existence.
MARTIN LUTHER KING, JR.

V30
We are effectively destroying ourselves by violence masquerading as love.
R. D. LAING

V31
Perseverance is more prevailing than violence.
PLUTARCH

V32
A good portion of the evils that afflict mankind is due to the erroneous belief that life can be made secure by violence.
COUNT LEO TOLSTOY

V33
Violent disorder once set in motion may spawn tyranny, not freedom.
CHARLES E. WYZANSKI

VIRGINITY
(See also CHASTITY, MODESTY and PURITY)
V34
Not because it is virginity is it held in honour, but because it is consecrated to God.
ST. AUGUSTINE OF HIPPO

V35
Neither widowhood nor virginity has any place in Heaven but that which is assigned to them by humility.
ST. FRANCIS DE SALES

V36
Virginity in the theological sense is basically an eschatological ideal which holds for all mankind equally, but not for all in the same way.
WALDEMAR MOLINSKI

V37
Virgins are thorns that produce roses.
ARTHUR SCHOPENHAUER

V38
Virginity is a life of angels, the enamel of the soul.
JEREMY TAYLOR

VIRTUE
V39
Virtue is like a rich stone, best plain set.
FRANCIS BACON

V40
Here and there people flee from public altercation into the sanctuary of private virtuousness.

But anyone who does this must shut his mouth and his eyes to the injustice around him . . . What he leaves undone will rob him of his peace of mind.

DIETRICH BONHOEFFER

V41

Love virtue rather than fear sin.

JEAN PIERRE CAMUS

V42

Virtue is not the absence of vices or the avoidance of moral dangers; virtue is a vivid and separate thing, like pain or a particular smell.

G. K. CHESTERTON

V43

So good a thing is virtue that even its enemies applaud and admire it.

ST. JOHN CHRYSOSTOM

V44

Many wish not so much to be virtuous, as to seem to be.

MARCUS TULLIUS CICERO

V45

Virtue and a trade are the best portion for children.

GEORGE HERBERT

V46

Some of the most virtuous men in the world are also the bitterest and most unhappy, because they have unconsciously come to believe that all their happiness depends on their being more virtuous than other men.

THOMAS MERTON

VOCATION

V47

Do not despise your situation. In it you must act, suffer and conquer. From every point on earth, we are equally near to heaven and the infinite.

HENRI FRÉDÉRIC AMIEL

V48

God chooses those who are pleasing to Him. He put a shepherd at the head of His people, and of the goat-herd, Amos, He made a prophet.

ST. BASIL

V49

Our vocation is to live in the Spirit – not to be more and more remarkable animals, but to be the sons and companions of God in eternity.

ANTHONY BLOOM

V50

When I have learned to do the Father's will, I shall have fully realised my vocation on earth.

CARLO CARRETTO

V51

It seems to me that it is the right thing for a director to discourage people who think they have a vocation. If it is real, it will vanquish all obstacles, and will stand out, not as a mere invitation, but as a categorical imperative.

JOHN CHAPMAN

V52

A good vocation is simply a firm and constant will in which the called person has to serve God in the way and in the places to which Almighty God has called him.

ST. FRANCIS DE SALES

V53

God has created me to do him some definite service; he has committed some work to me which he has not committed to another. I have my mission – I never may know it in this life, but I shall be told it in the next.

JOHN HENRY NEWMAN

V54

Many are stubborn in pursuit of the

path they have chosen, few in pursuit of the goal.

FRIEDRICH NIETZSCHE

V55
The test of a vocation is the love of the drudgery it involves.

LOGAN PEARSALL SMITH

V56
We must not forget that our vocation is so to practise virtue that men are won to it; it is possible to be morally upright repulsively.

WILLIAM TEMPLE

V57
The vocation of every man and woman is to serve other people.

COUNT LEO TOLSTOY

WAR
(See also PEACE and VIOLENCE)

W1
An infallible method of conciliating a tiger is to allow oneself to be devoured.

KONRAD ADENAUER

W2
For a war to be just, three conditions are necessary – public authority, just cause, right motive.

ST. THOMAS AQUINAS

W3
In peace the sons bury their fathers and in war the fathers bury their sons.

FRANCIS BACON

W4
The Church knows nothing of the sacredness of war. The Church which prays the 'Our Father' asks God only for peace.

DIETRICH BONHOEFFER

W5
There are many things worse than war. Slavery is worse than war.

Dishonour is worse than war.

SIR WINSTON CHURCHILL

W6
War can only be a desperate remedy in a desperate situation, used in order to spare humanity a still greater evil when all essentially reasonable and peaceful means have proved ineffective.

RENÉ COSTE

W7
How vile and despicable war seems to me! I would rather be hacked to pieces than take part in such an abominable business.

ALBERT EINSTEIN

W8
There is nothing that war has ever achieved we could not better achieve without it.

HAVELOCK ELLIS

W9
We must have military power to keep madmen from taking over the world.

BILLY GRAHAM

W10
Older men declare war. But it is youth that must fight and die. And it is youth who must inherit the tribulation, the sorrow, and the triumphs that are the aftermath of war.

HERBERT HOOVER

W11
For a Christian who believes in Jesus and his Gospel, war is an iniquity and a contradiction.

POPE JOHN XXIII

W12
It is becoming humanly impossible to regard war, in this atomic age, as a suitable means of re-establishing justice when some right has been violated.

POPE JOHN XXIII

W13
In modern warfare there are no victors; there are only survivors.
LYNDON B. JOHNSON

W14
Henceforth the adequacy of any military establishment will be tested by its ability to preserve the peace.
HENRY KISSINGER

W15
War is sweet to them that know it not.
ENGLISH PROVERB

W16
A great war leaves the country with three armies – an army of cripples, an army of mourners, and an army of thieves.
GERMAN PROVERB

W17
We (Christians in war) are called to the hardest of all tasks; to fight without hatred, to resist without bitterness, and in the end, if God grant it so, to triumph without vindictiveness.
WILLIAM TEMPLE

W18
To be prepared for war is one of the most effectual means of preserving peace.
GEORGE WASHINGTON

WEAKNESS

W19
Weak things united become strong.
THOMAS FULLER

W20
The acknowledgment of our weakness is the first step towards repairing our loss.
THOMAS À KEMPIS

W21
There are two kinds of weakness, that which breaks and that which bends.
JAMES RUSSELL LOWELL

W22
Men's weaknesses are often necessary to the purposes of life.
MAURICE MAETERLINCK

W23
The weak go to the wall.
ENGLISH PROVERB

W24
Weakness, not vice, is virtue's worst enemy.
FRANÇOIS DE LA ROCHEFOUCAULD

WEALTH
(See also MATERIALISM, MONEY and RICHES)

W25
Wealth is a good servant, a very bad mistress.
FRANCIS BACON

W26
Surplus wealth is a sacred trust which its possessor is bound to administer in his lifetime for the good of the community.
ANDREW CARNEGIE

W27
There is a time when a man distinguishes the idea of felicity from the idea of wealth; it is the beginning of wisdom.
RALPH WALDO EMERSON

W28
Great wealth and content seldom live together.
THOMAS FULLER

W29
Wealth is the relentless enemy of understanding

JOHN K. GALBRAITH

W30
The greatest wealth is contentment with a little.
ENGLISH PROVERB

W31
It is preoccupation with possession, more than anything else, that prevents men from living freely and nobly.
BERTRAND RUSSELL

W32
If a rich man is proud of his wealth, he should not be praised until it is known how he employs it.
SOCRATES

WHOLENESS
(See also BODY AND SOUL and HOLINESS)

W33
If a man is not rising upwards
to be an angel,
depend on it,
he is sinking downwards
to be a devil.
He cannot stop at the beast.
SAMUEL TAYLOR COLERIDGE

W34
Seek not every quality in one individual.
CONFUCIUS

W35
A weak person is injured by prosperity; a finer person by adversity, but the finest by neither.
PAUL FROST

W36
God does not ask of a person anything that is false or beyond his power. Rather, God invites what is most human in every person to become aware of itself.
LOUIS M. SAVARY

W37
Man must be lenient with his soul in her weaknesses and imperfections and suffer her failings as he suffers those of others, but he must not become idle, and must encourage himself to better things.
ST. SERAPHIM OF SAROV

W38
It costs so much to be a full human being that there are very few who have the enlightenment or the courage to pay the price. One has to abandon altogether the search for security and reach out to the risk of living with both arms. One has to embrace the world like a lover. One has to accept pain as a condition of existence. One has to court doubt and darkness as the cost of knowing. One needs a will stubborn in conflict, but apt always to total acceptance of every consequence of living and dying.
MORRIS WEST

WICKEDNESS

W39
The belief in a supernatural source of evil is not necessary: men alone are quite capable of every wickedness.
JOSEPH CONRAD

W40
No one ever became extremely wicked all at once.
DECIMUS JUVENAL

W41
A wicked man is his own Hell.
ENGLISH PROVERB

W42
Some wicked people would be less dangerous had they no redeeming qualities.
FRANÇOIS DE LA ROCHEFOUCAULD

W43
None of us feels the true love of God till we realise how wicked we

are. But you can't teach people that – they have to learn by experience.

DOROTHY L. SAYERS

WIFE
(See also MARRIAGE)

W44
A good wife and health, are a man's best wealth.

HENRY G. BOHN

W45
One shouldn't be too inquisitive in life
Either about God's secrets or one's wife.

GEOFFREY CHAUCER

W46
A wife is not to be chosen by the eye only. Choose a wife rather by your ear than your eye.

THOMAS FULLER

W47
Who lets his wife go to every feast, and his horse drink at every water, shall have neither good wife nor good horse.

GEORGE HERBERT

W48
The wife should be inferior to the husband; that is the only way to ensure equality between the two.

MARCUS MARTIAL

W49
Let us teach our wives to remain in the faith taught them and in charity and purity to cherish their husbands in all truth, loving all others impartially in complete chastity, and to bring up their children in the fear of God.

ST. POLYCARP

W50
The wife is the key of the house.

ENGLISH PROVERB

W51
In buying horses and in taking a wife, shut your eyes tight and commend yourself to God.

TUSCAN PROVERB

W52
A man too good for the world is no good for his wife.

YIDDISH PROVERB

W53
Try praising your wife, even if it does frighten her at first.

WILLIAM ASHLEY SUNDAY

W54
We always find it more acceptable to have God speaking to us directly rather than through our wives! But we may learn a great deal by listening to what He says to us through them.

PAUL TOURNIER

WILL OF GOD

W55
In his will is our peace.

DANTE ALIGHIERI

W56
The will of God is the measure of things.

ST. AMBROSE

W57
All Heaven is waiting to help those who will discover the will of God and do it.

J. ROBERT ASHCROFT

W58
Nothing, therefore, happens unless the Omnipotent wills it to happen: He either permits it to happen, or He brings it about Himself.

ST. AUGUSTINE OF HIPPO

W59
No one may prefer his own will to the will of God, but in everything we must seek and do the will of God.

ST. BASIL

W60

It needs a very pure intention, as well as great spiritual discernment, always to recognise the divine voice.

ROBERT H. BENSON

W61

The centre of God's will is our only safety.

BETSIE TEN BOOM

W62

If God sends us on stony paths, he provides strong shoes.

CORRIE TEN BOOM

W63

Self-will should be so completely poured out of the vessel of the soul into the ocean of the will of God, that whatever God may will, that at once the soul should will; and that whatever God may allow, that the soul should at once willingly embrace, whether it may be in itself sweet or bitter.

LOUIS DE BLOIS

W64

God's will is not an itinerary but an attitude.

ANDREW DHUSE

W65

There are no disappointments to those whose wills are buried in the will of God.

FREDERICK W. FABER

W66

Blessed are they who do not their own will on earth, for God will do it in heaven above.

ST. FRANCIS DE SALES

W67

A possibility is a hint from God.

SØREN KIERKEGAARD

W68

The hardness of God is kinder than the softness of men, and his compulsion is our liberation.

C. S. LEWIS

W69

Let your will be one with His will, and be glad to be disposed of by Him. He will order all things for you. What can cross your will, when it is one with His will, on which all creation hangs, round which all things revolve?

HENRY E. MANNING

W70

When we speak with God, our power of addressing Him, of holding communion with Him, and listening to His still small Voice, depends upon our will being one and the same with His.

FLORENCE NIGHTINGALE

W71

Prayer is no other but the revelation of the will or mind of God.

JOHN SALTMARSH

W72

Let each look to himself and see what God wants of him and attend to this, leaving all else alone.

HENRY SUSO

W73

It is God's will that is the proper measure of reality; and that is expressed in Christ, who is his Will.

SIMON TUGWELL

W74

The whole duty of man is summed up in obedience to God's will.

GEORGE WASHINGTON

WISDOM

W75

The first key to wisdom is assiduous and frequent questioning. For by

doubting we come in enquiry and by enquiry we arrive at truth.
ST. AMBROSE

PETER ABELARD

W76
Wisdom is the foundation, and justice the work without which a foundation cannot stand.
ST. AMBROSE

W77
Let your old age be childlike, and your childhood like old age; that is, so that neither may your wisdom be with pride, nor your humility without wisdom.
ST. AUGUSTINE OF HIPPO

W78
A prudent question is one-half of wisdom.
FRANCIS BACON

W79
Common sense, in an uncommon degree, is what the world calls wisdom.
SAMUEL TAYLOR COLERIDGE

W80
There is this difference between happiness and wisdom: He that thinks himself the happiest man, really is so; but he that thinks himself the wisest is generally the greatest fool.
CHARLES CALEB COLTON

W81
Fruitless is the wisdom of him who has no knowledge of himself.
DESIDERIUS ERASMUS

W82
He is not wise to me who is wise in words only, but he who is wise in deeds.
POPE ST. GREGORY I

W83
Wisdom is the ability to use knowledge so as to meet successfully the emergencies of life.

Men may acquire knowledge, but wisdom is a gift direct from God.
BOB JONES

W84
To have a low opinion of our own merits, and to think highly of others, is an evidence of wisdom. All men are frail, but thou shouldest reckon none as frail as thyself.
THOMAS À KEMPIS

W85
Only a fool tests the depth of the water with both feet.
AFRICAN PROVERB

W86
Wise men change their minds, fools never.
ENGLISH PROVERB

W87
The great wisdom in man consists in knowing his follies.
FRENCH PROVERB

W88
Wisdom comes by suffering.
GREEK PROVERB

W89
There is often wisdom under a shabby cloak.
LATIN PROVERB

W90
Nine-tenths of wisdom consist of being wise in time.
THEODORE ROOSEVELT

W91
Never be ashamed to own you have been in the wrong, 'tis but saying you are wiser today than you were yesterday.
JONATHAN SWIFT

W92
Wisdom is oftentimes nearer when we stoop than when we soar.
WILLIAM WORDSWORTH

WIT
(See also HUMOUR)

W93
Many get the name for being witty,
only to lose the credit for being
sensible.

GRACIAN

W94
Wit is the salt of conversation, not
the food.

WILLIAM HAZLITT

W95
A person reveals his character by
nothing so clearly as the joke he
resents.

GEORGE G. LICHTENBERG

W96
Wit is folly unless a wise man have
the keeping of it.

ENGLISH PROVERB

W97
Wit without learning is like a tree
without fruit.

ENGLISH PROVERB

WITNESS

W98
Witnessing is removing the various
barriers of our self-love to allow
Christ, living within us, to show
himself to our neighbours.

PAUL FROST

W99
The world is far more ready to
receive the Gospel than Christians
are to hand it out.

GEORGE W. PETERS

W100
If Christ lives in us, controlling our
personalities, we will leave glorious
marks on the lives we touch. Not
because of our lovely characters,
but because of his.

EUGENIA PRICE

W101
Our task as laymen is to live our
personal communion with Christ
with such intensity as to make it
contagious.

PAUL TOURNIER

WOMAN
(See also WIFE)

W102
There is no limit to the power of a
good woman.

ROBERT H. BENSON

W103
A man's good work is affected by
doing what he does; a woman's by
being what she is.

G. K. CHESTERTON

W104
Being a woman is a terribly difficult
trade, since it consists principally of
dealing with men.

JOSEPH CONRAD

W105
The society of women is the
foundation of good manners.

JOHANN WOLFGANG VON GOETHE

W106
No one knows like a woman how to
say things which are at once gentle
and deep.

VICTOR HUGO

W107
Women should remain at home, sit
still, keep house, and bear and
bring up children.

MARTIN LUTHER

W108
Woman is the confusion of man.

ENGLISH PROVERB

W109
Men shall always be what the
women make them; if, therefore,
you would have men great and
virtuous, impress upon the minds
of women what greatness and
virtue are.

JEAN JACQUES ROUSSEAU

W110
It was to a virgin woman that the birth of the Son of God was announced. It was to a fallen woman that his resurrection was announced.

FULTON J. SHEEN

W111
Christianity brings liberation through the Gospel in faith and action. But the Christian Church has not been a sufficiently liberating institution for women, in the sense of not opening up to them the full range of possibilities.

PAULINE WEBB

W112
Whatever women do, they must do twice as well as men to be thought half as good. Luckily, this is not difficult.

CHARLOTTE WHITTON

W113
The history of women is the history of the worst form of tyranny the world has ever known. The tyranny of the weak over the strong. It is the only tyranny that lasts.

OSCAR WILDE

W114
I think the great fault of the Catholic Church is that it has never really come to terms with women. What I object to, like a lot of other women in the Church, is being treated as Madonnas or Mary Magdalens, instead of being treated as people.

SHIRLEY WILLIAMS

WONDER

W115
You will find something far greater in the woods than you will in books. Stones and trees will teach you what you can never learn from masters.

ST. BERNARD OF CLAIRVAUX

W116
The man who cannot wonder is but a pair of spectacles behind which there is no eye.

THOMAS CARLYLE

W117
Wonder is the basis of worship.

THOMAS CARLYLE

W118
The world will never starve for want of wonders; but only for want of wonder.

G. K. CHESTERTON

W119
Men love to wonder, and that is the seed of science.

RALPH WALDO EMERSON

W120
To be surprised, to wonder, is to begin to understand.

JOSE ORTEGA Y GASSET

W121
Wonder rather than doubt is the root of knowledge.

ABRAHAM JOSHUA HESCHEL

W122
A wonder lasts but nine days.

ENGLISH PROVERB

W123
God made us and we wonder at it.

SPANISH PROVERB

W124
Wonder is especially proper to childhood, and it is the sense of wonder above all that keeps us young.

GERALD VANN

WORDS
(See also COMMUNICATION, CONVERSATION, GOSSIP and TALK)

W125
Our words are a faithful index of the state of our souls.
ST. FRANCIS DE SALES

W126
Words are nails for fixing ideas.
H. GIORNALE

W127
The words of God which you receive by your ear, hold fast in your heart. For the word of God is the food of the soul.
POPE ST. GREGORY I

W128
To the intelligent man a word is enough.
THOMAS À KEMPIS

W129
Words are, of course, the most powerful drug used by mankind.
RUDYARD KIPLING

W130
Cold words freeze people and hot words scorch them, and bitter words make them bitter, and wrathful words make them wrathful. Kind words also produce their image on men's souls; and a beautiful image it is. They smooth, and quiet, and comfort the hearer.
BLAISE PASCAL

W131
The world pays itself with words; there is little plumbing of the depths of things.
BLAISE PASCAL

W132
In love and divinity what is most worth saying cannot be said.
COVENTRY PATMORE

W133
A man of words and not of deeds is like a garden full of weeds.
ENGLISH PROVERB

W134
A word spoken is past recalling.
ENGLISH PROVERB

W135
Better one word before than two after.
WELSH PROVERB

W136
Little keys can open big locks. Simple words can express great thoughts.
WILLIAM A. WARD

WORK

W137
Nothing is really work unless you would rather be doing something else.
JAMES M. BARRIE

W138
It appears, on close examination, that work is less boring than amusing oneself.
CHARLES BAUDELAIRE

W139
He who labours as he prays lifts his heart to God with his hands.
ST. BERNARD OF CLAIRVAUX

W140
Without work, all life goes rotten. But when work is soulless, life stifles and dies.
ALBERT CAMUS

W141
The best worship, however, is stout working.
THOMAS CARLYLE

W142
Hard work is a thrill and a joy when you are in the will of God.
ROBERT A. COOK

Work

W143
No one has a right to sit down and feel hopeless. There's too much work to do.

DOROTHY DAY

W144
Work is love made visible.

KAHLIL GIBRAN

W145
Happiness, I have discovered, is nearly always a rebound from hard work.

DAVID GRAYSON

W146
Work is the greatest thing in the world, so we should always save some of it for tomorrow.

DON HEROLD

W147
God gives every bird its food, but he does not throw it into the nest.

JOSIAH G. HOLLAND

W148
I like work, it fascinates me. I can sit and look at it for hours.

JEROME K. JEROME

W149
Work is not a curse, it is a blessing from God who calls man to rule the earth and transform it, so that the divine work of creation may continue with man's intelligence and effort.

POPE JOHN PAUL II

W150
There is great fret and worry in always running after work; it is not good intellectually or spiritually.

ANNIE KEARY

W151
A dairymaid can milk cows to the glory of God.

MARTIN LUTHER

W152
It is our best work that he wants, not the dregs of our exhaustion. I think he must prefer quality to quantity.

GEORGE MACDONALD

W153
It is a sublime mystery that Christ should begin to work before he began to teach; a humble workman before being the teacher of all nations.

POPE PIUS XII

W154
Hats off to the past; coats off to the future.

AMERICAN PROVERB

W155
A man grows most tired while standing still.

CHINESE PROVERB

W156
Never was good work done without much trouble.

CHINESE PROVERB

W157
Work is worship.

FRENCH PROVERB

W158
Work is no disgrace: the disgrace is idleness.

GREEK PROVERB

W159
Nothing is denied to well-directed labour; nothing is to be obtained without it.

SIR JOSHUA REYNOLDS

W160
No amount of pay ever made a good soldier, a good teacher, a good artist, or a good workman.

JOHN RUSKIN

W161
When love and skill work together, expect a masterpiece.

JOHN RUSKIN

W162
Work is the natural exercise and function of man . . . Work is not primarily a thing one does to live, but the thing one lives to do. It is, or should be, the full expression of the worker's faculties, the thing in which he finds spiritual, mental and bodily satisfaction, and the medium in which he offers himself to God.

DOROTHY L. SAYERS

W163
A man can do only what he can do. But if he does that each day he can sleep at night and do it again the next day.

ALBERT SCHWEITZER

W164
Good for the body is the work of the body, and good for the soul is the work of the soul, and good for either is the work of the other.

HENRY DAVID THOREAU

W165
No nation can prosper till it learns that there is as much dignity in tilling a field as in writing a poem.

BOOKER T. WASHINGTON

WORLD
(See also CREATION and UNIVERSE)

W166
The very order, disposition, beauty, change, and motion of the world and of all visible things proclaim that it could only have been made by God, the ineffably and invisibly great and the ineffably and invisibly beautiful.

ST. AUGUSTINE OF HIPPO

W167
My habitual feeling is that the world is so extremely odd, and everything in it so surprising. Why *should* there be green grass and liquid water, and *why* have I got hands and feet?

JOHN CHAPMAN

W168
Man does not come to know the world by that which he extorts from it, but rather by that which he adds to it: himself.

PAUL CLAUDEL

W169
This world and that to come are two enemies. We cannot therefore be friends to both; but we must resolve which we would forsake and which we would enjoy.

ST. CLEMENT OF ALEXANDRIA

W170
The world is charged with the grandeur of God.

GERARD MANLEY HOPKINS

W171
The world has become a global village.

MARSHALL MCLUHAN

W172
The world is a sure teacher, but it requires a fat fee.

FINNISH PROVERB

W173
You cannot please both God and the world at the same time. They are utterly opposed to each other in their thoughts, their desires, and their actions.

JOHN VIANNEY

W174
Our very presence in the world gives a type of meaning to the world, but that meaning is the beginning and not the end of our lives.

A. A. VOGEL

W175
I look upon the world as my parish.

JOHN WESLEY

W176
We are citizens of the world; and the tragedy of our times is that we do not know this.

WOODROW WILSON

W177
The world is too much with us;
  late and soon,
Getting and spending, we lay waste
  our powers:
Little we see in Nature that is ours.

WILLIAM WORDSWORTH

WORLDLINESS

W178
The unalterable law of 'the world' is that evil is fought with evil, and that the devil is driven out by Beelzebub. And so long as that remains unaltered, Christianity is not victorious.

THEODOR HAECKER

W179
Whoever marries the spirit of this age will find himself a widower in the next.

WILLIAM RALPH INGE

W180
More men live regardless of the great duties of piety through too great a concern for worldly goods than through direct injustice.

WILLIAM LAW

W181
Be wisely worldly, be not worldly wise.

FRANCIS QUARLES

WORRY
(See also ANXIETY, DOUBT and TROUBLE)

W182
Worry does not empty tomorrow of its sorrow; it empties today of its strength.

CORRIE TEN BOOM

W183
When I look back on all these worries I remember the story of the old man who said on his deathbed that he had had a lot of trouble in his life, most of which never happened.

SIR WINSTON CHURCHILL

W184
There is nothing that wastes the body like worry, and one who has any faith in God should be ashamed to worry about anything whatsoever.

MOHANDAS GANDHI

W185
Worry is interest paid on trouble before it falls due.

WILLIAM R. INGE

WORSHIP
(See also LITURGY)

W186
We are told to sing to the Lord a new song. A new man knows a new song. A song is a thing of joy and, if we think of it, a thing to love. So the man who has learned to love a new life has learned to sing a new song. For a new man, a new song and the New Testament all belong to the same kingdom.

ST. AUGUSTINE OF HIPPO

W187
For the Christian who loves God, worship is the daily bread of patience.

HONORÉ DE BALZAC

W188
It is only when men begin to worship that they begin to grow.

CALVIN COOLRIDGE

W189
Glory to Christ. Come, let us offer him the great, universal sacrifice of our love, and pour out before him our richest hymns and prayers. For

he offered his cross to God as a sacrifice in order to make us all rich.

ST. EPHREM

W190
It is a man's duty to praise and bless God and pay him due thanks. Ought we not, as we dig and plough to sing, 'Great is God that He gave us these instruments wherewith we shall till the earth, great is God that He has given us hands to labour, and the power to draw our breath in sleep.' At every moment we ought to sing these praises, and, above all, the greatest and divinest praise, that God gave us the ability to understand His gifts and to use our human reason.

EPICTETUS

W191
The glory of God is a living man; and the life of man consists in beholding God.

ST. IRENAEUS

W192
A little lifting of the heart suffices; a little remembrance of God, one act of inward worship are prayers which, however short, are nevertheless acceptable to God.

BROTHER LAWRENCE

W193
A man can no more diminish God's glory by refusing to worship Him than a lunatic can put out the sun by scribbling the word 'darkness' on the walls of his cell.

C. S. LEWIS

W194
It cannot be that the instinct which has led to the creation of cathedrals, and of churches in every village, is wholly mistaken and misleading. There must be some great truth underlying the instinct for worship.

OLIVER LODGE

W195
It is a law of man's nature, written into his very essence, and just as much a part of him as the desire to build houses and cultivate the land and marry and have children and read books and sing songs, that he should want to stand together with other men in order to acknowledge their common dependence on God, their Father and Creator.

THOMAS MERTON

W196
Prayers travel faster when said in unison.

LATIN PROVERB

W197
Do not forget that even as 'to work is to worship' so to be cheery is to worship also, and to be happy is the first step to being pious.

ROBERT LOUIS STEVENSON

W198
Worship, then, is not a part of the Christian life; it is the Christian life.

GERALD VANN

YOUTH
(See also CHILDREN)

Y1
The principal trap which the Devil sets for young people is idleness. This is the fatal source of all evil.

JOHN BOSCO

Y2
Youth is not properly definable by age. It is a spirit of daring, creating, asserting life, and openly relating to the world.

MALCOLM BOYD

Y3
Young people will respond if the challenge is tough enough and hard

enough. Youth wants a master and a controller. Young people were built for God, and without God as the centre of their lives they become frustrated and confused, desperately grasping for and searching for security.

BILLY GRAHAM

Y4
The young want to be challenged by something sacrificial. They are rejecting phoney values and standards. The only hope is to create a community that doesn't live by false values.

TREVOR HUDDLESTON

Y5
You yourself know how slippery is the path of youth – a path on which I myself have fallen, and which you are now traversing not without fear.

ST. JEROME

Y6
When we are out of sympathy with the young, then I think our work in this world is over.

GEORGE MACDONALD

Y7
The real lost souls don't wear their hair long and play guitars. They have crew cuts, trained minds, sign on for research in biological warfare, and don't give their parents a moment's worry.

J. B. PRIESTLEY

Y8
Who that in youth no virtue useth, in age all honour him refuseth.

ENGLISH PROVERB

Y9
Youth and age will never agree.

ENGLISH PROVERB

Y10
Praise youth and it will prosper.

IRISH PROVERB

Y11
I was born in the wrong generation. When I was a young man, no one had any respect for youth. Now I am an old man and no one has any respect for age.

BERTRAND RUSSELL

Y12
One other thing stirs me when I look back at my youthful days, the fact that so many people gave me something or were something to me without knowing it.

ALBERT SCHWEITZER

Y13
Don't laugh at youth for his affectations; he is only trying on one face after another to find his own.

LOGAN PEARSALL SMITH

ZEAL
(See also ENTHUSIASM)

Z1
There are few catastrophes so great and irremediable as those that follow an excess of zeal.

ROBERT H. BENSON

Z2
Zeal without knowledge is always less useful and effective than regulated zeal, and very often it is highly dangerous.

ST. BERNARD OF CLAIRVAUX

Z3
Zeal without tolerance is fanaticism.

JOHN KELMAN

Z4
We are often moved with passion, and we think it to be zeal.

THOMAS À KEMPIS

Z5
Zeal dropped in charity is good;

without it, good for nothing; for it
devours all it comes near.
WILLIAM PENN

Z6
Misplaced zeal is zeal for God
rather than zeal of God.
WILLIAM PETTINGILE

Z7
Zeal, when it is a virtue, is a
dangerous one.
ENGLISH PROVERB

Z8
Zeal without knowledge is fire

without light. Zeal without
prudence is frenzy.
ENGLISH PROVERB

Z9
All true zeal for God is a zeal for
love, mercy and goodness.
ROBERT E. THOMPSON

Z10
Nothing spoils human nature more
than false zeal. The good nature of
an heathen is more God-like than
the furious zeal of a Christian.
BENJAMIN WHICHCOTE

INDEX

Index

Index

Index

Index

Index

Index

Index

Index

Index

Index

Prochnow, Herbert V.
C157, D54
Proust, Marcel (1871–1922)
C374, G187
Proverbs:
African
F149, W85
American
A161, E15, T13, W154
Ancient
C279
Arab
C304, G8, H58, J72, L178, O58,
O61, P242, U10
Belgian
E219
Bengalese
T49
Bulgarian
H25, P333, S204, T50
Chinese
A10, B57, C31, C317, D11, E197,
F65, F88, F95, F177, F197, G188,
G195, H161, L46, P42, P43, P99,
P118, P181, R121, R143, T26, W155,
W156
Croatian
P355
Czech
F127, F128, H9
Danish
A84, E105, E220, F96, G9, G26,
G37, H111, H222, H288, L41, L179,
M140, P243, S192
Dutch
H90
English
A40, A46, A70, A71, A129, A162,
B31, B32, B51, B90, B108, B113,
B117, B125, B142, B146, B163, C47,
C68, C69, C134, C166, C172, C250,
C305, C330, C331, C357, C362,
C420, C421, C432, D12, D19, D34,
D48, D59, D78, D89, D107, D120,
D155, E7, E70, E71, E85, E86, E87,
E106, E134, E135, E144, E177, F7,
F40, F55, F108, F150, F151, F198,
G10, G27, G38, G39, G50, G87,
G93, G94, G177, G204, H59, H74,
H169, H190, H196, H270, H271,
H279, H280, I10, I97, J2, J62, K40,
L10, L42, M19, M46, N11, O59,
O62, P5, P44, P74, P143, P149, P177,

P212, P334, P369, R63, R118, R128,
R137, S32, S56, S137, T27, T98, V6,
V16, W15, W23, W30, W41, W50,
W86, W96, W97, W108, W122,
W133, W134, Y8, Y9, Z7, Z8
Estonian
T63
Finnish
D108, W172
French
A130, B33, B114, C21, C135, C173,
C280, C348, D60, D95, D156, E72,
E120, E198, E199, F198, G11, G151,
G152, L69, P291, P370, R75, S33,
S182, T99, V7, W87, W157
German
A100, A111, A141, B58, D79, D80,
E107, E121, E136, E178, F129, F137,
G40, G95, G126, G196, H26, H75,
H91, H106, H170, H256, H289, I44,
M157, P75, P244, T160, W16
Greek
A112, D35, D157, F152, G170,
G171, O13, P269, S343, W88,
W158
Gypsy
F89
Hebrew
A142, L180, P191
Hindu
H112
Hungarian
A47
Irish
A26, E221, F138, L119, S150, Y10
Italian
B164, C332, C349, D36, G189, H41,
H61, M210, P192, P270
Japanese
D170, F153, K9, M176, P213
Jewish
A113, B85, B126, C221, C433, F66,
G12, G51, H197, H257, L21, L32,
L181, M177, M195, P193, P292,
R119, S93
Jugoslav
T161
Latin
C251, G137, H191, O14, P84, P194,
P356, S43, S169, S193, S232, T14,
T162, W89, W196
Malayan
K10

286

Index

Index

Index

Virgil, Publius (70–19 B.C.)
C72

Vogel, A. A.
W174

Voltaire, François Marie (1694–1778)
B86, G74, G206, P296, S184, S356

Von Balthasar, Hans Urs (b. 1905)
R114

Von Hildebrand, Dietrich
R123

Von Hugel, Friedrich (1852–1925)
C195, R56, S205

Von Weizsacker, Carl F. (b. 1912)
B129

Vos, Geerhardus
K28

W

Walcha, Helmut
M214

Walesa, Lech (b. 1943)
L34

Wallace, Lewis (1827–1905)
R66

Wallis, Arthur (b. 1928)
B148

Walton, Izaak (1593–1683)
B109, H63

Walworth, Clarence
A59

Wanamaker, John (1838–1922)
C119

Warburton, William (1698–1779)
E98, O70

Ward, Mary Augusta (1851–1920)
C388

Ward, Ted
L35

Ward, William A. (1812–1882)
A27, B110, F8, M14, O18, S206,
S287, T144, W136

Warner, Charles Dudley (1829–1900)
C268

Washington, Booker T. (1859–1915)
R81, W165

Washington, George (1732–1799)
C284, F205, H171, P362, R42, W18,
W74

Watson, David (b. 1933)
C424, D127, F31

Watson, John (*see* Maclaren, Ian)
(1850–1907)
K12

Watts, Alan W. (1915–1973)
K51

Watts, Isaac (1674–1748)
S48

Weaver, H. G.
L97

Webb, Pauline
W111

Webster, Daniel (1782–1852)
C142, C160, G127, L56, R82

Weil, Simone (1909–1943)
A244, D82, E210, H226, I32, I98,
M78, P377, R12, T167

Wellesley, Arthur (Duke of
Wellington) (1769–1852)
L129

Wells, Corrine V.
G13

Wells, H. G. (1866–1946)
A50, A228, C439, G75, J4, R8

Wesley, Charles (1707–1788)
D83

Wesley, John (1703–1791)
E166, H108, M181, O71, P102, P254,
P272, R57, S237, W175

West, Jessamyn
F156

West, Morris (b. 1916)
W38

West, Dame Rebecca (b. 1892)
M86

Whale, John S.
R97

Wharton, Edith (1862–1937)
E205

Whately, Richard (1787–1863)
C434, F42, H172, P144

Whichcote, Benjamin (1609–1683)
S115, Z10

Whipple, Edwin Percy (1819–1886)
C61

White, David
L196

White, Gustav J.
A74

White, William Allen (1748–1836)
L57

Whitehead, Alfred North (1861–1947)
I27, L110, O63, P134

Whitmell, C. T.
D14, L82

Whitney, Edgar A.
T16